ANCIENT MAN IN NORTH AMERICA

by

H. M. WORMINGTON

Curator of Archaeology

THE DENVER MUSEUM OF NATURAL HISTORY

Denver, Colorado

Popular Series No. 4   Fourth Edition, Revised 1957

Lithographed by The PEERLESS PRINTING COMPANY
Denver, Colorado

II

In Memory

of

Kirk Bryan

and

Edgar B. Howard

Fig. 1. Folsom point and associated fossil bison ribs imbedded in matrix, Type Station, Folsom, New Mexico.

PREFACE

When the first edition of this book appeared eighteen years ago, it was in the nature of an experiment. It was felt that there might be a great many persons who were keenly interested in archaeology, anxious to know something of the most ancient inhabitants of this country, but unable to obtain such information because of lack of training and of time. Many of the publications dealing with early man were highly technical papers almost unintelligible to the non-professional reader; and the ever increasing list of references made it necessary to read a far greater number of publications than was practicable for most amateurs.

The experiment has been most successful, for we have found that there are many thousands of persons, with no formal training in archaeology, who are eager to receive information about the subject if it is presented in a manner acceptable to the intelligent layman. It has been gratifying to discover that such books are also of use in the training of college and university students, and that such a synthesis may be of service to the professional anthropologist who specializes in another field and cannot devote a great deal of time to another subject but finds it desirable to keep abreast of new developments in the study of early man.

The present edition attempts to present a brief but comprehensive survey of the subject and to explain the many new developments since the third edition appeared in 1949. There have been many important changes, for the last eight years have been among the most fruitful for archaeologists concerned with the earliest inhabitants of North America; more geologists have become interested in the problems involved; and new dating techniques have been developed. Many gaps in our knowledge still exist, but tremendous progress has been made since acceptance was won thirty years ago for the association of artifacts with an extinct fauna in America.

Some idea of the increase in knowledge pertaining to the Paleo-Indians may be gained from the fact that when the first edition of this book appeared in 1939 it was possible to give an adequate summary in a publication that contained eighty pages and there were only ninety-two references in the bibliography, which was reasonably complete. This volume contains 309 pages, even though in many cases only a sentence or a paragraph has been devoted to major contributions, and some sites discussed in the earlier editions are now known to be of more recent age and are not considered here at all. There are 586 references in the bibliography, which consists largely of literature cited and which is far from exhaustive. Three hundred and eighty-three references have been added since 1949. Some publications that have appeared since January 1, 1957 have been listed, but reference to them will be found only in footnotes except in cases where I had access to manuscripts prior to publication.

This, like almost all archaeological publications, is essentially the result of collaboration. Each time I write a series of acknowledgments for the aid received in the preparation of a publication, I gain a fresh awareness of the magnificent cooperation provided by most of my colleagues, and I become more convinced that it is unlikely that any other profession can claim so great a concentration of thoroughly nice people, as can archaeology.

It is inevitable that there will be errors in any book that covers so wide a range as this one, but there are far fewer than there would have been had it not been for the kindness of various specialists who read and criticized this manuscript or portions of it. Those who have provided a variety of valuable suggestions are: Ernst Antevs, Ripley P. Bullen, Douglas S. Byers, Joffre L. Coe, L. S. Cressman, Herbert W. Dick, J. L. Giddings Jr., James B. Griffin, Robert F. Heizer, Frederick Johnson, J. Charles Kelley, Alex D. Krieger, Harold Malde, Irving Rouse, Reynold Ruppe, Waldo Wedel, Fred Wendorf and Joe Ben Wheat.

There are few more frustrating experiences than to summarize information available in existing literature while realizing that there are many new but unpublished data, derived from later work, that invalidate many of the older concepts. Fortunately, most archaeologists are extraordinarily generous in making the results of their research available prior to publication. The following individuals, to whom I am profoundly indebted, most unselfishly provided personal communications relating to work which had not yet been published when this book was being written: Luis Aveleyra A. de Anda, Ripley P. Bullen, Douglas S. Byers, Joffre L. Coe, L. S. Cressman, Herbert W. Dick, Robert F. Heizer, Allan Hudson, Frederick Johnson, Russell A. Johnston, Alex D. Krieger, Helge Larsen, T. M. N. Lewis, James MacGregor, Richard S. MacNeish, Hallam L. Movius, Jr., William Mulloy, Robert W. Nero, George I. Quimby, Irving Rouse, Reynold Ruppe, Linton Satterthwaite, Jr., J. M. Shippee, Fred Wendorf, Richard P. Wheeler, Stephen Williams, and F. V. C. Worman.

The assembling of illustrations for a book which deals with material found in many parts of the continent and now in the possession of various institutions is a major project, and one which can be successful only if one receives full cooperation from many individuals as well as institutions. Institutional credits will be found below each picture, but I should like to express my gratitude to the archaeologists who made it possible for me to obtain the required illustrations: Luis Aveleyra A. de Anda, Douglas S. Byers, Joffre L. Coe, Richard Daugherty, Herbert W. Dick, E. Mott Davis, J. L. Giddings, Jr., M. R. Harrington, Emil W. Haury, Frank C. Hibben, Helge Larsen, William A. Ritchie, Robert E. Ritzenthaler, Frank H. H. Roberts, Jr., William Roosa, E. B. Sayles, Linton Satterthwaite, Jr., E. H. Sellards, J. M. Shippee, Ruth D. Simpson, Fred Wendorf, Richard P. Wheeler, Lloyd A. Wilford and John Witthoft.

Many pictures were also provided by members of the Museum staff, to whom I am deeply grateful. With the exception of Figures 1, 4 and 13, which were taken by Albert C. Rogers, photographs not credited to other institutions are largely the work of Walker Van Riper. Figures 43, 44 and 63 were taken by the writer in the course of an archaeological survey of Alberta, sponsored by the Glenbow Foundation of Calgary, which will be reported upon in a later publication in the Museum's Pictorial Series. Drawings, unless otherwise credited, are by Mary Chilton Gray. Gertrude Pierce located sites on the map, which was painted by Miss Gray and lettered by George D. Volk. The cover design is by Arminta Neal.

Various other individuals also provided invaluable aid. The original typescript was prepared by Betsy Wright. Gertrude Pierce assisted with the compilation of the bibliography. Cynthia and Henry Irwin assisted with the preparation of the index. The book was proof-read by Dorothy Ellis. To all of them my sincere thanks, and a special note of thanks to Pat Wheat who edited the manuscript.

H. M. WORMINGTON

September 1, 1957

TABLE OF CONTENTS

LIST OF ILLUSTRATIONS

XV

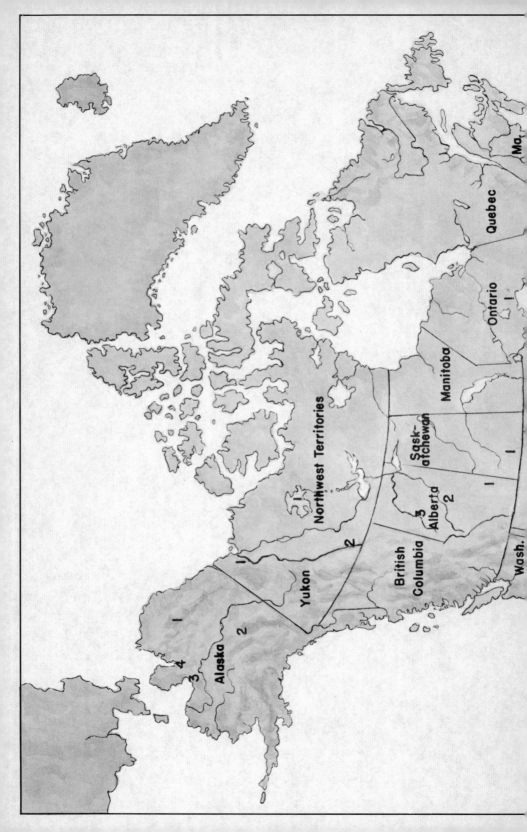

ANCIENT MAN

IN

NORTH AMERICA

Chapter I

INTRODUCTION

When Europeans first reached the New World they found the country already inhabited by groups of people who, although differing from one another in many respects, had certain physical traits in common. These people, whom we call American Indians, had yellowish- or reddish-brown skins, their eyes were black or dark brown, their head hair was usually black, straight, and coarse, their facial and body hair was very sparse. In general, they looked very much like Asiatics of the Mongoloid race.

This brings us to an important question, "Where did the American aborigines originate?" There is no belief on the part of any competent palaeontologist or physical anthropologist that man originated in the New World. No human skeleton has ever been found in North or South America which could be considered anything but that of Homo sapiens or modern man. Furthermore, all evidence indicates that evolutionary processes in the Western Hemisphere have produced no higher type of primate than the American monkeys, and these animals cannot be placed in the human line of development.

Therefore, it is in the Old World, where man has existed for hundreds of thousands of years and where his anthropoid predecessors lived, that we must seek the ancestors of the American Indian. There are two principal reasons for believing that Asia is the homeland of the American aborigine. First, there are strong physical similarities between eastern Asiatics and American Indians. Second, at Bering Strait, Asia and North America are separated by only fifty-six miles, and at certain times in the past the two continents were joined by a land bridge. Until watercraft suitable for oceanic travel was developed this was the only route by which man could have entered America.

Next we may ask, "When did man first reach this continent?" It was apparent that, at the time of the first European contact, people had already been living in the Western Hemisphere for some time. Ruined buildings, erected long before the birth of any man then living, were to be found in many parts of the country. Furthermore, there was great diversity among groups of living Indians as regards culture, language, and physical type, and many had adapted their culture to a remarkable extent to specialized environments. Certain discoveries were made in the nineteenth century which some scientists regarded as providing proof of great antiquity for man in the New World; but most anthropologists, although they realized that the country had been occupied for some time, were firmly convinced that the advent of man on this continent could not, at most, date back much farther than a few thousand years before the beginning of the Christian Era. Since 1926 enough evidence has been produced to convince students of the subject that man has been present in North America for more than 10,000 years. Recent evidence suggests that he may have been here for more than 20,000 years, but no one is certain when he first arrived.

As might be imagined, it is extremely difficult to assign exact dates to the earliest periods of occupation. In seeking to interpret the evidence of early cultures, archaeologists have been dependent not only upon the techniques of their own discipline, but also upon those of other sciences. In order to understand the problems involved, and to evaluate the contributions of the various disciplines, it is essential to know something of the periods immediately preceding the present. In the next two chapters will be found a highly simplified discussion of the Pleistocene and Recent epochs, and a brief explanation of some of the methods used in an effort to determine the conditions that prevailed in early prehistoric times and to assign dates to archaeological remains that cannot be dated through tree-ring records, ancient calendrical systems, or written records. Later chapters will tell of the tools and implements which indicate the presence of man in ancient times, the skeletal remains of presumed antiquity, and the routes which the earliest migrants may have followed.

In the fourth chapter various types of projectile points will be discussed. It should be noted that not all archaeologists would classify these points in exactly the same way. Ideally, an archaeological type should have "demonstrable historical meaning in terms of behavior patterns" (Krieger, 1944a, p. 272). Actually, however, a projectile point type is essentially an artificial construct, and in typology there are no eternal verities. An individual or a group of individuals may feel that certain traits characterize a sufficiently large number of points that a recurring pattern, believed to be culturally significant and delimited in time and space, can be recognized. In order to be able to communicate with others, it is necessary to assign a name to this group, and a type is thus created.

Not all archaeologists create types in the same way, however. Some are "lumpers" who recognize only a few types and allow a great variation within each category. Others are "splitters" who recognize a large number of types and insist on greater uniformity because they believe that certain relatively small differences may be significant. Even though archaeologists try to avoid both extremes, they must, if they are honest, admit that they tend toward one end of the scale or the other. The tendencies of the writer are, admittedly, on the splitting side.

If type names are to serve as a means of communication, it is essential that the reader and the writer attach the same meaning to the words. On pages 261 to 271 will be found pictures and definitions of certain key types. The purpose of this section is not to set up immutable categories but simply to indicate what the writer has in mind when using a type name in the following discussion. Obviously, not every point placed in a given category will be an exact replica of the point shown; there are too many variations as regards individual initiative, skill, materials used, etc. What is involved is that, when a type name is used, the specimen under discussion will, in the writer's opinion, conform to the definition and be more nearly like the specimen illustrated than like any of the others.

In order to keep the size of this volume within reasonable bounds, it has been necessary to set certain limits for the type of material to be discussed. In attempting to set such limits one is inevitably faced by terminological problems. Discussions of terminology are dull; unfortunately, they are essential. The term "Paleo-Indian" (Paleo = Old) is often used to refer to the earliest inhabitants of North America in order to differentiate them from the later peoples (Roberts, 1940). It is an undesirable term if we give it a racial connotation. The later American Indians were Mongoloids, but this is not necessarily the racial type of the first comers to the New World. Some physical anthropologists think that the Mongoloid race represents a relatively recent development in Asia. Since we do not know when men first reached this Hemisphere, we are not in a position to say what their racial type may have been. However, if we use the term Paleo-Indian simply in the sense of a designation for the oldest inhabitants it seems acceptable. It will be used here to refer to people who hunted animals which are now extinct, to the people who occupied the western United States prior to about 6,000 years ago, and to the makers of the fluted points found in the eastern United States. There are no firm dates for the latter, but there is reason to believe that some, at least, are quite old.

Most of the material to be discussed is attributed to the Paleo-Indian Stage but in a few cases there will be some consideration of complexes of more recent age because they are represented in multi-component sites containing earlier material, or because there is evidence of continuity from an earlier period. A few sites attributed to the Archaic Stage in the eastern United States will be discussed, either because there may be some Paleo-Indian connections or because materials found in them have yielded radiocarbon dates which indicate contemporaneity with the Paleo-Indian Stage in other areas. The use of the term "Archaic" which is found in most of the literature presents certain problems. This stage has generally been regarded as falling later in the developmental sequence than the Paleo-Indian, but new radiocarbon dates suggest that there was some overlap in certain areas. Additional complications arise because the name is not used in the same sense by all writers. There is general agreement that the people of the Archaic Stage, which preceded the Early Woodland Stage in the eastern United States, were gatherers as well as hunters and fishermen and some depended to a great extent on shell fish; their projectile points were usually fairly large notched or stemmed forms; they did not make pottery or practice agriculture. There is disagreement, however, as to whether only complexes with a polished stone technology should be referred to the Archaic Stage.

Alex D. Krieger (1953) applies the term Archaic only to pre-ceramic complexes which contain polished stone implements (polished or smoothed by intention, not by use). Gordon Willey and Philip Phillips (1955) define the Archaic Stage as one marked by the addition of grinding and polishing techniques, but they designate as Archaic certain complexes in which no ground or polished stone tools were represented. James B. Griffin (1952) uses the name Archaic for all pre-ceramic complexes in the eastern United States which are not referred to the Paleo-Indian stage. He recognizes an Early and a Late Archaic. The latter is characterized by the presence of polished stone implements, the former is not. In this publication the term Archaic will be used to refer to certain complexes that do not contain polished stone tools as well as to some that do.

Admittedly, the limits that have been set for the material to be discussed here are arbitrary and the inclusion of some Archaic sites and the exclusion of others may be questioned. However, limitations of space make it impractical to include a detailed summary of the Archaic Stage in this volume and, in any case, the writer does not feel qualified to provide such a synthesis. Some archaeologist who has first-hand knowledge of Archaic sites and materials and a full control of the literature could make a very valuable contribution by publishing a comparable summary of this stage.

Although every effort has been made to avoid the use of unfamiliar terms, this has not always been possible. A glossary of technical terms will be found in the back of the book. Numbers in parentheses after a writer's name refer to a publication listed under that name and date in the bibliography.

Chapter II

THE PLEISTOCENE AND RECENT EPOCHS

The period which is of interest to archaeologists covers the time from the present to the beginning of the Pleistocene, the latest of the great geological epochs, which probably began about one million years ago. Certain geologists place the end of the Pleistocene at about 7,000 or 10,000 years ago; others feel that it is still in progress.

The Pleistocene is also sometimes referred to as the Glacial Age or the Ice Age, for the earth experienced periods of intense refrigeration. There were times when nearly one-sixth of existing land was covered by ice sheets. Periods during which large areas were covered with ice are called glacial ages. Between these periods were warmer intervals when the ice retreated. These are called interglacial ages. During the last glacial stage, periods of somewhat ameliorated climate caused some recession of the ice. The frigid periods within a glacial age are called glacial subages; the warmer periods are known as interglacial subages or as interstadials. Not all areas were covered with ice during the glacial ages, but even in ice-free areas there was often an increase in precipitation, and evaporation was reduced. These times of wetter climate, known as pluvial periods, caused the formation or enlargement of lakes in some places, such as enclosed basins. In the intervening periods when there was less moisture, the lakes became smaller or disappeared altogether.

The question arises as to how geologists have been able to learn what was happening many thousands of years ago. In part, they are able to do so because deposits were formed and changes were made in the earth's surface as a result of glacial and pluvial action, and these can be interpreted by those trained to do so.

Studies of existing glaciers have brought knowledge of the deposits they leave and the changes they make in the landscape. When similar phenomena are observed in areas where there are no glaciers, it must be assumed that they existed at some time in the past. A glacier, which is a flowing mass of ice, carries great quantities of rock and earth. As it passes over bedrock it leaves polished and scoured areas. When the ice melts, the glacier's load is deposited. The rock material transported, deposited, or otherwise related to glaciers is known as drift. Sometimes erratic boulders may be deposited. These are large stones of non-local material that were carried far from their source. They may weigh in excess of 10,000 tons and could have been carried only by moving masses of ice. Around the margins of glaciers are ridges and embankments of earth and stones deposited and deformed through the thrust of glacial ice. These are called moraines.

In glaciated areas the weight of the ice may warp and deform the earth's crust. More widespread effects resulted in Pleistocene times from the fact that glaciations removed a great deal of water from the sea, and in some areas the sea bottom rose to some extent. Thus, coastal areas were extended, and in places where the sea is not very deep, such as Bering Strait, a land bridge was formed.

The melt water from glaciers also produced certain recognizable phenomena. These include terraces, bench-like features bordering a stream valley, that are remnants of former valley floors now dissected by the stream. During the glacial cycles of the Pleistocene there were times when streams carried great loads of debris, and as a result, they aggraded or deposited. There were other times when the load was decreased and the streams began to cut into the valley floors which they had built, thus forming terraces. Normally, each glacial stage will be represented by a terrace. Along some streams terraces occur in a step-like formation, the highest being the oldest.

Glacial melt water was sometimes impounded, and this resulted in the formation of lakes in which silts and clays were deposited. During the summer a coarse layer was deposited on the lake floor; and in the winter, when the water was less disturbed, a finer layer was put down. These paired laminations which formed each year are known as varves. Other lakes were formed in non-glaciated regions. Old beach levels, which indicate the former presence of great lakes, are found in areas now containing little water. It must be assumed that there were times when precipitation was far greater. Pluvial periods are often correlated with times of glaciation, for both lakes and ice sheets required a great deal of moisture in order to form. Cooler conditions also tended to reduce the rate of evaporation.

In glaciated regions and those adjoining them, the wind may also produce certain deposits. For example, there are beds of very fine buff-colored material, called loess. This is thought to have been taken by the wind from outwash plains, or from ground surfaces unprotected by vegetation, and deposited elsewhere. Massive beds of loess, sometimes reaching a thickness of more than 100 feet, are found in Nebraska. They are believed to indicate somewhat moister and cooler conditions in the past (Leonard and Frye, 1954).

Periods in which there is an increase of warmth and aridity also leave certain geologic evidence. In the upper reaches of streams deep channels, known as arroyos, may be cut, while farther downstream there may be filling of old channels. There is much wind erosion, and dune fields may be formed. Lakes fall to lower levels, forming new beach lines. Incrustations of calcium carbonate, called caliche, may form.

Although geologic data are the most important for interpreting the past, geology is by no means the only science that provides information as to the conditions that formerly prevailed. Studies of animal life, both vertebrate and invertebrate, and of plants, can be extremely useful, for some species can live only under certain climatic conditions. Bones and shells can indicate the type of climate that prevailed when the deposits in which they occur were being formed. Plant fragments, pollen grains preserved in peat deposits, and diatoms (microscopic plants with silicious skeletons) can be similarly utilized in studying climates of the past.

Evidence derived from various lines of inquiry has shown that during the Pleistocene there were four great glaciations in Europe and North America. They are believed to have occurred at essentially the same time in both continents. North American glacial stages have been named the Nebraskan, Kansan, Illinoian, and Wisconsin. It is only the fourth that need be considered in any detail here. During the Wisconsin, glaciers that originated from centers in Canada coalesced and spread southward across the Great Lakes into the upper Mississippi Valley. Another large ice sheet extended southward into the Pacific Northwest. In mountainous areas there were separate glacial masses. Evidence of pluvial periods has been found in the Southwest, the Texas High Plains, the Great Basin, California, and Mexico. Cold periods appear to have been dry in Nebraska. In Alaska, owing to low precipitation, only the mountainous parts were glaciated.

Geologists have usually divided the Wisconsin into four glacial substages: Iowan, Tazewell, Cary, and Mankato. Some geologists now prefer the term Valders for the last of these (Wright and Rubin, 1956). The term Mankato, which will be used here, is entrenched in geological and archaeological literature, but in later publications there will probably be an increased use of the name Valders. A post-Mankato ice advance, called the Cochrane, has been recognized, but it has been generally regarded as of less importance than the earlier ones. However,

Thor N. V. Karlstrom (1956), who has made an intensive study of the problem, believes that it is comparable to the earlier substage events of the Wisconsin and should be given equal rank within the standard Pleistocene chronology.

In the Great Basin, according to most geological literature, two main pluvial periods of Wisconsin age have been recognized. One, called the Bonneville, has been thought to correlate with the Iowan substage; the other, known as the Provo, has been regarded as correlative with the Mankato or with both Cary and Mankato. Recent Carbon 14 dates from the Lahonton and Bonneville Basins, however, suggest that the geologic history of these areas is far more complicated than has been realized and many believe that all previous interpretations may be incorrect.

After the ice had retreated for the last time, there was a relatively cool, moist period that became progressively warmer and was followed by a hot period. This in turn was succeeded by a period during which warmth decreased and moisture increased to some extent, resulting in climatic conditions such as we know today.

The period from the last retreat of the ice to the present has been called by a variety of names. The terms Post-Glacial and Post-Pluvial are sometimes used, but they are only locally applicable. Much confusion arises because of disagreement as to the time when the Pleistocene ended and the Recent began. R. F. Flint (1947) applies the term Pleistocene to all the time from the beginning of the epoch to the present, and uses the terms Post-Glacial and Post-Pluvial only for geographically limited areas. Ernst Antevs also extends the term Pleistocene to include the present, but designates as the Neothermal the relatively warm age that he believes began some 9,000 or 10,000 years ago (Antevs, 1948). He divides the Neothermal into three subperiods: the Anathermal, which was originally cool and moist but became warmer; the warm Altithermal, which was exceptionally dry in much of the western United States; and the Medithermal, the relatively cool, moist period which is still in progress.

C. B. Hunt (1953) bases his subdivision of the Pleistocene and Recent on a stratigraphic break in the western United States indicative of increased aridity that resulted in the desiccation of lakes, the disappearance of mountain glaciers, arroyo cutting, the formation of sand dunes, and the disappearance of certain Pleistocene mammals, particularly mammoth and camel. According to his definition, the Anathermal period would be regarded as part of the Pleistocene; the Altithermal and the Medithermal, which are characterized by modern fauna, would be assigned to the Recent. Krieger (1951a) and Sellards (1952) have made similar proposals.

Many theories have been advanced regarding the causes of the climatic fluctuations which occurred during the Pleistocene. Most of these need not be discussed here, for they have no direct bearing on problems pertaining to the coming of man to the New World. Those who are interested in the problem will find summaries of the principal hypotheses in Flint, 1947, pp. 501-520 and Martinez del Rio, 1952b, pp. 41-44. One recently developed theory, however, merits consideration here because of certain implications regarding conditions in the Arctic that would have affected human movements.

Utilizing data derived from radiochemical analyses of deep sea cores, Maurice Ewing and William L. Donn (1956) have come to the conclusion that there were fairly abrupt alternations between warm and cold conditions of the upper layer of the Atlantic and Arctic Oceans, and these regulated the climate of the land and produced the alternating warm and cold stages of the Pleistocene. They suggest that as an Arctic ice sheet melted there would be an increased interchange of water between the Atlantic and Arctic Oceans; the former would become cooler and the latter warmer and ice free. These changes would result in increased precipitation and changes in atmospheric circulation that would favor the growth of continental ice sheets. As these grew, sea level would be lowered, the interchange of water between the oceans would decrease, and conditions would be reversed. Arctic surface temperatures then would be reduced and freezing would occur, and continental glaciers would cease developing. As the latter waned there would be a rise in sea level, the Arctic ice would melt, and the cycle would be complete. According to this theory the Arctic Ocean was ice-free during periods of widespread continental glaciation, and at such times men could have lived along its margins. Some 11,000 years ago, at the close of the Wisconsin, however, conditions would have become unfavorable.

Chapter III

METHODS OF DATING

Knowledge of past climatic conditions is of great importance to archaeologists, but they are also much concerned with problems of chronology. Archaeologists keep hoping for an alchemist's stone that will unfailingly transform the base metal of the raw archaeological data into the gold of an exact correlation with the calendar; but these hopes have not been fully realized. They probably never will be; but new techniques will continue to be developed that will aid in answering the ubiquitous question, "How old is it?".

It is necessary to differentiate between relative and absolute dating. The former gives the age of certain objects or deposits in terms of whether they are older or younger or of the same age as other objects or deposits, but it does not provide dates in terms of years as does the latter. For relative dating, the principle of stratification is of the most widespread importance. In any undisturbed deposit, the lowest layer or stratum will be the oldest because it was laid down first; the overlying strata will be progressively younger as they approach the surface. If there are three layers, A the lowest, B the middle, and C the highest, we know that A is older than B and C, and that B is younger than A but older than C; but this does not give us the chronological age of any of these layers or the objects which they contain. However, if one of the layers can be dated, perhaps through correlation with some geological event or the finding of some object of known age, it may be possible to establish certain minimal and maximal dates for the deposits above and below. It must be noted, however, that for an object to be of the same age as the deposit in which it is found, it must be a primary inclusion. Streams, for example, may carry many things of widely differing age and deposit them together. Burial by human agency, or churning of material through the activities of burrowing animals, may also place fossils or artifacts in deposits of another age.

In addition to seeking to determine the relative ages of strata that contain objects of archaeological interest, it is sometimes possible to determine the relative ages of the objects themselves. The method for testing the fluorine content of bones, which has aroused so much interest in connection with the uncovering of the Piltdown hoax, is a case in point (Weiner, Oakley, and Clark, 1953). Buried bones receive free fluorine ions from the ground water. The fluorine combines with hydroapatite, which is present in all bones, and forms a mineral called fluorapatite. The older the bone, the more fluorapatite will be present. Unfortunately, some ground waters contain more fluorine than others; therefore, bones from different locations, or from different depths, cannot be compared. It is possible to determine the relative ages of bones only if they have come in contact with the same ground water. No exact dates can be obtained through the use of this method (Heizer, 1952). However, if human bones are shown to be of the same age as bones of extinct animals, some antiquity is indicated. The difficulty here is that the exact time when certain animals became extinct is not known. Few, if any, extinct Pleistocene forms, however, are thought to have survived the beginning of the warm period known as the Altithermal in America and the Climatic Optimum in Europe. This period began about 7,000 years ago. For such finds it is usually safe to assume an antiquity of more than 7,000 years; but this is entirely a minimal date, for some forms may have become extinct at an earlier date.

Efforts are being made to develop other chemical tests for bone which will be of value. Tests have been made to determine the water, carbon, nitrogen, calcium, and phosphorus content. S. F. Cook and R. F. Heizer have been studying chemical alteration in bones from archaeological sites in California, in the hope of discovering some chemical change that takes place in the course of fossilization which proceeds at a contant rate and is independent of external factors. They have learned that there is a progressive loss of organic matter, but, unfortunately, it does not appear to be independent of external conditions (Cook and Heizer, 1953 a and b).

In trying to assign absolute dates to the various periods of the Pleistocene and Recent, geologists have used a variety of techniques, but none has been developed which we can be sure is absolutely accurate. Many of the dates given are essentially estimates based on shrewd guesses, and they do little but express the general magnitude of the time involved. Even the newest and most promising technique, radiocarbon dating, may not be accurate in all cases, even within the range of specified probable error.

Many estimates have been based on what are believed to be rates of natural processes, but in most cases there are too many variable factors for them to be very satisfactory. Among the most commonly used are rates of erosion, particularly in the cutting of gorges and the reduction of drift sheets; the depths of leaching of sediments; and the rate of radioactive decay. An effort has also been made to utilize astronomical data, since glaciations, according to one theory, may have been caused by variation in solar radiation resulting from periodic changes in relationship between earth and sun.

Geological studies have proved very valuable. In general, the procedure of dating archaeological finds through geological studies includes the four main steps outlined by Ernst Antevs: "(1) study of beds and geological features, (2) climatic interpretation of beds and features, (3) assignment of the bed with the human record to a particular regional climatic age or phase, (4) correlation of the regional relative chronology with a dated climatic history." (Antevs, 1955a, p. 317). Most geologists believe that, since minor fluctuations within historic times were contemporaneous in both the Eastern and Western Hemispheres, earlier ones were, too; and that periods of glaciation were world-wide and approximately synchronous. Accordingly, dates obtained from studies in Europe have often been applied to American phenomena.

As might be expected, the farther back one goes in time, the scantier will be the evidence, and the more difficult it will be to determine the number of years that have elapsed. It is only natural that much attention has been devoted to the dating of post-glacial phenomena. Among the useful geochronological methods which have been developed is one introduced by Gerard De Geer. This involves the measuring of the paired laminations, known as varves, which formed in lakes in front of retreating glaciers. Since each varve represents one year, a count of these makes it possible to determine the number of years required to deposit any one body of laminated beds. Furthermore, if individual varves or distinctive patterns of relatively thick and thin varves can be recognized in two or more locations, correlation of deposits becomes possible and the chronology can be extended. The finding of pollen grains imbedded in dated varve sediments has made it possible to date levels in bogs that contain similar pollens and to determine periods of temperature change on the basis of the type of flora represented.

Unfortunately, personal judgment plays a large part in evaluating varves and making correlations. Also, ice fronts did not always lay down varves in the course of their retreat, because of lack of lakes, and there are certain gaps in the record that can be filled only by estimates. However, well-trained and experienced geochronologists develop great skill in measuring varves; and when sufficient caution is used in making correlations and interpolating dates, the method has real value.

A method for determining the age of organic matter by measuring the Carbon 14 content has been developed by W. F. Libby and his co-workers at the University of Chicago (Libby, 1955). It is based on the belief that the percentage of Carbon 14 is the same in all living organisms and that, after death, the radioactive carbon decays at a constant rate. The most recent attempts to establish a chronology for the Pleistocene and early Recent, and to date materials attributed to the very early inhabitants of this continent, have employed this radiocarbon dating technique. A brief explanation of the method follows.

Carbon 14 is produced by the action of cosmic rays on nitrogen. An equilibrium concentration is maintained in the atmosphere. Living organisms are similarly in equilibrium, because they constantly exchange carbon with the atmosphere. When they die they cease to receive Carbon 14, and that which they already possess disintegrates at a constant rate. If the rate of loss of Carbon 14 is known, it is theoretically possible to determine, through measurement of radioactivity, how much loss has occurred in the case of a given organic sample and, as a result, to compute the number of years that have elapsed since death occurred.

Various experiments have shown that half of the Carbon 14 atoms present in the organism at the time of death will have disintegrated after 5,568 ± 30 years. This period is called the half life of Carbon 14. In the course of the next 5,568-odd years, half of the remaining Carbon 14 will disappear and only a quarter of the original quantity will remain. The quantity will continue to be reduced by half during each succeeding half life.

The basic step in radiocarbon dating is to reduce the material to be dated to pure elemental carbon or a pure compound of carbon. Next, it is necessary to determine what percentage of carbon is Carbon 14. When the quantity of Carbon 14 has been reduced beyond a certain point, it is not possible to determine the exact amount which remains. Using the first technique that was employed, the solid carbon counting method, it was impossible to date samples that were much more than 20,000 years old. New techniques utilizing various gasses and liquids have made it possible to date samples more than 30,000 years old, and the dating of 50,000 year old samples is now believed possible. The use of gas also permits the use of smaller samples.

Obtaining the necessary samples presents certain problems. Suitable organic material is not present in all sites, and it does not always occur in sufficient quantities. Wood, either unburned or in the form of charcoal, and other plant remains are among the most desirable materials. Well-preserved shell can also be used. Bone, unfortunately, is not always datable, for the organic portion sometimes leaches out. Any material tested is, of course, destroyed in the process of reducing it to carbon, and archaeologists are reluctant to sacrifice key specimens, although the advantages of direct dating are great.

Further problems arise from the possibilities of contamination. If younger organic materials are incorporated in the sample, the dates obtained will be too recent. Contamination may occur in a number of ways. Fresh organic material may be introduced into material, while it is still in the ground, through root penetration, micro-organisms, fungal action, or the activity of burrowing animals. The intrusion of younger roots in the sample is particularly serious. In some cases they can be seen and removed with tweezers, but sometimes they become pulverized and, therefore, unrecognizable. Some errors may occur through the addition of dead carbon or inorganic carbonates, or through the exchange of Carbon 14 for Carbon 12. This will make the dates too old.

There is also danger of contamination after excavation. There have been times when laboratories using the solid carbon method have had to interrupt their activities because of the "fall out" of radioactive material following explosions set off in the course of testing fissionable materials many thousands of miles away. The use of gas counters has done much to minimize these difficulties in the laboratory, but stored samples, unless they are properly protected, may be exposed to various airborne contaminants. Some incorrect dates may be due to the attribution of material to the wrong geological or archaeological context.

Certain statistical problems must also be considered. The disintegrations of atomic nuclei are random events, and random errors are inherent in the process of measurement. Accordingly, it is necessary to obtain some quantitative measure of the degree of the error. This has been done by employing the formula for the standard deviation which is expressed in terms of a figure, preceded by a plus-or-minus sign, which follows the date obtained, as, for example, 2,000 $\pm$ 200 years. This means that sixty-eight percent of the time the correct date should fall in a 400-year span extending from 1,800 to 2,200 years ago. Thirty-two percent of the time, however, the correct date may be expected to fall outside of that range. This has serious implications for archaeologists who are, of necessity, concerned with a relatively short span of time; for in some cases a date may be off by as much as a thousand years (Driver, 1953).

Promising as this method is, and it is undoubtedly one of the most sensational developments in the field of chronology, it must be realized that not all Carbon 14 dates can be accepted as absolutely accurate. The method itself is sound, but various factors may produce erroneous dates. The fact that certain crucial dates obtained by the radiocarbon method are at variance with estimates obtained by other methods causes some difficulties. Also, certain dates are mutually inconsistent. However, with an increasing number of laboratories in operation, samples from important sites or localities can be submitted to more than one laboratory, which will help to eliminate the possibility of certain errors and insure greater accuracy. Also, experiments are now being undertaken that involve other radioisotopes. This may lead to a new method of dating that will provide a means of checking the accuracy of Carbon 14 dates.

One of the most important dates is for the Mankato substage. In Wisconsin is found an ancient spruce bog, known as the Two Creeks Forest Bed, which underlies the Mankato drift and which is believed to have formed very shortly before the last major ice advance. Five samples collected from this deposit, when assayed at the University of Chicago Laboratory, produced an average date of 11,404 ± 350 years ago (Libby, 1955). These and five other samples of comparable age, submitted to other laboratories, averaged 11,200 years ago (Suess, 1956).

Almost all geologists now believe that the Wisconsin lasted for a much shorter time than was previously estimated; they correlate the Two Creeks Forest Bed with the Alleröd period and the Mankato with the Fennoscandian substage in Europe. They are entirely willing to accept an age for the Mankato substage that is approximately half of that previously estimated (Flint, 1956; Horberg, 1955; Karlstrom, 1956). Radiochemical analyses of deep sea cores to determine past variations of ocean temperature provide support for the shortened chronology.

There are a few geologists who do not agree. Ernst Antevs, who has developed a varve chronology for the northeastern United States and who has worked intensively in the west, is convinced that the radiocarbon dates for the Two Creeks Forest Bed cannot be correct and that the Mankato maximum occurred some 18,500 years or more ago (Antevs, 1954b, 1955b).* This is a reduction from his previous

estimate of 25,000 years ago. Although there are some gaps in the varve records, Antevs feels that the estimates are low rather than high. He correlates the Cochrane with an ice advance in Europe which began some 11,000 years ago. Others would correlate this European advance with the Mankato.

Some radiocarbon dates indicate that the Cochrane must be more than 6,380 ± 350 years old. Thor N. V. Karlstrom and Meyer Rubin (1955) postulate that this glacial advance occurred between 9,000 and 6,500 years ago. George Quimby (1954a) originally equated the Cochrane with the Nipissing Stage of the Great Lakes and assigned to it a date between 3,000 and 4,000 years ago. He now has revised his opinion and accepts the dates of Karlstrom and Rubin (Quimby, Personal communication).

Antevs believes that some of the discrepancies between the Carbon 14 dates and those obtained through geochronological studies may be due to the fact that the former were obtained from material that had decayed under wet conditions and this would cause a change in the proportions of the radioactive Carbon 14 atoms and the normal stable carbon atoms. Charles B. Hunt (1955), who has undertaken extensive stratigraphic studies in the western United States, has come to essentially the same conclusion. He accepts a date of roughly 20,000 years ago for the Mankato.

Hunt points out that dates for samples from dry environments, such as arid regions and caves, sometimes conflict with those from wet environments. Both cannot be right. The accuracy of the former has been substantiated by written records in the case of Egyptian specimens, and by tree-ring dating in the case of material from the southwestern United States; but there is no proof of the accuracy of the latter. He believes that dates from humid deposits will be too young because fresh organic residues are incorporated in the samples through the activities of micro-organisms and through exposure to soil solutions that contain fresh Carbon 14. He also suggests that temperatures may be a conditioning factor. At lower temperatures the rate of

---

*Antevs has recently discussed this matter at greater length. See Antevs 1957.

decomposition of materials which may produce contamination is less than at high temperatures.

There has been fairly general agreement regarding the ages of the later Neothermal subdivisions. The Altithermal period, which is sometimes called the Thermal Maximum, or the Long Drought in the western United States and the Climatic Optimum in Europe, is thought to have begun some 7,000 to 7,500 years ago. It ended when the cooler Medithermal age, which is still in progress, began about 4,000 years ago.

Chapter IV

STONE INDUSTRIES

INTRODUCTION

In recent years there has been increasing evidence that, during the Paleo-Indian period, the people who lived on the eastern side of the Rocky Mountains and those who lived on the western side had somewhat different ways of life and produced different types of tools. In some areas, particularly in the Southwest, both ways of life were represented; but in general, we may recognize two different traditions —the Paleo-eastern, which emphasized big game hunting, and the Paleo-western, which placed a greater emphasis on food gathering (Quimby, 1954a). Projectile points, generally more or less lanceolate in outline, and usually finely flaked by pressure, characterized the former. Most tools were made from flakes. In the latter, projectile points were sometimes less important and were often stemmed or notched. Some flaked implements were crescentic in outline. Choppers, keeled scrapers, and grinding stones were characteristic tools. Cores were more commonly used. There was extensive use of percussion flaking. Not all of these traits characterize any one assemblage.

The term "Desert Culture" has been applied to manifestations of this tradition in the Great Basin (Jennings and Norbeck, 1955). Since the Southwest Seminar, sponsored by the Carnegie Corporation, was held in 1955 (Jennings, Editor, 1956) there has been an increasing tendency to use the term to refer to similar manifestations in an area extending from Oregon to the Valley of Mexico and from the Pacific Coast to the eastern foothills of the Rocky Mountains.

In Alaska and northern Canada there is a third tradition which may be designated the Paleo-northern. This is characterized by specially prepared cores, the prismatic flakes struck from them, small tools made from these flakes, and sometimes by a special type of grooving implement called a burin. This tradition did not begin so early as the other two, but it is the earliest known in the north. It shows cultural links with the Eskimo rather than with the American Indians.

FIG. 3—First fragmentary Folsom point found associated with bones of extinct bison, Folsom, New Mexico.

THE PALEO-EASTERN TRADITION

The Paleo-eastern tradition will be considered first because we have more information regarding it. The first complex of this tradition to be discussed will be the Folsom. This is not because it is the oldest, for it is not, but because it was the first to be recognized, it is better known, and it has become common practice to use it, in a sense, as a point of reference, thinking of other cultural manifestations as younger or older than Folsom.

THE FOLSOM COMPLEX

The First Discovery

A discovery that was to have the most far-reaching effects on the course of American archaeology was made in 1926, eight miles west of the little town of Folsom, New Mexico, on a small intermittent tributary of the Cimarron River (Cook, 1927, Figgins, 1927). Here, a party of palaeontologists from the Colorado Museum of Natural History (now known as the Denver Museum of Natural History) were excavating the bones of a type of fossil bison believed to have been extinct for thousands of years. These bones lay under clay and gravel varying in depth from four to thirteen feet. In the course of the excavations two pieces of chipped flint were found in the loose dirt of the diggings. Later, a third piece was uncovered, but this fragment was found still in position, imbedded in the clay surrounding a rib of one of the animals. The whole block of matrix, containing the bone and the flint, was shipped back to the laboratory and cleaned. It then became apparent that one of the fragments previously found fitted the piece of worked stone imbedded in the clay, and that the two pieces combined to form a readily distinguishable part of a projectile point. (Fig. 3)

The discovery of man-made objects in clear association with the articulated bones of long extinct animals, in an apparently undisturbed deposit which some geologists thought to be of Pleistocene age, was, of course, of the utmost importance, for it suggested a far greater antiquity for man in North America than had previously been believed possible. During the following winter, J. D. Figgins, who was then Director of the Museum, sought unsuccessfully to convince archaeologists of the validity of this association. Most of the scientists, however, inclined to the belief that, in spite of the appearance of clear association, there had been some mixing of the material and that the flaked stones were of a later date and were intrusive.

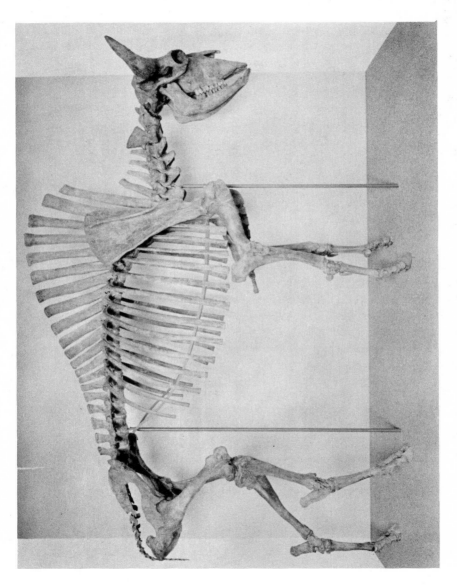

FIG. 4—Extinct Bison from the Folsom Type Station.

Still convinced of the authenticity of the association, Figgins ordered the excavation continued during the next field season. Four broken points were uncovered, but they were loosened from the matrix before their relationship with the bones could be determined. Finally a fifth point was found, still imbedded in the matrix. (Fig. 1) Immediately, all work was stopped, and telegrams were sent to leading institutions requesting that they send representatives to examine the new find. Barnum Brown, of the American Museum of Natural History, and Frank H. H. Roberts, Jr., of the Smithsonian Institution, responded and viewed the point *in situ*. Two days later A. V. Kidder, of Phillips Academy, Andover, arrived to examine the site. These three competent scientists accepted the authenticity of the association; but even after the facts had been made known, there was still a great deal of skepticism among their colleagues.

The following year a third expedition was sent to the Folsom Site. This was a joint expedition of the Colorado Museum of Natural History and the American Museum of Natural History. Again, points flaked by man were found with the bones of extinct bison. Again, telegrams were sent announcing the discovery, and this time numerous other specialists came to view the find. At last the evidence was considered conclusive. It was generally admitted that there could be no further doubt that the men who had flaked the weapon points were contemporaries of the extinct bison which, according to Harold J. Cook who published the first geological interpretation, were possibly of Pleistocene age. Thus, only a relatively short time ago, came the first widespread acceptance of the fact that man in America might lay claim to at least respectable antiquity.

In the three seasons of excavation, nineteen projectile points, all of the same distinctive type, were obtained from the Folsom quarry. Following the accepted rule of naming an artifact type after the type station, that is, the first site or station in which it was discovered, J. D. Figgins, who first described the finds, assigned the name Folsom to the new points. Associated with these artifacts were the bones of twenty-three large wide-horned bison of an extinct subspecies. The name *Bison taylori* was first assigned to this subspecies, and it will be found in much of the literature. On the basis of later studies, however, Morris F. Skinner and Ove C. Kaisen (1947) have shown that the name should be *Bison antiquus figginsi*. An interesting feature of these skeletal remains was the absence of the tail bones of most of the animals. This suggests that the animals had been skinned, for,

FIG. 5—Fragmentary Folsom Point with associated bison bones, Folsom, New Mexico.

as Barnum Brown has pointed out, in skinning, the tail goes with the hide.

Folsom points differ radically from most modern types found in America and show no close similarities to projectile points found in the Old World. They are pressure flaked and of excellent workmanship. They have an average length of about two inches, are thin, more or less leaf-shaped, with concave bases, usually marked by ear-like projections. There is frequently a small central nipple in the basal concavity. The lower edges and base normally bear evidence of grinding. The most important characteristic, however, which usually distinguishes the Folsom is the removal of a longitudinal flake from each face. This produces a fluted point with grooves or channels extending from one-third to almost the entire length of the point. Most Folsoms have a hollow-ground appearance when viewed in cross-section. Rare examples, including one from the type station, have been found with only one grooved face, and there are some points of the same shape as Folsoms that are ungrooved.

FIG. 6—Fragmentary Folsom point from the type station, fluted one face only.

FIG. 7—Folsom point and fragments from the Type Station, Folsom, New Mexico.

Many explanations have been advanced for the grooving of Folsoms, but none of them can be proved. The three theories that have been most often advanced are: (1) the grooves were designed to lighten the point so that it would carry farther; (2) they were made to facilitate hafting; (3) they were designed on the same principle as the bayonet, which permits a greater flow of blood from a wound than would an ungrooved blade. One might also consider the possibility that the grooving of projectile points was not functional and that it represents no more than a fashion. We do know that many people expended far more trouble on the production of certain stone artifacts than was necessary to make them effective.

The term point, which may refer to all types of projectile tips, is used rather than the term arrowhead, for it is believed that the earliest men used spears or atlatls (dart or javelin throwers) rather than bows. It is the general opinion that the bow was not introduced until a much later period.

Distribution and Origin of Folsom Points

Since the original discovery, Folsoms have been found in a great many other locations, often as surface finds where wind and water have eroded away the overlying material, or more rarely in excavated sites where further associations with the bones of extinct bison occurred. They have never been found with a still existing faunal assemblage. The greatest number of the classical type of Folsom, as exemplified by the artifacts from the type station, have been found in the area known as the High Plains, which extends along the eastern slope of the Rocky Mountains. Elsewhere finds have been much less frequent. A few are in collections from southern Alberta and Saskatchewan. Some examples have been found as far south as Uvalde County, Texas (Sellards, 1952).

A number of surface finds of Folsoms have been reported from the western slope of the Rocky Mountains. The late Clarence T. Hurst (1943) reported an interesting one in the San Luis Valley, in south central Colorado, which he called the Linger Site. In an old blow-out, fourteen Folsom points and fragments, blades, scrapers, two atypical points, and a channel flake were found together with the crumbled, disintegrating bones of five bison. It has been impossible to make any positive identification of these bison remains, but there is some reason to believe that they represent an extinct form, quite possibly *Bison antiquus*. A similar find was made later, about a mile away, and investigated by F. V. C. Worman (Personal Communication). This site, to which the name Zapata was assigned, is a blow-out area that yielded the remains of five animals, possibly an extinct species of bison. One complete and one fragmentary Folsom point, two scrapers, a graver, and a channel flake were associated with the bones. Hurst suggested that sites in this area were not necessarily so ancient as some other Folsom sites since the climatic conditions of late glacial times may have lasted longer in high altitudes and the fauna of the period may have survived for a longer time on the western side of the mountains.

There is reason to believe that Paleo-Indian sites may eventually be found on the Uncompahgre Plateau in west central Colorado. Two fragmentary Folsom points, one of which was apparently unfinished, were found there by Harold Huscher (1939). Both were made of quartzite which resembled local material. Julian Steward (1933) reported the discovery of a Folsom point near Grand Junction, Colorado. In Montrose County, Colorado, Albert Soderquist found the mid-section of a very finely flaked Folsom; and Orville Parson found a crudely flaked fluted point of quartzite, about two inches long.

Although true Folsom points are largely confined to the High Plains and the area immediately to the west, there are other points, to be discussed later, that possess enough characteristics in common with Folsoms to suggest a close relationship, and which are widely distributed. In earlier publications the terms "Folsom-like", "Folsomoid", and "Generalized Folsom" were commonly applied to such specimens. Following a symposium on terminology held in Santa Fe in 1941, it was decided to drop these terms and to refer to all points showing fluting or grooving on one or more faces as Fluted Points. The terms Folsom Point and Folsom Fluted Point were retained for the classic type. It was suggested that other grooved points exhibiting distinctive characteristics be given special designations, as, for example, Clovis Fluted Points.

These are also fluted points, but they are more generalized, exhibit less skilled workmanship, and are usually, although not always, larger than the true Folsoms. The grooves are generally more rudimentary and are often formed by the removal of more than one flake. The ear-like basal projections and the central nipple of the classic type are usually lacking. Some of the large fluted points, called Clovis points, have been found associated with the remains of mammoth, which would suggest great antiquity. Also, they have been found in a stratified site underlying a Folsom horizon, which shows that they are older. The true Folsom appears to be a specialization that developed from the

Clovis in the High Plains. The more generalized type, however, may have persisted for a long time in some areas, and not all specimens of this type are necessarily older, or even as old as true Folsoms.

The Lindenmeier Site

After the first discovery at Folsom, New Mexico, efforts were made to find more of the distinctive grooved points, and further examples were found in private and museum collections. Although there was evidence which indicated that the makers of these weapons had lived on this continent thousands of years ago and had hunted animals which no longer exist, we knew relatively little about these early hunters. Furthermore, it was impossible to assign even relatively definite dates to this period of occupation, for it is extremely difficult to determine when certain types of animals became extinct, and it was largely on faunal associations that a reasonable antiquity for man in the New World was postulated. The deposits at the original site did not lend themselves well to geological dating.

There was thus a great need for finding a site where the makers of Folsom points had actually lived and worked, so that we might learn more about their way of life. It was also highly desirable that Folsom artifacts be found in deposits of a type which would be favorable for geological interpretations and make possible more specific dating. Such a place was finally found in northeastern Colorado near the Wyoming State line, by Major R. G. Coffin, Judge C. C. Coffin, and his son A. L. Coffin, and was reported to the Smithsonian Institution in 1934. Here, at last, was a habitation site where it was possible for the first time to study the tools and implements which, in association with the characteristic grooved points, go to make up the Folsom Complex.

This location was named the Lindenmeier Site in honor of the owner of the land on which it was found. Excavations under the direction of Frank H. H. Roberts, Jr., were conducted from 1934 to 1938 on behalf of the Smithsonian Institution (Roberts, 1935, 1936). During the season of 1935 a party from the Denver Museum of Natural History, under the direction of John L. Cotter, joined in the investigation. Unfortunately, no physical remains which would have given information about the long sought "Folsom Man" were found, but there were further associations of man-made objects with the bones of extinct animals, notably an ancient type of big-horned bison and camel. Several thousand stone implements and a few pieces of carved bone were uncovered.

Courtesy Smithsonian Institution

FIG. 8—The Lindenmeier Site, viewed from the west.

Courtesy Smithsonian Institution

FIG. 9—Excavations at the Lindenmeier Site. Above, first excavations in the arroyo. Below, view of long trenches which led to discovery of first artifact concentration.

The site lies twenty-eight miles north of Fort Collins, Colorado, in a vestigial valley above a little stream which is an ephemeral tributary of the Cache La Poudre River. A deep arroyo or gully cuts through the terrace. Artifacts, charcoal and ash, and animal remains occurred in a dark soil zone overlain by some two to seventeen feet of alluvial material. Many specimens came from the deepest part of the site in an area believed to represent the edge of a shallow pond or marsh.

A large pile of bones, which contained the remains of nine or more bison of an extinct species, was found near the camp. It appears probable that the bison were killed there and only partially butchered. Camel bones were found with those of similar bison in other parts of the site.

The artifact assemblage includes a variety of forms. Unfortunately, only projectile points and two kinds of knives are entirely distinctive, and most of the implements, if found on the surface, could not be attributed to the Folsom Complex. Projectile points found in the lower artifact-bearing horizons were, with a few exceptions, of the Folsom Fluted type or represented points of the same shape but made from flakes too thin to have permitted the removal of channel flakes to form grooves. Although all the fluted points could be classified as true Folsoms, it is important to note that they occurred in two forms, one of which was relatively long and slender, the other relatively short and broad. These two forms, which appeared in approximately equal numbers, may have been used for hunting different types of game.

A small number of unfluted projectile points and fragments with parallel flaking occurred in the Lindenmeier Site. A few were found in a position which might indicate a late contemporaneity with Folsoms, but most of these specimens were found in a higher level, which would indicate a later survival. These points are discussed on page 126.

A great many knives were found and a variety of forms were represented, including some characterized by remarkably fine flaking and grooves. These resembled the points in many ways but the ends were blunt. It is thought that they were hafted. Certain other knives were finely chipped, but many were simply flakes with roughly formed cutting edges. The second distinctive type of knife was made by utilizing the long, thin flakes, known as channel flakes, removed in forming the grooves on points and fluted knives. These and the grooved knives are the only artifacts, besides the points, which show distinctive features.

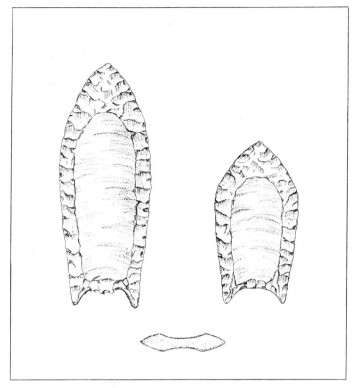

Fig. 10—Two forms of Folsom points found at the Lindenmeier Site. (After Roberts, 1935).

Scrapers were well represented in the site, and there was much variation as to form and quality of workmanship. In the greater number of cases the scraping surface was along the side, but in some it was at the end. Certain side scrapers had one concave edge. They are sometimes referred to as spokeshaves. An important category is that of the "snub-nosed scraper." These are characterized by the possession of one flat side and a thick round end, usually very carefully flaked. Minor types included small scrapers shaped like a thumbnail, and some with one convex and one flat side that are called "turtle-backs." Almost all tools and implements were made from flakes, but one core scraper was found. In addition to knives and scrapers, there were certain large leaf-shaped objects flaked on both faces, which combine the qualities of both these tools. All of these objects must have been useful in important activities such as shaping shafts for weapons, butchering animals, and preparing hides.

FIG. 11—Artifacts of the Folsom Complex from the Lindenmeier Site. Upper, Folsom point and snub-nosed scraper. Center, side scraper and knife. Lower, graver and fragmentary carved bone disc.

There were no polished stone tools and no true axes or celts, but a few choppers, usually made from cores, probably served the same purposes. Hammerstones and rubbing stones were also present. The former, which are thought to have been used for cracking bones and for knocking off large flakes, are usually unworked or only very roughly shaped. Rubbing stones did not occur in metate or mortar forms but there were small smoothed stones, often stained with red paint. Some are of unknown use, but it is thought that those marked by the pigment possibly served as implements for applying color to some material, such as hide, or as palettes. Numerous pieces of smoothed and striated hematite, which must have been an important source of pigment, are included in the collections. This material was also used for other purposes, for one hematite bead, ornamented with a simple carved design, was found. Another smaller fragmentary bead, which was undecorated, was made of lignite.

Among the most interesting flaked implements are objects sometimes referred to as gravers, although they do not resemble the European type of graver or burin. They consist of flakes or implements with minute, carefully worked points projecting from an edge. Their exact use is not known, but they could, perhaps, have been used for incising bone. A more definitely formed type, called a chisel-graver, consists of an implement or flake with a broader point which has a tip with a straight edge, markedly beveled.

The Lindenmeier Site also yielded examples of worked bone. Probably there was a greater use of this material than would be indicated by the rather small number of such objects in the collections because, through decalcification of the bones, much evidence of human workmanship was lost. The scanty evidence available shows that bone was used for the manufacture of awls, certain types of knives or fleshing implements, tubular beads, and possibly spear points. Among the most important finds of bone artifacts were three discs, two whole and one fragmentary, which were characterized by small incised lines around the edges, such as might have been produced by a graver. Since these objects were not perforated, it seems unlikely that they were ornaments, and it has been suggested that they may represent markers or counters used in some type of game.

The Making of Folsom Points

In addition to the data provided by completed artifacts, interesting information was obtained from studies of workshop debris. Since the first discovery of Folsom points, the question of how they were made and how the characteristic grooves were produced has often arisen. At the Lindenmeier Site was found workshop debris including uncompleted points, which made it possible to reconstruct the method of manufacture and to prove that, as many archaeologists had suspected, the major part of the shaping had been completed before the long spalls were removed to produce the grooves. Many long flakes, chipped on one side and smooth on the other, were found; one was uncovered which could be fitted into the groove of a certain point. This showed that the entire surface had been flaked prior to the striking off of the channel flake.

On the basis of the study of unfinished points, many of them broken in the process of manufacture, the method used, according to Roberts, was probably as follows: First, the major part of the shaping was completed, although the tip was left roughly rounded. Next, the base was prepared, leaving a hump in the center of the concavity for a striking platform. The next step was the removal of a long thin flake by percussion. The size of the platform makes it unlikely that a direct blow could have been struck, and it is probable that a bone or antler punch was used to transmit the blow indirectly. After the process had been repeated and the groove formed on the other side, the tip and edges were further shaped and sharpened by secondary chipping, using the pressure method of flaking. In a few cases it is possible that flakes which already possessed a groove on one side were utilized, but the groove on the other face appears to have been formed by the method described above. Such examples are rare.

Most Folsoms exhibit dull edges at the basal extremity and along the lower portion of the sides. This smoothing is thought to have been produced intentionally by grinding, after the completion of the point, in order to prevent the cutting of the sinew used in hafting. It is commonly found on projectile points of the Paleo-eastern tradition.

Geology of the Lindenmeier Site

Much of the importance of the Lindenmeier Site lay in the fact that its situation and the type of deposits involved were suitable for geological studies. Work undertaken by the late Kirk Bryan and Louis L. Ray (1940) indicated that the Folsom period must date from the closing phases of the Wisconsin.

In seeking to date the Lindenmeier Site the basic approach was to try to determine the relationship between the vestigial valley bottom, on which the site lay, with river terraces that could be correlated with glacial substages indicated by moraines in the mountains. Proceeding on the assumption that ice advances are essentially synchronous, the next step was to try to correlate the substages represented there with those known from other areas in North America, which had in turn been correlated with European substages dated by geochronological studies. Obviously, as Bryan and Ray freely admitted, there were many possibilities of both local and general error. Furthermore, they thought that Tazewell and Cary were regional manifestations of a single substage which they regarded as the second in the Wisconsin sequence. Geologists today believe the former was the second and the latter was the third. Bryan and Ray, however, were probably correct in concluding that the terrace which was of the same age as the Lindenmeier Valley was of Mankato age.

Since man could have occupied the Lindenmeier Site at any time after the valley floor was formed, it was desirable to determine how recently he might have done so. No evidence of Folsom man was found in the younger terrace, equated with the Cochrane ice advance by Bryan and Ray, so it was assumed that the makers of Folsom points were no longer present during the next substage. Also, there was evidence that when the Lindenmeier Valley was first formed, conditions were more favorable for man than they were later. The water table was higher and there were large swampy meadows. Such areas would attract an abundance of game, which would account for the presence of early hunters. Soon after the formation of the valley, dissection began and conditions became less swampy. This continued until a period when the grade was lowered to such an extent that springs no longer occurred. On the basis of this evidence, Bryan and Ray suggested that the Lindenmeier Site was occupied soon after the Mankato substage. They used the then accepted date of 25,000 years ago for the Mankato. The currently accepted date for this substage is about 11,000 years ago, and radiocarbon dates from a site in Texas indicate that Folsom points were being made some 9,000 or 10,000 years ago.

Other Folsom Sites in Northeastern Colorado

Near the village of Kersey, a good many classic Folsoms and snub-nosed scrapers were found in the top few feet of a sandy field (Roberts, 1937b). The deposit which originally contained the specimens was apparently destroyed by wind action. This site lay on the same terrace level as the Lindenmeier Site. It was named the Powars Site in honor of its discoverers.

Another minor Folsom site, the Johnson Site, lies near La Porte, Colorado, about fifteen miles from Lindenmeier. It was found by T. Russell Johnson and turned over to the Denver Museum of Natural History for excavation in 1936. This location was not particularly productive, but it did yield some Folsom points, scrapers, and workshop debris. Most of the artifacts duplicated the types found at Lindenmeier, but they differed in one important respect, for the predominant material was quartzite while chert and chalcedony were used most extensively at Lindenmeier. One distinctive type of scraper, not yet reported from other sites, was found. It was extremely thin, flat, and fan-shaped, and probably represents a variant of the ordinary snubnosed form.

The Lubbock Site

During 1948, 1950, and 1951, excavations were carried on by the Texas Memorial Museum in the valley of Yellow House Draw near Lubbock, Texas (Sellards, 1952). This site provides an excellent example of the problems encountered by workers in the Early Man field, for only six artifacts were found in place in the course of 529 man-days of labor. Despite the scarcity of artifacts, however, this is a most important discovery, for it is the first Folsom site to provide material suitable for radiocarbon dating. Charred bones from a diatomite stratum that contained five artifacts, four of which were Folsom points, were submitted to the University of Chicago Laboratory. They yielded a date of 9,883 ± 350 years ago (Libby, 1955). Freshwater snail shells from the same stratum, when assayed at the Lamont Laboratory, produced a date of 9,300 ± 200 years (Krieger, Editor, 1956). According to Griffin (1952b), Roberts believes that the Lindenmeier Site may be somewhat older than the Lubbock Site.

The Lipscomb Bison Quarry

Another interesting site, which was reported by C. Bertrand Schultz (1943), is the Lipscomb Bison Quarry, which lies eleven miles southwest of Lipscomb, Texas. Here were found fourteen articulated bison skeletons and nine skulls which, for the most part, are like those found at the Folsom Quarry. Eighteen artifacts were found scattered among the bones, and four were found in the quarry talus. They closely resembled those obtained at the Lindenmeier Site. They included Folsom points, scrapers, channel flakes, and utilized flakes that probably served as knives.

The MacHaffie Site

A stratified site with a Folsom component was found a few miles south of Helena, Montana (Forbis and Sperry, 1952). It was excavated under the direction of Richard G. Forbis. Three different occupation levels were recognized. The lowest contained Folsom points, the middle one yielded Scottsbluff points (discussed on page 122), and the upper level produced more recent notched points similar to those found in the second level at Signal Butte, Nebraska.

The Folsom material was found in a fine-grained, smooth-textured black soil that overlay sterile sands and was overlain by gray clay. One broken base of a Folsom point fluted on both faces, a fragment fluted on one face, and one nondescript point fragment were found. Associated with them were snub-nosed and turtle-back scrapers, bifacially flaked knives, and flakes with one or more worked edges that could have been used as knives or scrapers.

Bison bones were found in this level. The fragmentary nature of the remains and the absence of horn cores made it impossible to identify the species, but the animals appear to have been larger than modern bison. Other animal remains indicate the presence of deer, wolf, and rabbit.

Unfluted Folsom Points

As has been noted, a few Folsom points have been found that are fluted on only one side. Some sites have also yielded points that appear to be of approximately the same age and that have the same shape as classic Folsoms but are unfluted. In Ventana Cave, in southern Arizona, to be discussed in more detail on pages 177 to 180, were found deep deposits that yielded evidence of a number of complexes (Haury, 1950). The second level from the bottom, which consisted of consolidated volcanic debris, contained bones of extinct animals, some of which were split and charred, and a projectile point that closely resembled a Folsom point, but which was unfluted. It was very thin and was made of basalt, a material that does not flake easily, so it may have been impossible to flute it.

At the Scharbauer Site near Midland, Texas (discussed on pages 241 to 246), seven fluted Folsoms and twenty-one specimens that closely resembled them, but were unfluted, were found (Wendorf, Krieger, Albritton, and Stewart, 1955). They were made from materials that are easily fluted, so the type of stone used does not appear to have been a conditioning factor. The unfluted specimens, however, were extremely thin and flat, and fluting would probably not have been practical. The number of specimens recovered suggests that the thinness of the points was due to intentional preparation rather than to an accident which prevented the maker from producing a fluted point. Wendorf and Krieger were at first reluctant to give them formal status as a type, and referred to them as "unfluted Folsoms", but in a forthcoming report on more recent work at this site they will call them Midland points.

OTHER FLUTED POINTS

As has been previously mentioned, there are certain fluted points that have many of the same characteristics as the classic Folsom but which are more generalized, have less well developed grooves that were often produced by the removal of multiple flakes, generally lack the ear-like basal projections, and rarely show fine secondary chipping along the edges. They are usually, although not always, considerably larger and heavier. In the High Plains and in southern Arizona such specimens, called Clovis Fluted points, have been found associated with mammoth bones. Similar points are widely distributed over the whole of the United States, but they have not been found associated with an extinct fauna in other areas. There are certain marked areas of concentration in the eastern part of the country. Some fluted points have been found in California, in the Pacific Northwest, and in the Great Basin.

Four specimens have been reported from Mexico, and one was found in a museum collection under circumstances that suggest it could have come from Costa Rica. Some true Folsoms have been found in the collection assembled by Kenneth Jones near Mortlach, Saskatchewan, and a similar specimen was found near Cereal, Alberta, by Russell A. Johnston; but the less specialized form of fluted point, so widely distributed in the United States, appears to be lacking in the prairie lands of western Canada*. A number of fluted points closely resembling those from the eastern United States have been found in Ontario (Kidd, 1951). The majority come from the southwestern part of the Province. Five fluted points have been reported from Alaska, north of Bering Strait. One was found near the Utukok River by Raymond M. Thompson (1948), and one was found by J. L. Giddings

---

*In June 1957 a good example of a Clovis Fluted point was found sixty miles east and thirty miles north of Edmonton, Alberta. At an earlier date James MacGregor found a fluted point near Edmonton that was essentially triangular in outline. (MacGregor, Personal communication).

(1951) associated with material of the Denbigh Flint Complex which is discussed on page 208. Three were found in the Brooks Range (Solecki, 1951b). A fluted lozenge-shaped point has been reported from Labrador (Harp, 1951).

The Llano Complex

E. H. Sellards (1952) has suggested that the tools and implements, including Clovis Fluted points and some unfluted specimens, scrapers, bone implements, and hammerstones, found associated with mammoth bones in the High Plains and in southern Arizona, be recognized as a complex. He has proposed that the name Llano be assigned. This name is derived from the "Llano Estacado," the Staked Plains of Texas and New Mexico, where some of the most important sites, including the type station for Clovis points, are located. A discussion of the sites containing material attributed to this complex follows.

The Angus, Nebraska, Find

In 1931, J. D. Figgins reported that a fluted point was found in association with an articulated mammoth skeleton which was being excavated near Angus, Nebraska, under the direction of the late A. M. Brooking of the Hastings Museum (Figgins, 1931). Geologists who have examined the site, however, are convinced that the deposits in which the find was made are of mid-Pleistocene age and, since it seems impossible that such points were being made at so early a period, it appears that the association was not authentic. The point itself has always been something of an anomaly, for it is much cruder and thicker than most similar specimens, and it is possible that it was made from a piece of stone which was already grooved. It seems possible that it was a forgery, deliberately introduced into the deposits by some unknown individual. There cannot be the slightest doubt that Figgins and Brooking acted in all good faith and were honestly convinced of the authenticity of the association.

The Dent Site

The first generally accepted discovery of a fluted point unmistakably associated with articulated mammoth remains was made near Dent, Colorado, in 1932 (Figgins, 1933). Following a flood, masses of very large bones could be seen outcropping in the bank of a small gully some 500 feet south of the railroad station. Frank Garner, a section foreman for the Union Pacific Railroad, reported this to the late Father Conrad Bilgery, S. J. of Regis College. Father Bilgery investigated, found that the bones were those of mammoths, and began excavations with the aid of some of his students. He found a large point with rudimentary grooves lying under the pelvis of one of the animals (Fig. 12, No. 1).

Very generously, Father Bilgery offered the Denver Museum the privilege of continuing the excavations during the following year. The bones of a dozen mammoths were removed from the quarry. One was a large individual, presumably a male, and the others were females and immature individuals. A second point, clearly associated with articulated mammoth bones, was found (Fig. 12, No. 2). This specimen, which is more markedly fluted than the first, was noted while it was still imbedded in the matrix surrounding the bones. Still and motion pictures were taken on this occasion, and the find is among the most fully documented. It is interesting to note that a great many large stones were found with the mammoth remains, although boulders of comparable size are extremely rare elsewhere in the vicinity.

In 1955, Mr. Garner presented to the Museum a third specimen which he found in 1932 lying about one foot from the teeth of one of the mammoths (Fig. 12, No. 3). The photograph gives a false impression of a single-shouldered specimen, but examination of the artifact itself indicates that this apparent shouldering is the result of the fortui-tous removal of a large flake, and this is almost certainly the tip of a projectile point of virtually the same size and shape as the first one discovered.

Regrettably, the stratigraphy of the Dent Site has been largely if not entirely destroyed. However, in 1954, Harold E. Malde, of the U. S. Geological Survey, examined the site and talked with Mr. Garner, who had visited the quarry at the close of each day's excavations. Malde feels that the bones and artifacts were emplaced during a glacial phase, possibly the Mankato, or an early phase of glacial recessional time.

Texas Finds

Further evidence of the contemporaneity of man and mammoth was obtained at two localities in Texas that produced points of the type now designated Clovis Fluted. Near Miami, in Roberts County, three good sized fluted points and a scraper were found in a deposit

FIG. 12—Clovis Fluted points and fragment found in association with articulated mammoth remains at Dent, Colorado.

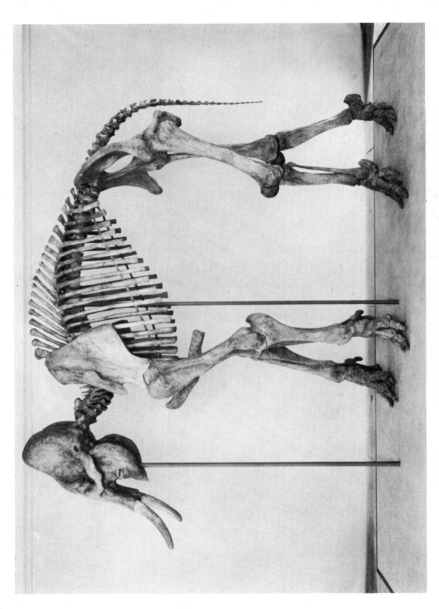

Fig. 13—Mounted skeleton of one of the Dent Site mammoths.

which contained the bones of five or more elephants (Sellards, 1938, 1952). One point lay less than three inches from a vertebra, and the scraper was found near the left humerus of an elephant. The skeletal remains and artifacts were found in a sink, thought to represent a former water hole.

At the McLean Site, thirty miles southwest of Abilene, Cyrus N. Ray and Kirk Bryan (1938) reported the finding of a similar fluted point imbedded in an alluvial deposit near the lower jaw of a mammoth. They believed that the artifact was carried by the same current that deposited the bones and the alluvial cap, which lay on bedrock.

At the Doering Site, a midden of the Archaic Stage, which lies near Houston, Joe Ben Wheat (1953) found two fragments of a Clovis Fluted point which fitted together. One lay in the midden and the other was found in the stream bed. This was probably an old point picked up and reused by the later occupants.

The Clovis Finds

One of the most important areas investigated by students of Early Man is a section between Clovis and Portales in New Mexico which contains the remains of ancient lake beds. Work has been carried on here at intervals since 1932, first by the Academy of Natural Sciences of Philadelphia and the University of Pennsylvania Museum, and later by the Texas Memorial Museum.

The section investigated lies near the Texas-New Mexico border in the flat, arid region of the old Llano Estacado or Staked Plains, a large elevated plateau. It contains over twenty dry basins hollowed out by wind action to form what are known as blow-outs. Here George O. Roberts and A. W. Anderson found bones and artifacts weathering out of some of the deposits that the wind had exposed. They brought their finds to the attention of the late Edgar B. Howard, who first examined the sites in 1932. In the same year a gravel pit was started by a road construction company, seven miles north of Portales and fourteen miles southwest of Clovis.

During 1933, Howard worked here and in Anderson Basin, a series of three erosion basins separated from each other by sand dunes (Howard, 1935 a and b). Further investigations, reported by John L. Cotter (1937a, 1938) were undertaken there and in another nearby area, known as Beck Forest Basin, during 1936 and 1937. A party from the Texas Memorial Museum, under the direction of E. H. Sellards, undertook additional excavations during 1949 and 1950 in the gravel pit, which was designated Blackwater No. 1 locality (Sellards, 1952). Geological investigations have been conducted by Chester Stock and Francis Bode (1937), Ernst Antevs (1935a, 1949), and Glen Evans (1951).

The first discoveries at Blackwater No. 1 were made by workmen who plowed up a large, extremely thin, leaf-shaped artifact and a mammoth tooth. A smaller but similar implement, and a finely flaked unfluted projectile point were found in the dumps at the pit. The first *in situ* finds in this locality were made in 1933 when three flake knives or scrapers and two snub-nosed scrapers were found in association with burned bison bones and charcoal.

Some of the most important discoveries were made in 1936 and 1937 when Cotter found artifacts in unmistakable association with mammoth remains in a sand deposit overlying bedrock gravels. Two of these were grooved points. These are the type specimens from which the name Clovis Fluted is derived (Fig. 29). One lay one inch below a mammoth vertebra and the other was found between two leg bones. The first is a little over four inches in length and the other is a little over three inches long. Both are grooved about halfway up the face. Other stone artifacts found in this horizon at this time included a smaller point which has not been illustrated, a fragmentary point or knife, a scraper, several retouched flakes, and some unworked chips.

In addition to the stone artifacts, two extremely important polished bone pieces were found *in situ*. One lay near the foreleg of one of the mammoths, the second lay near the tusk of another. These are tapering cylindrical bone shafts with a beveled end. It is interesting to note that other somewhat similar finds have been reported. In muck deposits, believed to be of Pleistocene age, near Goldstream, Alaska, were found similar bone artifacts (Rainey, 1940). Others were found in deposits at Lower Klamath Lake in northern California which also yielded remains of extinct fauna (Cressman, et al 1942). Some similar examples were recovered at the Lind Coulee Site in Washington (Daugherty, 1956a). Three other smaller specimens were found in the bed of the Itchtucknee River in north-central Florida (Jenks and Simpson, 1941). One appears to have been made of manatee bone and the other two are thought to be ivory, presumably from mammoth or mastodon. It was first thought that these specimens represented foreshafts. However, a recent discovery of this type of tool in the abdominal cavity of a skeleton suggests that they may have served as projectile points (Cressman, 1956).

In and on dumps at the Clovis gravel pit, and at the base of erosion islands, were found classic Folsoms and unfluted lanceolate points, some of which had fine parallel flaking. Since these were found in disturbed deposits, their exact position could not be determined; but there was every reason to believe they were associated with bison bones and that they came from a higher level than the larger fluted points associated with the mammoth, and, accordingly, were younger.

More clear-cut proof might have been available had it not been for a local collector who later reported finding a small true Folsom imbedded in a bison vertebra lying in position in an upper level. Instead of bringing it to the attention of a trained observer, or even removing the matrix containing the bone so that the association could be seen, he removed the vertebra and pulled the Folsom point from it. This is a perfect example of the harm that can be done by a "relic hunter" who is concerned only with adding to his collection and not with contributing to scientific knowledge. It should be noted, too, how short-sighted such a policy is. The value of any collection will be immeasurably enhanced by the addition of a well-documented specimen; but the same specimen, no matter how fine it may be, is practically valueless if it has been torn from its context without being properly studied.

During 1949 and 1950 additional artifacts were found in position by the Texas Memorial Museum party, and further stratigraphic studies were undertaken by Glen Evans (1951), who was investigating prehistoric wells in the area. Seven different strata were recognized (Sellards, 1952). The lowest deposit consisted of bedrock gravels that contained no artifacts. Above this lay a bed of speckled gray sand in which were found mammoth remains and artifacts of the Llano Complex. In this level, the same which contained the mammoth bones, Clovis points, and bone tools reported by Cotter, were found two smaller points with basal thinning but no true fluting, a hammerstone, a core, a scraper, bone tools, and split bones.

The gray sand was separated by a disconformity from a brown sand wedge which contained no artifacts. There was another disconformity and then a layer of diatomaceous earth which ranged in color from almost white to dark blue-gray. This stratum yielded twelve artifacts and the bones of hundreds of bison. The latter have not been definitely identified due to the absence of good skulls, but they are of the same size as those of the extinct species found elsewhere in association with Folsom points. No elephant or horse bones, such as were found in the underlying stratum, occurred in this horizon. Seven whole and fragmentary projectile points of Folsom shape were found. Three were fluted on both sides, one was deeply fluted on one side and imperfectly fluted on the other, one was barely fluted on both sides, one was barely fluted on one side and unfluted on the other, and one, which is of the same general shape and size, showed no evidence of fluting. The latter was made of a material that is difficult to flake.

No dates have been obtained for this horizon, but it seems probable that it may be of the same age as the similar diatomite horizon at the Lubbock Site in Texas, which yielded comparable material and has been dated at about 10,000 years ago by the radiocarbon method. The material of the Llano Complex, which lay below, is obviously older, but how much older remains a question. Antevs (1949) has suggested a maximum date of 13,000 years.

Artifacts younger than Folsom points were also found. The diatomaceous earth which contained the Folsom artifacts was separated by a disconformity from a carbonaceous silt that lay above it. The latter contained points with fine parallel flaking reminiscent of types made elsewhere in the Plains some 7,000 years or more ago. These artifacts, attributed by Sellards to a complex which he calls the Portales, are discussed on page 112. Above this stratum lay a jointed sand which contained only a few artifacts of no diagnostic value, and a sterile aeolian sand.

The presence of extensive lake and pond deposits in what is now a very dry part of the High Plains indicates the existence of a pluvial period when the climate was considerably more moist than it is today. Lower temperatures as well as greater precipitation are thought to have been necessary to form these lakes and glaciers in the mountains (Antevs, 1954b). The presence of disconformities between the various strata in the Clovis beds has presented certain problems. The first idea that comes to mind is that they represent periods of greater aridity when there was extensive wind action. Some of the upper ones undoubtedly do. Ernst Antevs (1955a) does not believe that there were dry periods during the Pluvial. He has suggested that during the wet period the depression which contained the lake at the gravel pit locality (Blackwater No. 1) was closed by an artificial dam built by men or beavers, and that three times the dam was destroyed and then rebuilt after stream erosion had occurred. This seems unlikely in view of the fact that significant faunal and artifact changes may be recognized in the strata separated by the disconformities. Furthermore, geologic studies at the Scharbauer Site in Texas, described on pages 241 to 246, suggest that periods marked by wind erosion and a major drought preceded the Altithermal. Similar conditions probably prevailed in this area which lies only about 200 miles away.

Burnet Cave

Other interesting discoveries were made by Edgar B. Howard (1935a) in a dry cave in the Guadalupe Mountains of New Mexico. This cave, which lies about thirty-two miles west of Carlsbad, was named in honor of its discoverer, R. M. Burnet. In the first three feet of deposit were found five human cremations in baskets and twined woven bags. Associated with them were atlatl fragments, sandals, cordage, and a small stemmed projectile point. There was no corn or pottery. Similar artifacts have been found in various parts of the Great Basin, the Southwest, and Mexico. Some of this material is attributed to the Christian Era, but it is thought that some may date from one or two millenia earlier.

Two and a half feet below the deepest of the cremation burials, and unassociated with artifacts of the type found in the upper level, was found a point fluted on both faces. It is somewhat smaller than most of the Clovis specimens, but in general appearance it resembles them closely and it may be placed in that category. Also below the level of the human burials were found three bone awls and some hearths containing charcoal and burned bones. There were many varieties of unburned animal bones, including some extinct forms, in the lower levels. Among them were a caribou-like animal and one that resembled a musk ox. There were also some marmot bones.

At the present time marmots are found only at higher elevations. Antevs (1954b) has suggested that, if the marmots came from within fifteen miles of the site, the period in which hunters brought them into the cave must have been one when life zones stood some 2,500 feet lower than they do today. Caribou and musk ox are now found living only in cold climates, and it is reasonable to suppose that when similar forms lived in the Guadalupes the temperature was lower than at present.

Courtesy Arizona State Museum

FIG. 14—Excavation of mammoth bones at the Naco Site, Southern Arizona. Left, John Lance. Right, Emil W. Haury.

Charcoal obtained some three feet below the level of the fluted point provided a Carbon 14 date of 7,432 ± 300 years ago (Libby, 1955). The faunal evidence seems to indicate greater age, and similar points found elsewhere in the Southwest are thought to be more than 10,000 years old. The Burnet Cave date is probably too recent.

The Naco Site

Two extremely interesting sites containing mammoth remains and projectile points have been excavated by archaeologists from the Arizona State Museum, and important geological and palaeontological studies have been undertaken (Haury, 1953). The first site lies very close to the Mexican border, eight miles southeast of Bisbee and one mile northwest of Naco, Arizona. It was discovered in 1951 by Marc and Fred Navarette, who removed two Clovis points and some mammoth bones from an arroyo bank. Instead of doing further digging, which might have destroyed important evidence, they very wisely reported their find to archaeologists at the Arizona State Museum.

Excavations were carried out in 1952 under the direction of Emil W. Haury. The excavators first removed recent surface deposits in order to determine the exact extent of the previous excavations; then they removed the overburden down to the bone layer in order to learn the extent of the bone deposit. The bones were then exposed and covered with a jacket of plaster-soaked burlap, which made it possible to remove the bones and the matrix in position and transport them to the Museum laboratory. A block one meter square, containing mammoth ribs, vertebrae, and scapula, and five projectile points, was removed intact and is now on exhibition at the Museum.

Most of the bones of a mammoth, exclusive of the hind legs, pelvic girdle, and lumbar vertebrae, were recovered. Perhaps the missing portions were carried away by the hunters, or perhaps they were moved some distance away in the butchering process and left in a section that was later eroded away. There certainly can be no doubt that this animal was hunted by man, for eight projectile points were found in unmistakable association with the bones. Another was found upstream in the arroyo.

The exact position of some of the points could not be determined, but one point lay at the base of the skull, one near the left scapula, two were wedged between ribs, and one rested against the surface of the atlas vertebra. It seems probable that it was the latter which caused the animal's death by severing the spinal column. If this

FIG. 15—Clovis Fluted points found in association with mammoth remains, Naco, Arizona.

were the case, the hunters presumably succeeded in getting their prey; it did not escape and die elsewhere from its wounds. The latter possibility has been suggested because of the apparent waste in leaving undamaged points in the carcass. No tools used in butchering were found.

The size range of the points is of particular interest. It had been generally believed that only large points were used in hunting elephants; yet, although some of the points were large, two were of the size of Folsom points, used, so far as is known, only in hunting bison and smaller game. All the points, however, could be classed as Clovis Fluteds, for they lack the specialized Folsom features. All were fluted on both faces. In some cases a single large flake had been removed, but in some instances the grooves had been formed by the removal of several smaller flakes. All had ground edges at the basal end.

The bones and points lay on top of a rust-colored pebbly sand deposited by an essentially perennial stream. They were buried by laminated beds formed in a pond. Above was a layer believed to have formed in a wet meadow. Overlying beds consisted of channel and flood plain deposits which indicate progressively more arid climatic conditions. Ernst Antevs (1953a), who studied the geology, attributes the stream and pond deposits to the last pluvial culmination in the region, which he correlates with the Cochrane ice advance, dated by him at 11,300 ± 1,150 years ago. Geologists who accept a date of about 11,000 years ago for the Mankato believe that the Cochrane was more recent, and, in view of the faunal evidence, would question this correlation. Many would, however, probably admit that Antevs' estimate of an age of between 10,000 and 11,000 years for the Naco mammoth may be somewhere near the right order of magnitude.

The Lehner Site

In his report on the Naco discovery, Haury indicated that other similar finds might be expected in the same area, and stated: "It would be folly to believe that the Naco elephant was the only such evidence." He was certainly correct, for in 1955 a second site containing mammoth remains was found (Haury, 1956). This site was on the Lehner Ranch, one and one-half miles southwest of Hereford, Arizona. Lehner had reported earlier to the Arizona State Museum that he had found fragments of mammoth bones in a black deposit eight feet below the surface, in the bank of an arroyo tributary of the San Pedro River.

In the summer of 1955, heavy rains exposed more bones in the arroyo bank, and intensive excavation was begun by archaeologists from the Arizona State Museum.

Thousands of tons of earth were removed with mechanical equipment, and a large bone bed was exposed. Among the bones, which included mammoth, tapir, extinct bison, and probably horse, were found weapons and tools left by the ancient people who had killed and butchered these animals. There were thirteen Clovis points, some of which were quite small, and eight stone tools designed for cutting and scraping. Three of the small points were made of quartz crystal. Two hearths were also found in the bone bed. They contained charcoal which provided a Carbon 14 date of about 8,500 years ago. This seems too recent. Ernst Antevs' estimate of an age of 10,000 to 15,000 years, which is based on geological evidence, is probably closer to the correct date.

Courtesy Arizona State Museum

FIG. 16—Small fluted points made of quartz crystal, found in association with mammoth remains at the Lehner Site, Arizona.

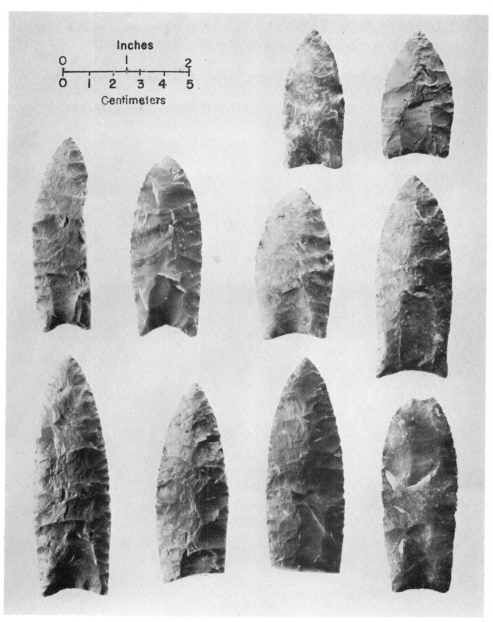

FIG. 17—Clovis points found with mammoth remains at the Lehner Site, Arizona.

The Lewisville Site

Near Lewisville in Denton County, Texas, nineteen hearths were uncovered in the course of dragline operations in a large borrow pit.* They lay in the lower portion of a geological formation, known as the Upper Shuler, which is believed to derive from the latter half of the Wisconsin. The hearths contained the remains of elephant, extinct bison, horse, and camel, various small animals such as coyote, prairie dog, and rabbit, that are still found in the area, snail and mussel shells, and hackberry seeds.

In the largest hearth, excavated by Wilson W. Crook, Jr., R. K. Harris, and members of the Dallas Archaeological Society, were found a Clovis point and a large piece of charred wood. It was believed that a radiocarbon date on the wood would date the Clovis point, and a sample was submitted to the Humble Oil Company Laboratory. When it was found that the sample was beyond the range of the laboratory technique, which would indicate an age in excess of 37,000 years ago, it seemed probable that there was some error. On the basis of other Carbon 14 dates it is believed that, even in the Old World, chipped stone projectile points were not being made at so early a date, and most archaeologists thought that Clovis points were probably less than 18,000 years old. Furthermore, if the 10,000 year date generally accepted for the Folsom Complex is correct, this would indicate that the tradition of fluting persisted for more than 27,000 years, which seems highly unlikely. However, when a second sample from another hearth was tested, it produced the same results.

Archaeologists are reluctant to accept this date for the Clovis Fluted point, and it is completely at variance with dates obtained from other sites containing this type of point. Material from Burnet Cave gave a date of 7,432 ± 300 years, and charcoal from the Lehner Site gave a date of approximately 8,500 years ago. These appear to be too low. It is difficult to explain, however, where the error may lie.

It has been suggested that the Clovis point may have been "planted" in the hearth, but archaeologists who have worked closely with the individuals involved in the excavation are completely convinced of their integrity and competence. Furthermore, Alex Krieger, who saw the hearth before it was excavated, states that there was no evidence of disturbance in the hard-packed clay surface such as

---

*Originally listed as a personal communication by Alex Krieger, but now published. See Krieger, 1957a.

would have been present had an object been intentionally introduced into the hearth. This also appears to preclude the possibility that the point reached this location through the dragline operations.

There is the possibility of a laboratory error; but this is an extremely good laboratory, and samples from two different hearths were checked. When dates are too recent, there is always the possibility of contamination by younger organic matter. Possibly there are also factors, not yet fully understood, that permit contamination or replacement by dead or inorganic carbons.

At present it is still impossible to date Clovis points accurately. It is highly unlikely that the Lewisville, Burnet Cave, and Lehner Site dates can all be right. In the opinion of the writer, it is quite probable that all three are wrong and that a date somewhere between 10,000 and 15,000 years ago would be of the right order of magnitude for the Llano Complex.

The Lake Cochise Find

Willcox Playa, which lies twenty-five miles northeast of Benson, Arizona, is a salt flat which is the remnant of pluvial Lake Cochise. In 1952 a projectile point was found in position in the lake gravels, which are thought to date back to the last pluvial (Haury, 1953). This point is crudely flaked, essentially triangular, and has some basal thinning but no true fluting. It could not be classified as a Clovis Fluted, but it is quite possibly of the same age as the Naco specimens. Grinding stones, commonly found in Cochise sites (discussed on page 169) but not reported from sites containing fluted points, were found nearby at the same depth.

Surface Finds of Fluted Points in Arizona

A number of fluted points have been found on the surface in southeastern Arizona. Marc Navarette found a Clovis point about one-quarter of a mile above the Naco Site. Sayles and Antevs (1941) reported finding a fragmentary Clovis point, apparently an intrusive artifact, in a Chiricahua Cochise site near Benson. One Clovis point was found on the surface in Texas Canyon northwest of Bisbee; and one was found in a blow-out near Willcox, on an old lake terrace that had been exposed by wind action (Di Peso, 1953). Both were grooved on two faces and exhibited basal grinding.

Fluted Points in the Great Basin

Scattered finds of fluted points in the Great Basin have been reported; but only in one location, in southeastern Nevada, have they been found in sufficient numbers and in such an association with other artifacts that a specific area could be designated as a site (Campbell and Campbell, 1940). This site lies on a sandy ridge close to the shore of an extinct lake. The lake could have existed only in a time of more moist climate than at present, but its exact age has not been determined (Antevs, 1948). It is known that hundreds of artifacts were found scattered over the surface, but, unfortunately, this site has not been fully reported upon, and only a few of the implements have been illustrated.

Most of the points are fairly small and fall into the normal size range of Folsom points. Only one of those illustrated, however, has a base like a true Folsom, and it is not fluted. Most of the others look more like Clovis Fluted points. Grooving was produced by the removal of several flakes, and the grooves do not extend very far from the base. One point is essentially pentagonal in shape, as are certain eastern specimens. The presence or absence of basal grinding is not noted. Among the associated artifacts shown in the plates are well-flaked end and side scrapers, flakes with tiny graver points, and one implement that resembles those found at the Lindenmeier Site called "chisel-gravers."

Fluted Points in the Pacific Northwest

Douglas Osborne (1956) has reported that three Clovis points have been found in the Northwest. One was found in eastern Oregon, one in the Black Hills area west of Olympia, and one on the Washington side across the Columbia River from The Dalles, Oregon. The first was of red obsidian, the other two of an obsidian verging toward a glassy basalt.

Fluted Points in California

Approximately one hundred miles northwest of Berkeley, California, at the western edge of Clear Lake, lies an old lake bed known as Borax Lake. It is dry the greater part of the year, save for a small pond of saline water, but in the winter portions of it contain some fresh water. Here Mark R. Harrington (1948c) and his associates at the Southwest Museum excavated a site in an alluvial fan. When the site was first discovered, the presence of fluted points on the surface, which

Harrington erroneously called Folsoms, suggested that the lower artifact-bearing levels represented a "Pre-Folsom" occupation. In the
course of later excavations, however, it became apparent that the situation was far more complicated than had first been thought.

Fig. 18—Fluted point from the Borax Lake Site, California.

Twenty fluted points and fragments were found. Fifteen specimens lay on the surface, and five were recovered in the course of
excavation. Of the sixteen that were sufficiently complete to be evaluated, the length varied from two and a half inches to four inches. Two
were fluted on one face only, and fourteen were fluted on both faces.
The fluting was accomplished by the removal of three or more flakes.
In a few instances the removal of a final broad flake tended to obliter-
ate the scars left by the first flutes. In many cases the channels were
not centered in the basal concavity. All lacked the characteristic
Folsom base. There was grinding along the base and lower edges.
One specimen was made of chalcedony and one of jasper; the others
were of obsidian. On seven of the latter there are what appear to be
scratches in the channel area. It was assumed that these had been
intentionally produced. A photographic enlargement of one of the
specimens, prepared by Walker Van Riper, however, revealed that
these marks were curved and that there was no superimposition of the
lines such as would be expected if some abrasive had been rubbed back
and forth over the surface. (Fig. 18.)

The site also yielded a variety of other point types. One is called Borax Lake Stemmed. This is a broad-shouldered form, sometimes barbed, with a broad, relatively long, straight stem. The blades are fairly short and may have straight or slightly convex sides. They have an average length of two inches. A percussion technique was often employed in flaking these artifacts. Bases sometimes show evidence of thinning by the removal of longitudinal flakes; they are usually square but may sometimes be concave. Some specimens exhibit basal grinding. Other interesting types include thick, narrow, unstemmed forms, usually pointed at both ends, which Harrington calls willow-leaf points, and a type with an elongated contracting stem. Some specimens resemble Silver Lake, Lake Mohave, and Pinto Basin points, which are discussed on pages 161 and 165. There were also some small triangular side-notched forms classified as arrow points. In addition, there were various associated implements including flaked crescent-shaped objects, sometimes serrated; knives, scrapers, drills, gravers, hammerstones, choppers, mortars, pestles, milling stones, manos, and charm stones.

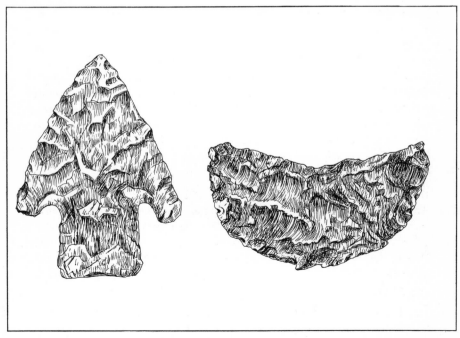

FIG. 19—Borax Lake Stemmed point and Crescentic implement from the Borax Lake Site, California.

There was no stratification to indicate a sequence of cultures, and accounting for such a heterogeneous assemblage presents very definite problems. The nature of the deposits has suggested to some that these artifacts represent mixed materials washed in from some other area. Harrington, however, felt that he had definite habitation layers indicated by charcoal and groups of stones apparently placed by man. He suggested that this was a location visited by many groups, with different types of stone industries, who were attracted to this locality by nearby obsidian quarries, and who camped on the far side at the edge of the lake where they had access to water. In an effort to postulate the order in which the different peoples might have arrived, an attempt was made to work out a possible sequence by applying statistical methods to a chart showing the depth at which various types of artifacts were found. This was not successful, however.

More recently, Clement Meighan (1955b) has suggested that some of the artifacts found here represent a single complex for which the diagnostic traits are Borax Lake Fluted points, Borax Lake Stemmed points, and chipped crescentic objects. On the basis of evidence from surface sites, he feels that this complex is widely distributed throughout the North Coast Ranges.

In the Napa Valley, Robert Heizer (1953c) found a site similar to Harrington's that produced points with basal thinning, willowleaf points, and manos. Other artifacts represented in the Borax Lake assemblage, notably stemmed and notched points, were not found here. Heizer has suggested that chronologically this site may represent a part of the time period of the Borax Lake Site. He has also pointed out that many of the artifacts found at Borax Lake closely resemble those of the Middle Horizon of the Sacramento Valley, which probably does not date back beyond 1,000 B. C.

Some geological studies have been undertaken in an effort to date the Borax Lake Site. It was first thought by Carl Sauer and Ernst Antevs that the alluvial fan in which the artifacts occur must have been formed in a period when precipitation was heavier than it is at present. It was assumed that it must have been laid down during the Provo Pluvial, which was thought to have ended some 10,000 years ago, and, accordingly, the age of the artifacts was believed to be in excess of 10,000 years.

In the light of the more recent studies, however, Antevs (1952) has decided that the fan was not built up during a period of increased precipitation. He now thinks that such deposits would be formed, not during a rainy period when there would be a dense growth of vegetation that would check erosion and therefore prevent fan building, but rather during a dry age in which vegetation was reduced because of lack of moisture. Due to the scantiness of the plant cover there would be a rapid run-off of such rains as did occur. On this basis he places the formation of the Borax Lake fan in the dry age, known as the Altithermal, which dates at about 7,000 to 4,000 years ago.

As yet, fluted points have been found in California only on the surface or in sites where the stratigraphy was far from clear. Evidence from other sites, where sound stratigraphic studies can be made, is needed before we can be sure that the fluted points are part of the same complex as the other types found with them. It may be that the fluted points from Borax Lake are pieces picked up locally and brought to a later site by the inhabitants, but, as yet, no fluted points have been found under conditions suggestive of great antiquity. Present studies provide only the information that the tradition of fluting spread as far west as California. No date can now be assigned to this manifestation. It seems possible, however, that these fluted points will prove to be younger than those found farther east in association with extinct fauna, and that they may date from the Altithermal period or later.

Fluted Points East of the Plains

Fluted points have been reported as surface finds from every state, but in only a few sites east of the Plains have they been found in position. None has been found associated with extinct fauna, and the nature of the sites has precluded dating by geological studies. Except at Graham Cave, there has also been a lack of material suitable for radiocarbon dating. There seems little doubt, however, that these artifacts are relatively ancient, for in most cases they pre-date those of the Archaic Stage which began many thousands of years ago.

Graham Cave

Graham Cave was excavated by Wilfred D. Logan (1952), students of the University of Missouri, and members of the Missouri Archaeological Society. It is a large shelter, some eighty feet wide and sixty feet deep, that lies a few miles north of the confluence of the Loutre and Missouri rivers.

Excavations were carried to a depth of six feet in one-foot levels. There were three broad levels of occupation. The bulk of the material belongs to the Archaic Stage, which is beyond the scope of this book. Some fluted and basally ground points were found, however. Certain specimens resemble the Clovis points found farther west, but others are more nearly triangular and the bases are more deeply concave. Most were found in Levels 5 and 6, but one was found in position in Level 4. Associated with these were straight-based lanceolate projectile points, and unifacially beveled steeple-shaped specimens with concave bases similar to Meserve points discussed on page 113. In this area the latter, which are usually serrated, are sometimes called Dalton points. There were also notched and stemmed forms. Other artifacts included drills, scrapers, knives, mortars and pestles, thin flat milling stones, awls made from split bones, and a flaked hematite adze.

The materials found in Levels 4 through 6 are attributed to a single culture complex which was changing from the Early Man stage, with emphasis on hunting, to the Archaic stage, with greater emphasis on food gathering (Chapman *in* Crane, 1956). Organic material from a fireplace on the original floor of the cave gave a carbon date of 9,700 ± 500 years ago. A sample from Level 6 was dated at 8,830 ± 500 years ago, and one from Level 4 at 7,900 ± 500 years ago (Crane, 1956).

Another cave, in Callaway County, Missouri, which is being investigated by members of the Missouri Archaeological Society, also contains points of types normally attributed to the Paleo-Indian horizon, as well as artifacts of more recent origin (Shippee, 1955). Preliminary excavation in the talus area in front of the cave produced projectile points like the lanceolate forms found in Graham Cave, and Meserve points. They could not be ascribed to any specific cultural horizon, but excavations within the cave, where it may be possible to determine stratigraphic relationships, will doubtless provide much interesting information.

Bee County, Texas

In Bee County, which lies in the Coastal Plains region of Texas, E. H. Sellards (1940b) found six sites which contained artifacts and fossils. The bones and artifacts were in stream-laid sediments in a terrace of the Mission River drainage system. The terrace was named after a nearby town and is called the Berclair. The lower horizon contained the bones of numerous fossil vertebrates including mammoth, mastodon, horse, bison, camel, and sloth. In this same zone were found the base of a Clovis Fluted point, two well-flaked lanceolate points, a fragmentary specimen resembling a Scottsbluff, and a corner-notched point.

To the writer, this mixture of types, that elsewhere were made at different times, would seem to indicate secondary deposition. However, the artifacts were not water-worn, and Sellards, who is a capable geologist, considered this possibility but decided, on the basis of studies in the field, that the association was probably a primary one. If he is correct, this may, like Graham Cave, represent a transition from Paleo-Indian to Archaic.

Sites with Fluted Points in Kentucky

In the course of excavating the Carlson Annis Site, a great shell mound in Butler County, Kentucky, which contained Archaic material, two fluted points were found at the base of the midden (Webb, 1950). It is thought that they represent chance inclusions and pre-date the Archaic material dated by the radiocarbon method at more than 4,000 years ago. Both points show grinding on the base and lower edges. One has one very jagged and uneven edge and appears to have been retouched at a later time.

At the Parrish Village Site, near Nebo, in Hopkins County, investigated by William S. Webb (1951), three fluted points were found on the surface and four more were found through excavation. The fluted points occurred throughout the deposit, which also contained Archaic artifacts. The stratification of this site had been lost due to disturbance through soil erosion, cultivation, and the digging of grave pits, so the stratigraphic position of these specimens could not be determined. Webb believed, however, that the fluted points were older and that two cultural manifestations of different ages, one Paleo-Indian and one Archaic, were represented in this site.

Of the fluted specimens found through excavation, two are basal portions with broad flutes extending the full length of the fragment. There is a complete point which is not really grooved, but apparently an unsuccessful attempt had been made to flute both sides. The fourth is short, virtually triangular, and side-notched. Four long slender projectile points with fine oblique parallel flaking reminiscent of Angostura points (see page 139) were also found.

In addition to the projectile points, there were a number of other tools that Webb felt differed from normal Archaic types. He tentatively attributed these to the assemblage of the early hunters. They include snub-nosed scrapers; a variety of fairly large flakes retouched on one face, that could be classified as side scrapers; scrapers with one concave side, sometimes called spokeshaves; and some tools flaked on both faces, apparently cutting implements. There were also tools with small needle-like points, and others with small drill-like points, classified as gravers and chisel-gravers. Some heavy, crudely flaked tools may have been used as choppers. These were attributed to the earlier horizon. Certain specimens appear to have served more than one purpose. In some cases there were two different scraping surfaces; in some, scraping and cutting edges were represented; and in one instance the basal end of a drill had been flaked to form a snub-nosed scraper.

On the basis of a re-examination of the artifacts, Raymond H. Thompson (1954) came to the conclusion that the collection was basically homogeneous and he noted the possibility of two alternative interpretations. 1) Only an Archaic occupation was represented and the specimens that resemble Paleo-Indian types are out of context, presumably having been brought in by later people. 2) This site may represent a period of transition between Paleo-Indian and Archaic. Without stratigraphic evidence one cannot be sure, but the presence of a notched and fluted point, which is similar to some found at the Hardaway Site discussed on page 72, suggests that the latter may be correct.

The Enterline Chert Industry (The Shoop Site)

Interesting work has been done in eastern Pennsylvania by John Witthoft (1952) who has undertaken typological studies of eastern fluted forms. At the Shoop Site, near Enterline, Pennsylvania, has been found an assemblage of artifacts, including fluted points, to which Witthoft has given the name Enterline Chert Industry.

The site was discovered some fifteen years ago by George Gordon, a collector. For some time he concealed the location, but he finally showed it to the late Edgar B. Howard, who visited the site and put down a number of test pits. These, however, were unproductive. In 1942 Gordon revealed the location of the site to Frank J. Soday, who began to collect there. Witthoft met Gordon in 1950 and examined his collection, which contained forty-one fluted points and fragments, and several hundred other artifacts. He visited the site and found two fluted points and a number of other tools. Witthoft has also worked with Soday's collection, which contains 120 distinctive tools and many chips.

Worked stone was spottily scattered over an area some twenty acres in extent, on an irregular plateau bounded by small streams. A very thin sandy soil lies over the bedrock, which consists of red shale. With the exception of a very few artifacts, probably lost by later hunters, all the material appears to belong to a single complex. There is no geological or palaeontological proof of antiquity, but the artifacts are more deeply weathered than are more recent types made of the same materials, and there are strong typological similarities between these artifacts and some found farther west that are known to be ancient.

Although most fluted points found in Pennsylvania are made of local jasper or a fine-grained black flint, only a very few specimens made of these materials were found at the Shoop Site. Over 800 specimens collected from this site were of Onondaga chert, for which the source beds lie in western New York some 200 miles to the north. Witthoft has suggested that this shows that the people brought the material with them, in the form of finished tools and blanks, as they migrated southward. The scarcity of chips and rough rejects at the Shoop Site does suggest, as Witthoft has indicated, that much of the basic flint work was not done at this site. However, as Krieger (1954) has pointed out, this does not necessarily provide proof of migration.

In many areas throughout the United States and Canada the earliest artifacts were made of exceptionally fine material that often could be obtained only from a source hundreds of miles away, while some later artifacts were made of poorer, but readily available, local materials. The early hunters who produced magnificently flaked points were fine craftsmen. They expended far more energy on the production of their weapon tips than was necessary for purely functional purposes, and aesthetic factors were certainly taken into consideration. The choice of a material that would enable them to create fine examples of their skillful workmanship must have seemed sufficiently important to justify making a real effort to obtain it. Some later groups, with other aesthetic drives, were more likely to be concerned purely with the production of a serviceable weapon and were content to use inferior materials that were easily obtainable. Others, who were concerned with the production of fine stonework, made an effort to get good flints.

The finding of twelve unfinished points, as well as forty-eight completed points and fragments, helped Witthoft to analyze the techniques used in the production of the fluted points. The usual

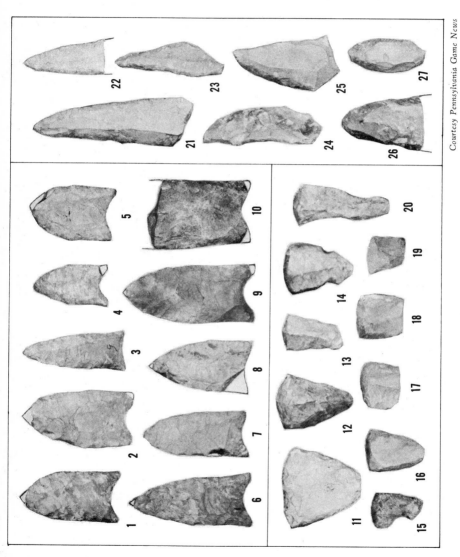

Courtesy Pennsylvania Game News

FIG. 20—Artifacts from the Shoop Site, Pennsylvania. Nos. 1-10 Fluted Points. Nos. 11-20 End Scrapers. Nos. 21-27 Side Scrapers. (Witthoft 1954, p. 12)

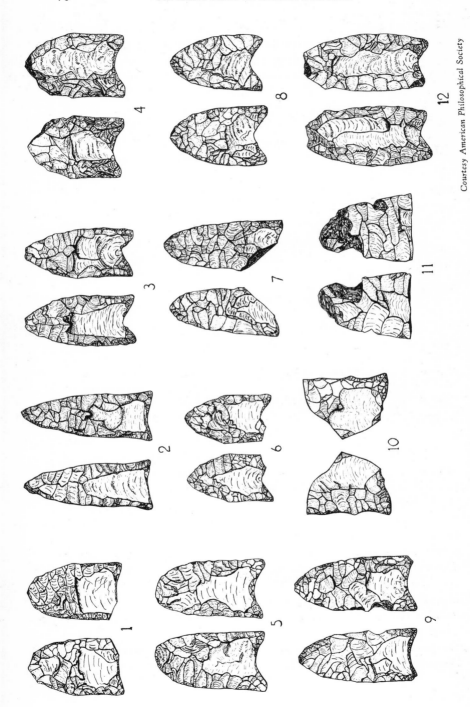

FIG. 21—Fluted points from the Shoop Site, Pennsylvania. (From Plate I, p. 469, Witthoft, 1952).

method, apparently, was to thin the base by removing two longitudinal flakes, and then removing the final channel flake. This sometimes obliterated evidence of the smaller flutes, but in some cases the earlier flake scars are still readily apparent. The point was then shaped and retouched along the edges and the basal edges were ground. Some of the Clovis points found with mammoth remains at Naco, Arizona, were evidently prepared in the same way. Most of the Shoop Site points are widest at the mid-section, but in some cases the greatest breadth is at the base.

A few tools chipped on both faces, apparently used as knives, were found. Most of the other tools were flakes chipped on one face to form side and end scrapers. There were a few flakes and tools with small acute points or gravers.

There are three other sites, the Williamson, Quad, and Hardaway (St. 4) that Witthoft has assigned to the Enterline Chert Industry.

The Williamson Site

In 1947, Ben C. McCary and members of the Archaeological Society of Virginia began a survey of fluted points found in the State. Nine years later, 263 such specimens had been recorded and plotted on maps (McCary, 1947, 1954, 1956). This is a fine example of the major contributions that can be made by serious, well-organized, nonprofessional groups. Early in the course of the survey it became apparent that there were three major areas of concentration for such specimens. One of these was in Dinwiddie County where a fluted point site has now been discovered (McCary, 1951).

The site, which lies on the farm of Joshua S. and John E. Williamson, covers a long, narrow, ridge-top area approximately a mile long. Scattered over the surface have been found thirty-three fluted points and a few larger fragmentary specimens with some fluting that were probably used as knives. The latter lack the basal grinding found on most of the points. Among the 198 scrapers recovered there were a few side scrapers, but the majority were of the snub-nosed variety. There were also a few implements that resembled gravers. The area was littered with many cores and unutilized flakes, and it seems probable that many of the implements were made here. Interestingly enough, the non-local material most commonly used was a Pennsylvania jasper. Most of the specimens closely resemble those found at the Shoop Site. There are some pentagonal points reminiscent of those found at the Reagan Site in Vermont, discussed on page 79.

The Quad Site

On two deeply eroded ridges near Decatur, in central Alabama, is a site which contains a Paleo-Indian as well as an Archaic component. This is the Quad Site, discovered in 1951 by Frank J. Soday (1954). Stratigraphic evidence was lacking, but nearly 1,000 artifacts believed to belong to a fluted point complex were sorted on the basis of typology, weathering, and choice of materials. Most of the artifacts assigned to the Paleo-Indian horizon were made of a material not used by the later people, a mottled blue chert indistinguishable from the Onondaga chert from New York.

Artifact types include all those found in sites assigned to the Enterline Chert Industry as well as some reported from the Parrish Site but not from the others. In most cases the points were prepared by the multiple fluting technique, but some appear to have been grooved by the removal of a single flake. There is considerable variation in size. All the specimens have basal grinding. Unfinished points, channel flakes, and chipping debris were found on the site. The assemblage includes many end and side scrapers, some spokeshaves, drills, and possibly choppers. There were also some simple gravers and gravers combined with other tools. A radiocarbon date from Russell Cave, discussed on page 149, suggests that, in this area, Paleo-Indian occupation dates back more than 8,000 years.

The Hardaway Site (St. 4)

No detailed report is yet available on a site in North Carolina investigated by Joffre Coe, but some information in regard to it has been published by Witthoft (1952) and Coe has very generously provided additional data through a personal communication. This site, which was first designated St. 4 and called the Hardaway Site, lies at the Fall Line where the Yadin River enters the Coastal Plains. Fluted points were found on the surface by the discoverer, H. M. Doerschuk. Excavations by Coe revealed the presence of tools and implements similar to those found at the Shoop Site as well as types found in lower levels of a deep stratified site across the river from the Hardaway Site. Some of the projectile points were side-notched. Coe feels that a transition from fluting to notching is represented. One of the points shown in Fig. 22 shows both fluting and notching. Many of the tools were made of a local stone which does not flake well, and this has led to an appearance of crudeness. There was some use of an imported flint that is also found at the Williamson Site. The Hardaway Site yielded a larger number of gravers than did any of those previously described. This, however, may be due to the fact that they were found in undisturbed deposits and fewer of the tiny, delicate points had been destroyed.

Courtesy Research Laboratories of Anthropology
University of North Carolina

FIG. 22—Artifacts from the Hardaway Site, North Carolina. Note fluting on notched point, lower right.

The North Carolina Sequence

On the basis of his work in North Carolina, Coe recognizes eight pre-ceramic complexes as well as Woodland and Historic manifestations. His sequence is based primarily on the excavation of four stratified sites; the Hardaway, Doerschuk, and Gaston, which are close together, and the Lowder's Ferry which lies 150 miles away. The complex with fluted points, to which the name Hardaway has been given, is the oldest. Next in order of age are the Palmer, Stanley,

Morrow Mountain I, Morrow Mountain II, Guilford, Halifax, and Savannah River. The Doerschuk Site contained material ranging from the period of the Stanley Complex to Historic times. The Hardaway and Palmer Complexes were represented only at the Hardaway Site, where they were found in position. Morrow Mountain, Guilford, and Savannah River artifacts were found there in the overlying plowed soil. The Gaston and Lowder's Ferry Sites had a range from Guilford to Historic.

Information relating to the point types which characterized some of the complexes is not available at the present time, but it is interesting to note that artifacts of the Morrow Mountain I Complex include points with contracting stems that resemble those found at Gypsum Cave (discussed on page 158) and that points similar to the Lake Mohave type (discussed on page 162) were found redeposited in flood sand between the Morrow Mountain I and Stanley levels at the Doerschuk Site. Characteristic points of the Guilford Complex (Coe, 1952) are long, slender lanceolate forms. They are usually thick and sometimes almost diamond-shaped in cross-section. The bases are usually concave but are sometimes straight or slightly convex. Some are basally ground and the flaking on many specimens is reminiscent of the oblique type. They resemble the Nebo Hill points discussed on page 146. Small notched axes, polished through use but not intention, are commonly found with Guilford points. A radiocarbon sample from the Halifax horizon at the Gaston Site was dated at 5,440 ± 350 years ago at the University of Michigan Laboratory. Six complexes are still older and those which include specimens that resemble Paleo-Indian forms found farther west must be quite old. Polished stone implements also appear to have considerable antiquity here for a polished atlatl weight is attributed to the Stanley Complex.

The LeCroy Site

At a site on the Tennessee River above Chattanooga, A. L. LeCroy has found thousands of artifacts including nine fluted points and one which resembles a Meserve as well as Archaic and Woodland specimens (Lewis and Kneberg, 1955, 1956). Associated tools which may be of Paleo-Indian origin include gravers and snub-nosed scrapers. Unfortunately, the site is often covered by the waters of Lake Chickamauga and no excavations had been undertaken by the spring of 1956, although it was hoped that a test trench might be put down at a later date.

The Bull Brook Site

Farther north is another site that has much in common with those previously discussed. The Bull Brook Site, which lies near Ipswich, Massachusetts, was discovered by William C. Eldridge and Joseph Vaccaro. The first find was a fluted point picked from a surface exposed by a bulldozer. Between 1951 and 1957 this site, which covers some ten or twelve acres, yielded more than 3,000 artifacts, more than 100 of which were fluted points and fragments (Douglas Byers, Personal communication). They were made of materials for which no local sources have yet been identified (Byers, 1956). The site lies

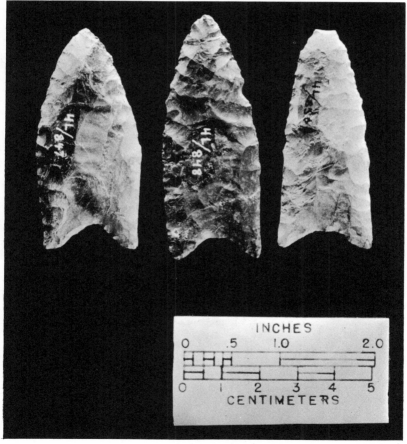

Courtesy Robert S. Peabody Foundation for Archaeology

FIG. 23—Fluted points from the Bull Brook Site, Massachusetts.

on a kame terrace. Some sandy loam overlies eighteen to thirty inches of structureless sand which rests on cross-bedded sand. The first twelve to sixteen inches below the loam are fairly compact. The sand which lies below is somewhat softer and lighter in color. It was in the latter section that the fluted points and other implements occurred. Douglas Byers and Frederick Johnson visited the site on a number of occasions but found no artifacts in position (Byers, 1954). In 1955,

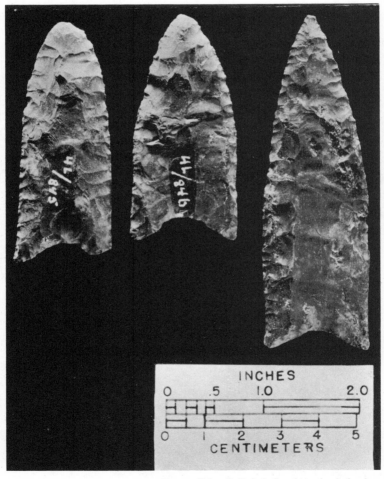

Courtesy Robert S. Peabody Foundation for Archaeology

Fig. 24—Fluted points from the Bull Brook Site, Massachusetts.

INCHES

FIG. 25—Scrapers from the Bull Brook Site, Massachusetts. Above, snub-nosed **end** scrapers. Below, side scrapers.

Byers revisited the site and undertook some excavations. Although he did not find any fluted points *in situ,* he did find a number of scrapers, gravers, and worked flakes made of the same material as the fluted specimens and with similar flaking (Byers, 1955).

One of the confusing factors was that there was no evidence of an old land surface, and it was difficult to understand how the artifacts had been buried. The later excavations, however, indicated that there had been a good bit of disturbance and that this zone had been unstable for a long time. Matching fragments of artifacts were found separated by some distance both vertically and horizontally. There was probably some trampling of the sand by the makers of the implements and later disturbance by frost action and wind throw of trees. Such a site is not suitable for geological dating, and no material has been obtained which could be utilized for radiocarbon dating.

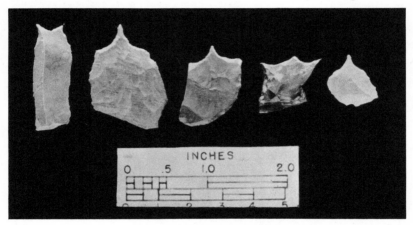

Courtesy Robert S. Peabody Foundation for Archaeology

FIG. 26—Gravers from the Bull Brook Site, Massachusetts.

The points range in length from one and one half to three and three-eights inches. A fragment of point which must have been much longer was also found. Some have parallel sides below the mid-point, but some are more nearly triangular. In most cases grooving was achieved by the removal of multiple flakes. Other specimens in the collection include end scrapers of the snub-nosed variety, side scrapers, drills, flaked knives, and tools with small needle-like projections. Some of these little graver tips occur on the cutting edge of end scrapers. Some examples of rubbed graphite, which may have been used to provide pigment, were found.

Courtesy New York State Museum and Science Service

FIG. 27—Artifacts from the Reagan Site, Vermont.

The Reagan Site

Another fluted point site lies six miles south of the Quebec border near Shawville, Vermont. It is called the Reagan Site (Ritchie, 1953)*. Over a period of more than twenty years, William A. Ross and Benjamin W. Fisher have amassed collections from this site which they have made available for study to William Ritchie, who visited the site in 1950 and put down some test pits. The site lies in an area of shifting dune sands, and all the specimens have been recovered through surface collecting over a section approximately two miles in extent. The site is no longer productive, and the test pits did not reveal the presence of any habitation zone.

---

*William Ritchie has recently published further details pertaining to this site and an excellent summary of Early Man finds in the northeastern United States. See Ritchie, 1957.

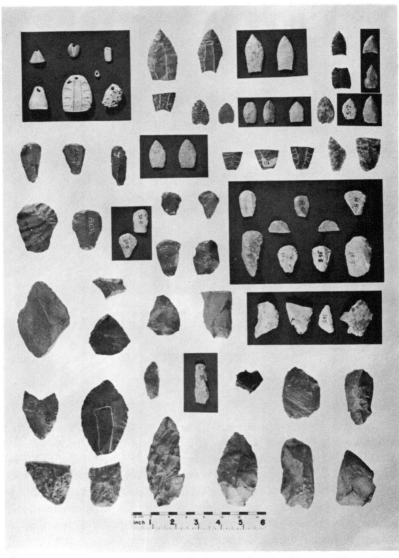

Fig. 28—Artifacts from the Reagan Site, Vermont. Note talc pendants shown against black background in upper left hand corner. (Fig. 89, p. 252, Ritchie, 1953.)

The 179 artifacts available for study were made of a wide variety of materials, most of which are not known in this locality. Some are deeply weathered. Certain specimens are made of a material which may be Onondaga chert from New York State, which was so commonly used at the Shoop Site. The abundance of flint debris indicates that artifacts were made here.

The collection contains forty-seven projectile points and fragments. An unspecified number are fluted on one or both sides. Many are ground on the basal edges. Triangular, lanceolate, and pentagonal shapes, and forms with incipient sloping shoulders, are represented. Most of the bases are concave, but some are straight. Among the associated artifacts are end scrapers, some with constricted stems; side scrapers; spokeshave scrapers with small, delicately flaked graver tips; and knives. Some of the latter are simply retouched flakes, while others are well flaked on both surfaces and are lenticular in cross-section. Six specimens have a single shoulder which is reminiscent of Sandia points discussed on page 86. There are some puzzling artifacts made of talc and presumably worn as pendants. They are perforated, and some show wear produced by being suspended from a cord. Some are decorated with grooves, reminiscent of the flutes on the points, but in this case the effect was produced by abrasion instead of by flaking.

Ritchie believes this complex, although it probably stems from the Enterline Chert Industry, contains other elements. He thinks it is somewhat more recent although dating back more than 6,000 years.

Distribution, Characteristics, Age, and Derivation of Eastern Fluted Points

Although every state has produced some fluted points, it is only in certain states that intensive work has been done, and, accordingly, more is known in regard to the typology and distribution of fluted points in some areas than in others. Reference has already been made to the fine work being done by the Archaeological Society of Virginia. A similar project has been undertaken by the Tennessee Archaeological Society, and good photographs of the specimens have been published (Lewis and Kneberg, 1951, 1954, 1955, 1956). The records gathered by this group have shown that there is a marked concentration in the Highland Rim area around Nashville. A site has been discovered in eastern Tennessee (Lewis and Kneberg, 1955, 1956). The Alabama Archaeological Society is also active, and one member, E. C. Mahan (1954, 1955, 1956), has reported upon and illustrated a large number

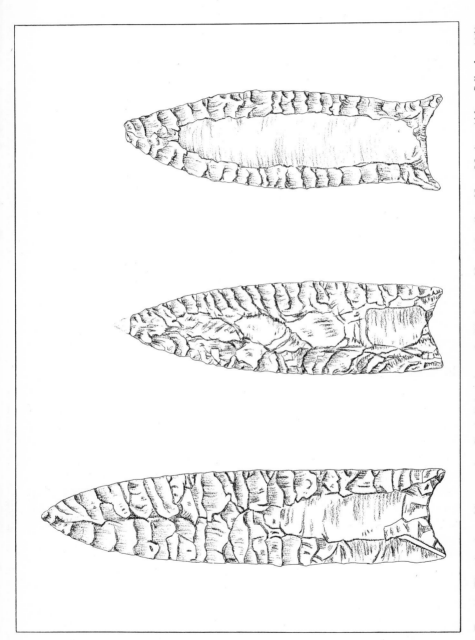

Fig. 29—Fluted points. Nos. 1 and 2 Clovis Points from the Blackwater No. 1 locality, New Mexico. (After Sellards, 1952, Fig. 17, p. 35.) No. 3. Point with constricted base, flaring ears, a type commonly found in the eastern United States. Sometimes designated "Ohio" or "Cumberland" Fluted points.

of fluted points found in that state. Malcolm W. Hill and Arthur George Smith are collecting data pertaining to fluted points in a number of areas. The latter has particularly good records for the state of Ohio.

As more such data are recorded and reported, it is hoped that more typological studies, such as Witthoft's of the Shoop Site material, will be undertaken. Only then will it be possible to evaluate the different patterns and determine the regional variations which undoubtedly exist.

Even a cursory check of published illustrations reveals certain characteristics of eastern fluted points. Grooves were most commonly produced by the removal of multiple flakes and often did not extend very far up the face of the point. Some examples, however, were grooved by the removal of single flutes which sometimes extended almost to the tip of the point. Although quite a few points are widest at the mid-section, or are parallel-sided to the mid-point, as are most Clovis points found farther west, there are many that are essentially triangular in outline and many that are constricted at the base and have flaring ears. The latter are sometimes called Cumberland points (Kneberg, 1956). Some writers have called them Ohio points. Many of them tend to be longer and narrower than other fluted points. Some specimens are pentagonal in outline. A greater number of eastern points have deeply concave bases than do the western forms.

The age of many eastern types can be determined only when sites are found that can be dated geologically or through radiocarbon tests. However, since in most areas the fluted point horizon appears to pre-date the Archaic, it is certainly ancient in the east. Witthoft has suggested that the Enterline Chert Industry may be the oldest in the United States. He believes that it may be related to earlier Alaskan manifestations, which in turn can be related to Asiatic patterns. There are a number of objections to this hypothesis (Krieger, 1954). First, no fluted points have been reported from Asia. Second, even the earliest date that might be assigned to the few fluted points found in Alaska would be far too recent.

It seems virtually certain that the tradition of fluting developed in the New World. From some as yet undetermined center it spread in various directions. The writer, while inclined to believe that this center lay in the Southwest or in the Plains, recognizes that it may be more than coincidence that others who have worked in the west usually have similar ideas, while those whose field work has been done in the east are equally likely to favor an eastern source for this and many other traits. Despite all efforts to be entirely objective, an area that one knows intimately may tend to assume greater importance than one known largely through the literature. Actually, no one has sufficient data to say where, or when, fluted points were first made.

Fluted Points in Mexico and Central America

Homer Aschman (1952) found a fluted point in a collection owned by a family in San Joaquin, Baja California. It was reportedly found in the central part of the peninsula. The point is of virtually the same shape and size as one found with the Naco mammoth. It has a long, broad groove on one face and a shorter narrower groove on the other. Along the shores of now extinct lakes in the same region have been found bison bones that appear to have been intentionally split, and there are reports of the finding of camel and horse bones that show evidence of burning.

Charles Di Peso (1955) has reported the finding of two fluted points in Sonora. They lay on an old beach margin some thirty miles north of Guaymas. One of the points was complete, the other fragmentary. They were fluted on both faces, and the basal edges were ground.

The finding of a fluted point in Durango by J. Charles Kelley has been reported by José Lorenzo (1953). It was a surface find and there was no association with other material. It differs from most points of the Llano Complex in that it tapers toward the base and then widens again in a manner reminiscent of the more markedly indented "fish tail" forms of fluted points found in the eastern United States. It is only two inches long, but it appears to have been broken and then had a new tip chipped on. The grooves on both faces were formed by the removal of two flakes. There is some slight evidence that the lower edges were smoothed.

William J. Mayer-Oakes (1952) has described a point, fluted on one side, with basally ground edges, which may have come from Costa Rica. It was found in the Carnegie Museum in a collection purchased in San José in 1904. The box had been opened only twice before the point was observed in 1950, and it seems possible that the artifact is part of the original collection.

SANDIA POINTS

Sandia Cave

A site known as Sandia Cave, which lies on the northern end of the Sandia Mountains in Las Huertas Canyon, New Mexico, yielded evidence of a culture older than Folsom. This is a large tunnel-like limestone cave, 150 yards long with an average width of ten feet. There was an exceptionally well-defined stratigraphy, and there was no deposition from the outside nor redistribution of material, so that objects were found where they were originally deposited. The excavation was sponsored by the University of New Mexico. Frank C. Hibben (1941) published the final report.

The top level, known as the Recent layer, consisted of wind-blown dust, bat guano, and pack rat dung. In it were found a few potsherds, a metate, and a deer antler. These were found near the mouth of the cave. They are all late and indicate only brief and intermittent occupation. Animal bones found in this stratum included not only those of the expected modern fauna, but also ground sloth remains. This was a Pleistocene animal, but some students have thought it might have survived into comparatively recent times. Charles B. Hunt (1953), however, has failed to find sloth remains in any of the recent deposits of the Rocky Mountain area. He believes that the bones found at Sandia Cave are of the same age as the stalagmitic layer that lies below. He thinks that men or rodents were responsible for their introduction into the younger bed.

Below this top layer was a crust of calcium carbonate that sealed off the lower levels. This varied from less than half an inch to six inches in thickness. Underneath the crust lay the level known as the Folsom layer because of the occurrence of Folsom artifacts within it. It was made up of cave debris which was originally loose and unconsolidated but was later consolidated into a cave breccia almost like a friable concrete. Throughout this layer, but with marked concentration toward the mouth, were found artifacts, flakes, and charcoal. Included among the artifacts were two classic Folsoms and two bases. Other points included four unfluted specimens. Hibben stated that, in outline, three of these were much like Folsoms, but the two that are illustrated exhibit only slightly concave, almost straight bases, and lack the ear-like projections of the true Folsoms. They more nearly resemble Plainview points discussed on page 108. Another unfluted lanceolate point narrows markedly toward the base and is leaf-shaped.

It is strongly reminiscent of one of the specimens found associated with mammoth in Mexico which is discussed on page 97.

There were also large bifacially flaked implements like those found at the Lindenmeier and Clovis sites, and five small gravers of the type reported from Lindenmeier. A wide range of scrapers, including snub-nosed, side, and concave forms, also occurred. With these artifacts were found a number of flakes, both utilized and waste, but no channel flakes were uncovered to indicate that Folsom points were manufactured within the cave. Three pieces of worked bone also came to light, and it is possible that one of them may be a splinter of ivory. Animals represented by skeletal remains included horse, camel, bison, mammoth, ground sloth, and wolf.

Below the Folsom layer and separating it from the lowest level was one of the most interesting features of the site, a water-laid layer of finely laminated yellow ochre which was entirely sterile. This deposit varied in thickness from two inches to two feet.

Under the sterile yellow ochre lay a stratum of cave debris much like the higher Folsom layer but less consolidated. It was here that the oldest artifacts, which included nineteen examples of the distinctive points, to which the name Sandia has been assigned, were obtained. All were characterized by an inset on one side only, which produced a single shoulder, but two subtypes may be differentiated. Type 1 is rounded in outline and lenticular in cross-section while Type 2 has more nearly parallel sides, a straight or slightly concave base, and in cross-section is somewhat diamond-shaped. The bases of the latter were commonly thinned through the removal of longitudinal flakes, and one specimen, from which a single large flake was removed, is reminiscent of fluted forms. Type 2 points tended to occur a little higher in the deposit, and there may be a slight difference in age between the two forms. The more rounded forms, which occurred lower in the level, are the least well flaked. Both types have ground edges. Neither type exhibits the fine flaking which characterizes Folsoms. Other stone implements included scrapers, preponderantly of the snub-nosed variety, utilized flakes, and crude nondescript points. The snub-nosed scrapers are somewhat larger than those of the Folsom level. None of the stone tools found associated with the distinctive points could be attributed to either of these ancient complexes if they were found out of context. Cultural remains also included two charcoal-filled hearths, one of which was surrounded by a ring of limestone boulders.

Of particular interest was the occurrence of two bone artifacts somewhat resembling Sandia points in outline and quite possibly
used as projectile tips. The bone of which they were made cannot be
definitely identified, but it appears to be the leg bone of an extinct
form of camel. For the most part, bones found within the Sandia
layer were poorly preserved, but occasional partly articulated skeletons
occurred. The fauna represented included extinct forms of horse, bison,
camel, mastodon, and mammoth.

The geological interpretation of Sandia Cave was undertaken by
Kirk Bryan. This study was complicated by the fact that there was
no physical connection between the cave deposits and others in the
locality outside the cave, and this made correlation with other sequences
difficult. The only alternative lay in seeking correlations with climatic
fluctuations.

The fact that the Sandia layer was partially solidified indicated the
presence of greater moisture than at present. Since the structure of
the cave is such that it was impossible for water to have come in from
the outside, it must have come from the roof. The fact that the layer
is more solidified toward the top suggests that the drip from the roof
increased during the period of deposition. Since the only way in which
this drip would increase would be through a greater fall of rain or snow
on the ridge over the cave, it may be assumed that this indicates a
progressively wetter climate.

For the formation of the yellow ochre layer the cave must have
been very wet, and evaporation must have been at a minimum. It is
probable that during this time the mouth of the cave was closed, which
would tend to reduce the rate of evaporation. Under these conditions
the formation of the ochre, which is an oxide of iron, may be explained
on the basis that the greater precipitation would stimulate the forest
growth above the ridge, and this would add to the iron content of the
water dripping through the roof.

It is believed that, during the period of the deposition of the
Folsom layer, water continued to drip from the roof, solidifying the
material, but that the entrance to the cave was open. Following this,
there appears to have been another period during which the mouth of
the cave was closed and the dripping water formed the stalagmite crust
which seals off the lower levels. The formation of this calcium carbonate deposit, rather than another layer of ochre, was presumably the
result of a decreased iron content of the water.

Fig. 30—Sandia points from the Lucy Site, New Mexico. Note fluting on specimens 4 and 5. Scale in centimeters.

Courtesy University of New Mexico

If it is assumed that this period of humid climate may be correlated with a glacial substage, the problem arises as to which glacial substage is the one in question. The answer was based on the previous work done at the Lindenmeier Site. If we attribute the Folsom layer of Sandia Cave to the closing stages of the Mankato substage, where the Lindenmeier Site was placed by Bryan and Ray, the yellow ochre deposit below may be correlated with the climax of this substage. On this basis the Sandia layer would be regarded as of pre-Mankato age.

There is much confusion in regard to a Carbon 14 test on charcoal from Sandia Cave, allegedly run in 1948 at the University of Chicago but not published.* There has also been some question about the meaning of the dates from ivory samples, ascribed to the Sandia level, which were submitted to the University of Michigan. They produced dates in excess of 20,000 years ago (Crane, 1955). No exact date can be given yet for Sandia points, but the writer believes they will prove to be among the oldest of the Paleo-Indian projectile point types, quite possibly exceeding Clovis Fluted points in age.

The Lucy Site

In 1954, K. W. Kendall discovered another site that contained Sandia points. It was named for the railroad siding of Lucy, New Mexico, which lies seven miles north and one mile east of the site. Excavations conducted during 1954 and 1955 were under the general direction of Frank C. Hibben. William B. Roosa (1956 a and b) was in charge of work at the site.

The Lucy Site consists of a series of blow-outs. It apparently represents the remnants of a series of ponds that lay above the shoreline of Pleistocene Lake Estancia. Surface finds included both fluted and unfluted Folsoms, Clovis points, Sandias, one of which was fluted, and stemmed points, as well as biface and uniface knives, scrapers, gravers, and metates. Mammoth and bison remains were observed weathering out on the surface.

While outlining a portion of a long bone, probably of an elephant, Hibben found a Type 2 Sandia lying beside it. In the course of later trenching operations, Roosa and his crew found six Sandia specimens. One complete point and one base had deeply concave bases and were fluted. The others are of Type 1. Bases and lower edges were ground.

---

*It has now been established that no material from Sandia Cave was submitted to the University of Chicago Laboratory. Johnson and Hibben (1957).

The grinding sometimes extended beyond the shoulder. Associated with them were three biface implements and a scraper. The latter has a rounded tang with a constricted neck, and closely resembles some forms found in Asia. A similar specimen was found by Russell A. Johnston in Alberta, Canada, in a locality which also yielded a Sandia point.

No Folsom or Clovis points were found in position. The makers of the fluted points were undoubtedly in this area but, in the absence of stratigraphic evidence, their chronological position in relation to the Sandia people here cannot be determined. Points which resemble the Pinto Basin type (see page 165), thin slab metates, small one-hand manos, and fire pits were found *in situ* in a level well above the Sandia layer and must be considerably more recent.

The nature of the deposits, the stratigraphic placement of the Sandia artifacts, the association with the bones of an elephant and their concentration in a limited area, suggest that the animal was killed on the edge of an ancient pond. Preliminary investigations of the geology have been undertaken by Jerry Harbour (1956). Clay layers lie above the sand in which the Sandias were found *in situ*. Harbour believes these clays may date from the Mankato. The nature of the sediments in which the Sandias were found would indicate a period of increasing rainfall, such as might be expected at the end of an interstadial.

Distribution of Sandia Points

It cannot be stressed too strongly that not every single-shouldered point is a Sandia. Many unfinished specimens and some aberrant forms of more recent types are reminiscent of the Sandia point, but they are not the same thing. Only a relatively small number of specimens have been found that are virtually identical to those found at the type station, and an even smaller number have been found under conditions that provide some evidence of antiquity.

Five years after the publication of the original Sandia Cave report, Hibben had received some 180 communications purporting to deal with the discovery of Sandia points, but he had recorded only thirty-eight specimens that he felt reasonably certain could be placed in this category (Hibben, 1946). In fourteen instances there appeared to be an association with the bones of extinct animals, but in no case was there controlled excavation. Eight specimens came from southeastern New Mexico and southwestern Texas. Eleven were found in the area that includes the northern half of Oklahoma, western and southern

Missouri, and southern Iowa. Two were found in the Texas Panhandle, one near Abilene, Texas, one in eastern Colorado, and one in Oregon. The location of the others is not given. In the Museum in Mesa Verde National Park are several specimens found in the Four Corners area that Hibben has classified as Sandia points.

Doubtless other points which resemble the Sandia specimens have been found during the ensuing years, but a search of the literature has revealed only a few further examples that are adequately illustrated. One is a point reported by Harold K. Kleine (1953) as coming from a site in northeastern Alabama which also produced fluted points. These were surface finds. The point illustrated appears to be a good example of a Type I Sandia. Another example, also a surface find, was reported by Keith A. Dixon (1953). It was found in Long Valley, Mono County, California, near the shore of an ancient lake. Biface leaf-shaped knives were made in this area in relatively recent times, and it is entirely possible that this is simply an aberrant example of that type, but it does closely resemble specimens from Sandia Cave. Not far from the Lucy Site, in the southern half of the Estancia Basin, which is now arid but which once contained many lakes, C. V. Haynes, Jr. (1955) has found, on the surface, a large number of projectile points of types attributed to the Paleo-Indian Stage. One of the specimens illustrated could be classified as a Sandia Point, Type II, and three others are reminiscent of Sandia forms.

The writer has seen at least one hundred specimens that were regarded as Sandias by their possessors, but there are only three of those examined that she would not hesitate to place in that category. These were all collected in eastern Alberta by Russell A. Johnston. As has been previously noted, one of these points was found in the same locality as a tanged scraper similar to that found at the Lucy Site. There are a number of other single-shouldered specimens in Johnston's collection that may or may not be related to those classified as Sandias. A point that may be a Sandia was found near Mortlach, Saskatchewan, by Kenneth Jones.

ARTIFACTS ASSOCIATED WITH MAMMOTH IN MEXICO

A number of important discoveries have been made near the town of Tepexpan, which lies some twenty miles northeast of Mexico City. Some of these discoveries are discussed on pages 199 to 202 and pages 238-241. In this area are found lake and marsh deposits laid down during a wetter period when Lake Texcoco was very large. In two instances stone tools have been found in unmistakable association with mammoth remains. As early as 1884 M. E. T. Hemy, a French scientist, reported finding simple stone tools in deposits which contained mammoth teeth and bones. In 1945 a waste flake of obsidian was found beneath a mammoth skull near Tepexpan by A. R. V. Arellano (1946). It was not until 1952, however, that the discovery of well-made artifacts in association with elephant remains provided incontrovertible proof of the contemporaneity of men and mammoths in the Valley of Mexico (Martinez del Rio, 1952a; Aveleyra A. de Anda and Maldonado-Koerdel, 1952, 1953).

Courtesy Direccion de Prehistoria
Museo Nacional de Antropologia Mexico, D. F.

FIG. 31—Bones of the first mammoth found at Santa Isabel Iztapan, Mexico. Left, Manuel Maldonado-Koerdel; right, Luis Aveleyra A. de Anda.

When an irrigation ditch was dug near the village of Santa Isabel Iztapan, which lies about a mile and a half south of Tepexpan, workmen uncovered bones and tusks of mammoth in a stratum assigned to the upper Pleistocene. In March of 1952 work was begun under the auspices of the Direccion de Prehistoria of the Instituto Nacional de

Antropologia e Historia. Luis Aveleyra, assisted by Arturo Romano, started the excavations while Manuel Maldonado-Koerdel undertook stratigraphic and palaeontological studies. After four days of work a projectile point was found lodged between two mammoth ribs. Further work revealed the presence of three more artifacts. Work was halted while telegrams were sent to various specialists inviting them to view the finds *in situ*. Many distinguished Mexican scientists responded; and three archaeologists arrived from the United States, E. H. Sellards, Alex D. Krieger, and the writer. The superbly excavated site was visited and the artifacts were viewed in their original position by a large number of qualified archaeologists and geologists. In the course of later work, two more artifacts were uncovered in association with the bones, by Senora Sol Arguedas R. de la Borbolla and Don Pablo Martinez del Rio.

The bones have been identified as those of an imperial mammoth (*Mammuthus* (*archidiskodon*) *imperator* Leidy). Most of the elephants found with artifacts in the United States were of another species, the columbian mammoth (*Mammuthus* (*parelephas*) *columbi*). About eighty percent of the total skeleton was recovered. Unfortunately, most of the skull had been lost in the course of the earlier ditch digging activity. One femur lay more than six feet away from the rest of the skeleton. It is probable that it was moved there during the butchering process. The bones were imbedded in a lake deposit, a fine green muck, that is assigned to the Upper Becerra formation. At the Tepexpan locality discussed on page 238 this formation was dated at between 11,000 and 12,000 years by geological methods (De Terra, Romero, and Stewart, 1949). Radiocarbon dates obtained from Upper Becerra samples ranged from 11,003 ± 300 to more than 16,000 years ago (Libby, 1955).

The projectile point found with the mammoth is quite unlike any of the points previously found with elephant bones. All the others were fluted points, while this one was unfluted and slightly stemmed. It bears a general resemblance to the Scottsbluff points of the United States, which are discussed on pages 118-123. The latter, however, have been found only with bison and are believed to be of somewhat more recent age. The Mexican specimen, which is made of a grayish chert, lacks the tip. Its estimated length is between two and three-quarters and three inches. It is thin and well-made, with rather broad flake scars roughly parallel to each other. There is a fine pressure retouch along the edges. Fig. 32, No. 1.

Courtesy *Direccion de Prehistoria*
Museo Nacional de Antropologia Mexico, D. F.

FIG. 32—Artifacts associated with the first mammoth found at Santa Isabel Iztapan, Mexico. Scale in centimeters.

The second artifact to be uncovered was a broken obsidian scraper flaked along the edges on one face. It lay near a mammoth rib. Another artifact, also of obsidian, seems to have served a double function. One edge appears to have been prepared for use as a normal scraper while the other has three concavities. Similar specimens have been called spokeshaves. It is thought that they were used in rounding and smooth· ing wooden shafts. The fourth artifact is of a silicious stone. It is triangular in outline. A steep bevel along the base indicates that it may have been used as an end scraper.

Of the two artifacts found in the course of later work, one is a long prismatic flake knife of obsidian with pressure retouched edges. Such blades, which were removed from specially prepared cores, were still being made at the time of the Spanish Conquest. The second specimen is an elongated implement of gray flint with fine marginal retouching along the edges on one face. At one end is a sort of curved beak or hook. It may have been used for working bone.

In June of 1954 members of the staff of the Direccion de Pre-historia, under the direction of Luis Aveleyra, excavated a second fossil mammoth of the same species, which lay less than half a mile from the first, in the same geological horizon (Aveleyra A. de Anda, 1956). The second skeleton was more nearly complete than the first, but there was even clearer evidence that the animal had been butchered. The skull was overturned and the base smashed, probably in order to extract the brains. Many of the other bones showed cuts and grooves made by stone tools.

Three artifacts were found in direct association with the bones. The first, which lay close to a rib, was made of a dark red igneous stone. It is lanceolate in form with an essentially straight base. The maximum breadth is at the mid-point. It has broad overall flaking on both faces and an extremely fine marginal retouch. Aveleyra has classified it as an Angostura point (described on page 269), but the writer would not put it in that category because of differences in shape and flaking. Neither would Richard P. Wheeler (Personal communication) who conducted the most extensive excavations in the Angostura Reservoir area and who has completed but not published a detailed report on the type station.

The second point found by Aveleyra lay under a mass of ribs and vertebrae. The illustration might suggest that the upper portion of a point is shown upside down, but grinding along the edges serves to indicate that this is the basal portion and that the specimen was pointed

Courtesy *Direccion de Prehistoria*
Museo Nacional de Antropologia Mexico, D. F.

FIG. 33—Bones of the second mammoth found at Santa Isabel Iztapan, Mexico.

at both ends and is of the type to which the name "laurel-leaf" is often given. These are also called Lerma Points. It is made of dark brown chert and is characterized by the removal of broad irregularly placed flakes; there is a delicate retouch along the edges that produces a slightly serrated appearance. The third specimen, a broken bifacial implement of light gray chert, is apparently the remnant of a knife or a larger point. Aveleyra believes that in its original form it may have been pointed at both ends. The bones and specimens will be exhibited in a specially constructed museum in the exact place where they were found.

Courtesy Direccion de Prehistoria
Museo Nacional de Antropologia Mexico, D. F.

FIG. 34—Artifacts associated with the second mammoth found at Santa Isabel Iztapan, Mexico.

Courtesy Direccion de Prehistoria
Museo Nacional de Antropologia Mexico, D. F.

FIG. 25—Point No. 1 *in situ* with associated mammoth rib; second discovery at Santa Isabel Iztapan, Mexico.

Further information regarding the distribution and age of the doubly pointed "laurel-leaf" forms is urgently needed. They occur as far north as Canada. A considerable number have been found in Alberta under circumstances that lead the writer to suspect that they may be an early form there. It is not impossible that they could have been one of the types, brought from Asia by early migrants, that one would expect to find along a migration route. Proof of age in the north is lacking, however. Similar specimens were found in the Agate Basin of eastern Wyoming, (discussed on page 141) but they were associated with bones attributed to modern bison (Roberts, 1943). It is possible, however, that the bones were incorrectly identified (Forbis, 1956).

As has been previously mentioned, one such leaf-like point was found in the Folsom layer at Sandia Cave. The finding of one of these specimens in association with mammoth remains in Mexico shows that this type was in use there at an early date. Also, the Lerma Complex in Tamaulipas (discussed on page 202), which contains similar points has been dated by the radiocarbon method at the University of Michigan at 9,270 ± 500 years ago.

Recent work by J. M. Cruxent at El Jobo in the State of Falcon, northwestern Venezuela, has revealed the presence of a series of camp sites which contained laurel-leaf forms with the same type of flaking that occurs on the points found with the second Santa Isabel Iztapan mammoth (Cruxent and Rouse, 1956). These are quite unlike other specimens found in this area, and it seems quite possible that the makers of these leaf-like forms moved farther south than Mexico at an early period. Unfortunately, only surface finds are represented, and the age of the South American specimens cannot be determined.*

An Implement of Elephant Bone From Manitoba, Canada

Douglas Leechman (1950) has reported the discovery of an implement made from the fibula of a mammoth or a mastodon in Manitoba. It was found by a farmer in the course of plowing a field some fifty miles northeast of Winnipeg. The distal end of the specimen,

---

*Rouse and Cruxent (1957) have published some further comments on the El Jobo discoveries. They note that Rex Gonzalez (1952) illustrated some points quite similar to those from El Jobo among the artifacts of the Ayampitin Complex of Central Argentina, dated at Yale by the radiocarbon method at 7970± 100 years ago. Leaf-shaped points are also constituents of three other non-ceramic complexes in South America, but, according to Rouse and Cruxent, they bear only a general resemblance in shape to the El Jobo and Ayampitin points.

which is seventeen inches long, has been tapered to a point, apparently with an adze. The proximal end is unworked. There is no proof that the bone was worked while it was still green. It showed little or no mineralization and could probably have been cut at any time. The fact that a grooved stone maul lay immediately above and in direct contact with the bone does not suggest great age, for such mauls, which are very common in the Prairie Provinces, are usually associated with late sites that contain pottery.

SOME POSSIBLE ASSOCIATIONS WITH MASTODON

Certain sites which have yielded mastodon remains are discussed elsewhere in the text: Bee County, Texas, page 65, Sandia Cave, page 85, Potter Creek, California, page 164, Friesenhahn Cave, page 218, Vero and Melbourne, Florida, pages 226 and 228. Others will be considered here. It has been most generally believed that mastodons became extinct at an early date, (Eiseley, 1946) although a few anthropologists and palaeontologists, (Montagu, 1944, and Scott, 1937) have suggested that they may have survived into relatively recent times. On the basis of the more recent age now generally accepted for the Mankato, it is reasonable to assume that climatic conditions that might permit the survival of a Pleistocene fauna may have continued in some areas into a more recent period than had previously been thought possible, and radiocarbon dates obtained at the University of Michigan (Crane, 1956) provide some support for those who favor the latter theory.

Wood reportedly in association with the mastodon remains found near Cromwell, Indiana, sometimes called the Richmond Mastodon, produced a radiocarbon date of 5,300 ± 400 years ago. There is, however, an unconfirmed report that a later run on this sample provided a considerably older date.* According to E. R. Burmaster (1932) and John T. Sanford (1935) charcoal was found on the clay on which the skeleton rested and under the bones. Two corner-notched points lay on the clay within twenty feet of the skeleton. Partially mineralized fragments of a mastodon tusk found in Washtenaw County, Michigan, were dated at 6,100 ± 400 and 6,300 ± 500 years ago. Wood that lay immediately above a mastodon tusk in Lenawee County, Michigan, provided a date of 9,568 ± 1,000 years ago. Wood collected immedi-

---

*Williams (1957) states that James B. Griffin (Personal communication) has indicated that a second run of the sample produced a date nearly twice this age.

ately below a mastodon skeleton and in the muck surrounding it at Orleton Farms, Madison County, Ohio, produced dates ranging from 8,420 ± 400 to 9,600 ± 500 years ago.

The Koch Discoveries

One of the first finds that suggested a contemporaneity between man and elephant in the New World was made in Missouri in 1838 by Albert C. Koch, a trader in fossils (Koch, 1860). In the bottom-lands of the Bourbeuse River in Gasconade County, he found the charred skeleton of a mastodon and some stone artifacts. In 1840 Koch found an almost complete mastodon skeleton near the Pomme de Terre River in Benton County, Missouri. Three projectile points were apparently found near the bones. The only one which has been illustrated is a stemmed form that resembles Archaic specimens (Rau, 1873). Koch believed that the animals and the men who made the artifacts were contemporaneous. He sold the bones and the artifacts found in Gasconade County to the Royal Museum of the University of Berlin.

M. F. Ashley Montagu and C. Bernard Peterson (1944) suggested that the animal found by Koch might have been a ground sloth. However, after the end of World War II, a German scholar, Hugo Gross, succeeded in finding some of the bones sold by Koch to the Berlin Museum and they proved to be those of mastodon. He also found eight artifacts, four of which he believes were those found with the bones (Gross, 1951). They resembled artifacts of the Archaic stage and were unlike any of those found in proven association with elephant remains. Gross has suggested that the skeleton could have been exposed by water action and that later Indians sought to destroy it by fire and by throwing stones at it. As he has noted, hunters usually roast certain parts of an animal rather than burning the whole carcass, and, in this case, the whole skeleton had been exposed to fire.

We still do not know exactly when mastodons became extinct, nor do we know how far back in time the Archaic may go. However, radiocarbon dates indicate that some Archaic sites date back more than 8,000 years and that some mastodons may have survived until that period or even later. It seems probable that certain Archaic people may have been contemporaries of the mastodon. In connection with the Koch discovery, it is worth noting that large stones lay upon and within the ash level associated with the bones. It is difficult to see why throwing stones at so huge an animal would be particularly effective, except perhaps to drive it into an area where it would become mired, but it is a curious coincidence that at the Dent Site (page 43), where there is unmistakable evidence of the association of man and mammoth, many large stones, which were scarce in the rest of the deposit, lay among the bones. At this late date there is no hope of obtaining proof of the authenticity of the association reported by Koch. It is possible that the bones and artifacts found by him are of different ages, but it is by no means certain.

The Island 35 Mastodon

Another early claim for contemporaneity of man and mastodon has recently been reinvestigated by Stephen Williams.* At the beginning of the century, Island 35, which has since disappeared, lay in the main channel of the Mississippi River in Tipton County, Tennessee near the Arkansas border. In 1900 part of a sand bar at the head of the island was destroyed by a rise in the river and, as the waters subsided, a mastodon skeleton was exposed. Curiosity seekers damaged many of the bones, but some were still in position when the locality was visited by Dr. James K. Hampson, who excavated them. Under what remained of the pelvis he found a large scraper and a broken projectile point. The former is a crudely flaked implement with no diagnostic value; the latter appears to have been stemmed and resembles two of those believed to have come from Koch's Gasconade County locality and the one reportedly found by him in Benton County. Again, there is no absolute proof of association between Archaic artifacts and mastodon bones, but there does seem to be a reasonable chance that Archaic people did hunt these animals. Better evidence may be available when a report is published on the 1949 discoveries at Orleton Farms, Ohio, for which the Carbon 14 dates derived from wood associated with mastodon bones are given above. Williams mentions a personal communication from Robert S. Goshin, who excavated the bones, to the effect that a projectile point with a contracting stem lay a few inches from the mastodon femur.

Jacob's Cavern

In 1921 a partially decayed left humerus of a deer was found in loose dirt in Jacob's Cavern in McDonald County, southwestern Missouri. On one side was an incised design that appeared to represent a mastodon. On the basis of physico-chemical studies, Vernon C. Allison (1926) came to the conclusion that the carving and the bone must

---

*The data in this section were obtained from a manuscript kindly provided by Williams. He has since published it. See Williams, 1957.

be at least some 14,000 years old. N. C. Nelson (1933), who excavated in Jacob's Cavern, however, came to the conclusion that the mastodon carving was not authentic. Most archaeologists who have seen the specimen have shared Nelson's opinion.

SOME PROBLEMS OF TERMINOLOGY

In the following section various sites will be discussed that have yielded the tools and implements of prehistoric men who, like the Folsom people, were hunters of bison now extinct. Their finely flaked projectile points were originally called Yuma points. It would have been difficult to make a more unwise choice of a name, for in the southwestern United States there is a well-known linguistic family which is called Yuman, and there is a Yuma tribe in the Colorado River area. Accordingly, there are archaeological remains which are legitimately referred to as Yuman, but there is not the slightest connection between these and the finely flaked projectile points first found in the Colorado county named for the historic Yuma Indians of Arizona. Doubtless one should be grateful that the first specimens were not found near Pueblo, Colorado.

The unfortunate choice of a name, however, marked only the beginning of the confusion. Far more serious was the fact that marked typological differences, some of which certainly have cultural and chronological significance, were overlooked. This category became a catchall in which to place any well-flaked point that was unfluted and lacked the notches and barbs that characterize many more recent types. When one name is assigned to a variety of forms, one would expect that there must be unmistakably clear evidence that all of these forms belong to the same complex. This is not the case. On the contrary, there is good evidence that several complexes are included.

In addition, unsubstantiated assumptions have been made about the relationships with Folsom. Much nonsense continues to be written about a "Folsom-Yuma Complex" although there is now ample evidence that a number of complexes are represented in the so-called Yuma category, and not one of these has been shown to be directly linked with Folsom. One bit of evidence has suggested a late contemporaneity between the makers of Folsom points and the people who produced some of the finely flaked points first found in Yuma County; but no relationship between the two groups has been established. Furthermore, there is evidence that many of the unfluted points belong to a more recent period than do Folsoms. The situation is so confused that it seems desirable to review briefly the history of the discoveries and studies of the various types of artifacts that have been so unfortunately lumped together.

Following the discovery at Folsom, New Mexico, many persons began searching for points of the type found there. In Yuma County, Colorado, Perry and Harold Andersen found a number of Folsom points on the surface of large bowl-shaped depressions, known as blow-outs, which had been denuded of top soil and scoured by wind action. They also found other long slender points, characterized by fine parallel flaking, and devoid of the barbs and notches that characterize most modern forms found in the area. The Andersens brought these finds to the attention of the late A. E. Jenks, who reported them to Harold J. Cook.

Cook visited the area investigated by the Andersens and reported finding similar specimens lying in the bottom of blow-outs with Folsom points (Cook, 1931). He also stated that one artifact was found in a grayish stratum which, in some areas, contained bones of extinct bison and mammoth. It was described only as "a large and spendidly wrought flint point." It was largely on the basis of this scanty evidence that it was first assumed that parallel flaked points were of great age and were related to Folsoms. The association of Folsoms and other points on the surface of blow-outs, of course, was not necessarily meaningful, for there was no way of determining from which levels the various artifacts were derived.

Later, a series of finely flaked unnotched points of the type found in the Yuma County blow-outs were examined by E. B. Renaud, who undertook the first typological studies (Renaud, 1931, 1932). Following the usual practice of assigning the name of the type locality to a newly described form, he called them Yuma points. This is an accepted way of naming a new type, but under the circumstances, it was a most unfortunate choice.

These points were divided into groups by Renaud on the basis of blade shapes and types of base. Included were some parallel-sided forms, others which reached a maximum breadth above the base, triangular shapes, and stemmed forms. Bases were straight, concave, and convex. The distinctive flaking he described as follows: "On the best pieces the flaking is rather narrow and long, ribbon-like, parallel and oblique, usually upward from the right edge and even reaching skillfully from edge to edge, while on others the flaking was completed by similar chipping, usually smaller, from the other side" (Renaud,

1931, p. 10). He also pointed out that in many cases the base had been thinned by the removal of vertical flakes and that there were more marked medial ridges on the narrower pieces.

Naturally, many difficulties arose because so many widely divergent types were placed in a single category, and various efforts were made to define the term "Yuma" in such a way as to include all of them. One such effort is represented by the definition submitted by the Committee appointed by the Chairman of the round table discussion of Folsom and Yuma points at the International Symposium on Early Man held in Philadelphia in 1937. "A Yuma point is triangular. It runs from triangular through parallel-sided to leaf-shaped. Its base is either straight or convex or concave. It is frequently stemmed but when stemmed has parallel sides . . . the sides of the stem are parallel. It is never fluted. It is pressure flaked from both sides, the flakes being parallel."

This definition was virtually meaningless. It made it possible to include a heterogeneous assortment of types under a single term without differentiating between them. In an effort to develop a more satisfactory form of classification, the writer and Betty Holmes undertook a study of 500 points, including many from the Andersen collection gathered in Yuma County, which would have been classified as Yumas under any then existent definition. It was found that 305 of these points could be placed in two main categories. In the first were placed unstemmed points which were more or less parallel-sided and usually had a concave base. They were characterized by the removal of narrow ribbon-like spalls which were parallel and ran obliquely across the face of the blade. This was called the Oblique Yuma type. The second group consisted of points which were often stemmed, although the basal insets were commonly very shallow. They usually had straight bases and were characterized by horizontal parallel flaking. This was called the Collateral Yuma type.

One hundred ninety-five specimens remained to be classified. They conformed to the definition of the modal type, but the flaking, although roughly parallel, was shallow and less regular. These points occurred in shapes characteristic of both the horizontally and obliquely flaked forms, and some had shapes similar to those of fluted points, although they lacked the distinctive grooves. Admittedly, this did not appear to be a homogeneous group, but the practice of calling such points Yumas was so well-established that those who were working on the project hesitated to suggest removing them from that category.

Accordingly, they were called Indeterminate Yumas.

This classification helped to clarify the situation to some extent, but it left much to be desired, particularly since the Indeterminate category still provided a catchall for many divergent types. As a result, when a conference on terminology and typology of early points was held in Santa Fe in 1941, it was decided to abandon this term, and synonyms such as Generalized Yuma and Unfluted Folsom, and leave such points, which were known only from surface finds, unnamed until type stations were found.

The term Parallel Flaked points was selected as an over-all designation for the types which remained. The term Oblique Yuma was retained; but the horizontally flaked points, which had been called Collateral Yumas, were named after a site in the Eden Valley of Wyoming where they had been found *in situ,* and were called Eden Yumas. Later it was pointed out that the horizontally flaked group included two subtypes, one of which was broader and more markedly stemmed (Howard, 1943). Since such an artifact had first been found in a quarry near Scottsbluff, Nebraska, these were named Scottsbluff Yumas.

Again the situation was improved, but difficulties still arose. There were important typological differences between the various types that bore names with a Yuma modifier, and horizontally and obliquely flaked forms were not found together. Furthermore, the term Yuma was still very loosely used, and references were still made to a "Folsom-Yuma" culture or horizon, although evidence was now available which indicated that there was, at best, only a late contemporaneity between the two groups and that the unfluted lanceolate forms apparently persisted into more recent times.

In 1948 the writer proposed that the term Yuma be dropped altogether and that the term Parallel Flaked replace it as a general designation (Wormington, 1948). This term simply describes the flaking technique and has no connotation of age. It was also proposed that the points formerly known as Eden Yumas and Scottsbluff Yumas be known only as Eden points and Scottsbluff points; and that the former Oblique Yumas, for which a type station had not yet been found, be left unnamed and simply be referred to as points with oblique parallel flaking. The name Browns Valley points, which had been previously suggested by Roberts (1940), was proposed for certain specimens with such flaking, found at a site of that name in Minnesota.

Since the Santa Fe conference, a number of types previously placed in the Indeterminate category have been found in excavated sites. They have been called Plainview points, Long or Angostura points, Agate Basin points, and San Jon points. These and a variety of points found in the Clovis-Portales area will be discussed in the following section. All other types which have previously been loosely categorized under the term "Yuma" but which are known only from surface finds are left unnamed pending the discovery of type stations.

In more recent publications the term "Yuma" is being less and less frequently used, although there is some persistence of the regrettable practice of putting the word in quotation marks and then continuing to use it in the same unwarranted fashion. This certainly does nothing to clarify the situation, and it is to be hoped that this term will be abandoned altogether.

Although points with parallel flaking can be divided into two broad groups—those with horizontal, and those with oblique flaking—Davis (1954) has pointed out that a further subdivision should be made in the former category. Two types of horizontal parallel flaking may be recognized. (1) Collateral—broad conchoidal spalls were removed beginning at either edge, and extending to the mid-section, producing a dorsal ridge. Artifacts formed in this manner have a diamond-shaped cross-section. (2) Transverse—narrow flakes, starting at either edge, were removed in such a manner that the scars met smoothly to form a single flake scar. These scars lie at right angles to the long axis of the point. Artifacts formed by this technique have an essentially lenticular cross-section. Obliquely flaked specimens bear similarly formed flake scars and have the same type of cross-section, but the scars are directed diagonally across the face of the blade. They usually slant downward from left to right.

The Plainview Site

One type of point, perhaps more than any other, contributed to the practice of linking unfluted points with Folsoms. These points, which were commonly called "Yumas," were ungrooved, but they had shapes reminiscent of fluted forms. In 1945 a site was finally discovered where such artifacts were found *in situ* in unmistakable association with the remains of extinct bison (Sellards, Evans, Meade, 1947).

This most important site lies in the High Plains of northwestern Texas near the town of Plainview. A great bed of bison bones was uncovered in a pit dug to obtain road material in 1944. In the following year excavations were begun by geologists from the Texas Memorial Museum. They found the remains of approximately one hundred bison, which appear to be of the same species as those from the Folsom type station. They were larger than the largest individuals of modern species.

This great mass of bones raises the question of how such an accumulation could have been formed. Since projectile points have been found in position in the deposit, we must assume that man was at least a contributing factor. One possible theory is that the bone bed may indicate a bison stampede, perhaps deliberately caused by man, which resulted in the trampling of many fallen animals by the onrushing herd. Dart points might have been shot into the herd to begin the stampede, or they might have been used to kill some of the fallen and crippled animals. There is also a possibility that the bones may have accumulated over a period of time as animals repeatedly sought a water hole, perhaps during a period of drought. Under such conditions some individuals might die of natural causes while others would fall an easy prey to man.

In any case, we can at least be sure that some of the bison must have been killed by man; and it is the association of extinct animal remains with projectile points that makes this site of great archaeological significance. The artifacts from the Plainview bison bone bed have been described by Alex D. Krieger. Twenty-two artifacts were found in position with the bones, and five others were almost certainly associated but they were disturbed in the course of excavations. Included are eighteen whole and fragmentary projectiles of a distinctive type; these are now called Plainview points. They are lanceolate in outline and have concave bases. They somewhat resemble Clovis Fluted forms, but they are ungrooved. In general, the flaking is rather irregular, but some specimens have parallel flaking at the distal end. Basal edges are smoothed, and there is some basal thinning produced by the removal of vertical flakes. (Fig. 69, p. 264.)

Two Carbon 14 samples from the Plainview Site were tested at the Lamont Laboratory. Bone fragments that had lain on or near the surface from the time when the excavation ended in 1945 until they were collected in 1955 had been subject to contamination by plant rootlets. They gave a date of 7,100 ± 160 years ago. Shells of freshwater snails that had been kept free of contamination in glass containers since they were collected in 1953 produced a date of 9,170 ± 500 years ago.*

---

*Originally listed as a Personal Communication, but now published. See Krieger, Editor, 1957a.

Distribution of Plainview Points

Plainview points are widely distributed throughout the Plains and have been found as far north as Alaska and as far south as Mexico. One Plainview point, reported by Froelich Rainey (1940), was recovered in the Tanana Valley of Alaska, in muck deposits believed to be of Pleistocene age. Another was reported by Frank Hibben (1943). It was found by a miner in muck deposits in the vicinity of Circle, Alaska. The origin of these deposits is not definitely known, but Hibben has suggested that they are probably wind-blown material from outwash plains of local glaciations. A third specimen was found by J. L. Giddings, Jr., (1951) north of Bering Strait with the Cape Denbigh material discussed on page 208.

Richard S. MacNeish (1953, 1956b) has reported on a site on a bench some forty feet above Great Bear Lake in the Northwest Territories which yielded two complete and two fragmentary projectile points. Two well-flaked specimens with basal grinding could be classified as Plainview points. One tip fragment is not sufficiently complete to be assigned to any type, but it does bear parallel flake scars. One complete point has a shape much like that of a Plainview, but it is considerably smaller and the edges are not ground. Snub-nosed end scrapers, side scrapers, ovoid knives, disc choppers, together with the points, make up the complex to which MacNeish has given the name Franklin Tanks.

At the Brohm Site in the Thunder Bay District of Ontario, excavated by MacNeish (1952) six Plainview points were found. Associated with them were lanceolate points with straight and rounded bases, triangular forms, a point with a contracting stem, a drill, biface knives, pick-like objects, a variety of scrapers, including snub-nosed types, choppers, hammerstones, and a grooved piece of sandstone that may have been used for abrading. The artifacts lay in gravels attributed to a high beach of Lake Algonquin. Peat samples, collected on the east shore of Lake Michigan and dated at the University of Michigan, averaged 7925 ± 350 years ago. These are thought to provide a minimum date for Lake Algonquin. The beach gravels must be older.

A number of Plainview points have been found in Alberta in the vicinity of Edmonton, Red Deer, and Cereal. In the latter locality finds made by Russell A. Johnston suggest that here, as in the Plains sites farther south, they were sometimes associated with the alternately beveled forms called Meserve points, which are discussed on page 113. A point with basal thinning and basal grinding, which apparently could be placed in the Plainview series, was found in the Chehalis River Valley west of Olympia, Washington (Osborne, 1956).

The basal portion of a good example of Plainview point was found by Sol Arguedas R. de la Borbolla on the Mexican side of the reservoir basin of the Falcon Dam two miles northeast of Ciudad Guerrero, Tamaulipas. It apparently came from a buried zone that lay some twenty inches below the surface (Borbolla and Aveleyra, 1953). Another Plainview point was found with artifacts of the Nogales Complex in Tamaulipas discussed on page 204.

The Lone Wolf Creek Finds

Although the Plainview type was not defined until 1947, a Plainview point had been found with extinct bison at a much earlier date, but the evidence was not conclusive. At a site on Lone Wolf Creek, near Colorado City, Texas, was made one of the earliest discoveries in America of man-made implements associated with the bones of an extinct animal. It antedated the Folsom discovery by two years (Cook, 1927; Figgins, 1927).

Articulated bones of an extinct bison were found overlain by seven feet of a solidly cemented mixture of sand, gravel, and clay. Instead of clearing the skeleton in the field, large blocks of matrix, containing the bones, were removed and prepared for shipment to the laboratory by being incased in plaster-soaked burlap. As the matrix was being cleared from the underside of the blocks, two whole and one fragmentary projectile points were found. One of the complete points was lost and no adequate description is available, although it is said to have resembled the other two specimens (Fig. 36). The fragmentary piece has a concave base and conforms perfectly to the definition of the Plainview type. The whole point has a very slightly convex base and would now be classified as a Milnesand point described below.

The fact that the Lone Wolf Creek discovery was made at a time when there was great skepticism about the antiquity of man in America, added to the manner in which the points were uncovered, militated against widespread acceptance of the association. Now, however, since similar points have been found nearby, unmistakably associated with extinct bison possibly of the same subspecies, there is no reason to doubt the authenticity of the association. J. D. Figgins (1935a), who was convinced of its validity, suggested at an early date that the Lone Wolf Creek points should not be confused with either Folsoms or the so-called Yumas.

FIG. 36—Point and fragment found with extinct bison on Lone Wolf Creek near Colorado City, Texas. Left, Plainview, right, Milnesand point.

The Milnesand Site

In a sand dune area three miles northeast of Milnesand, New Mexico, E. H. Sellards (1955) found a bone bed which contained bison bones and artifacts. The bison skulls were not preserved, so species identification cannot be made. However, on the basis of the size of certain bones, it is thought possible, but not certain, that a fossil bison is represented. The associated artifacts include projectile points and scrapers. Of the former, eleven were found in position in the bone bed and twelve were found on the surface. They are characterized by transverse parallel flaking, but some have a fairly pronounced median ridge. They somewhat resemble Plainview points, but the bases are square and thinning was accomplished through the removal of more and smaller flakes in such a manner as to produce a bevel. Basal grinding is present on all specimens and often extends one half or more of the length of the point. The name Milnesand has been assigned to this type.

Since it is only recently that this type has been defined, relatively little is known of its age and distribution. The discovery near Colorado City, Texas, has suggested that it was contemporaneous with Plainview. At the Lime Creek Site in Nebraska, discussed on page 120, two points that closely resemble those found at Milnesand were found in the same zone as a Scottsbluff point. Here a Plainview point was found in a higher zone. Finds in Iowa indicate that the Milnesand type spread farther east. The writer has seen two splendid examples from there, and it is reported that twenty-seven similar points have been found in Mills County. Artifacts that closely resemble points from the Milnesand Site have also been found in the north. There are many good examples in collections from Alberta and Saskatchewan. A similar specimen was found near the University of Alaska at Fairbanks (Skarland and Giddings, 1948).

The Portales Complex

At the Blackwater Draw No. 1 locality near Clovis, New Mexico, described on page 47, there were three horizons which contained artifacts. The lowest produced Clovis points, and Folsom points were found in the second. The uppermost contained a few scrapers and worked flakes, and twenty-three whole and fragmentary projectile points, most of which have transverse parallel flaking. Some of these points have concave bases and some are long and narrow, but the great majority closely approximate the Milnesand type although grinding does not extend so far up the edges. Sellards (1952) has proposed the name Portales Complex for this assemblage.

Bones from the Portales horizon at the Sanders Gravel Pit on the Charles Baxter ranch near Portales were tested by the radiocarbon method. A sample consisting of uncharred bones, submitted to the Lamont Laboratory, produced a date of 6,300 ± 150 years ago, while another sample made up of partially charred bones was dated at 6,230 ± 150 years ago.* The close similarity of these dates would suggest

---

*Originally listed as a Personal Communication, but now published. See Krieger, Editor, 1957a.

that the use of charred bones for Carbon 14 dating is not so essential as was originally thought.

The San Jon Site

A site which lies on the south side of the Canadian River near the town of San Jon, New Mexico, was excavated under the direction of Frank H. H. Roberts, Jr. (1942). In the lowest of four stratigraphic horizons recognized at the site was found a single thick, roughly flaked, square-based point to which Roberts assigned the site name, calling it a San Jon point. The writer, who does not feel that a type can be defined on the basis of a single specimen, would now regard it as probably belonging to the Portales Complex. Associated with this point, which lay in deposits indicating the former presence of a lake or pond, were the completely fossilized bones of a large bison, probably of an extinct species. At another part of the site a Folsom fragment was found weathering out of the same layer, together with similar fossilized bones. Mammoth remains, although not found with artifacts, occur nearby in what appears to be the same stratum. A discussion of the specimens, reportedly of the Scottsbluff type, found in an alluvial deposit that lay disconformably on this stratum, will be found on page 122.

The Meserve Site

In 1923, near Grand Island, Hall County, Nebraska, Charles and Earl Foster found a bison skull in the bank of the Platte River (Barbour and Schultz, 1932). They brought their find to the attention of F. G. Meserve who visited the site during the following summer. He found two skulls of extinct bison and many skeletal parts. The species represented is thought to be *occidentalis*. A projectile point lay under a scapula in the matrix, associated with the fossil bison bones. The quarry was reopened in 1931 (Schultz, 1932) and a second artifact of the same general type was found in the matrix in a cluster of ribs and vertebrae.

Both specimens have concave bases and prominent basal thinning scars. The basal edges are ground. The first found has the greatest breadth at the mid-section; the second has essentially parallel sides for approximately a third of its length and the remainder of the blade is steeple-shaped. Both are unifacially beveled, the bevel being on the right side when the point is viewed with tip upward. A similar specimen was found in a deeply buried site near Abilene, Texas. Cyrus

N. Ray (1940) applied the name Gibson point to it, but the use of this term might cause confusion with an unrelated complex that bears the same name. Davis (1953) has suggested that the Meserve Quarry, where these points were first found, should provide the type designation, and they have been called Meserve points. Similar points have been found in Oklahoma, Arkansas, Missouri, Iowa, Illinois, and Canada, as well as in Nebraska and Texas. At the Dalton Site in Cole County, Missouri, similarly shaped points were found some five to eight feet below the surface in a road borrow pit (Logan, 1952). Many of these were serrated. The name Dalton points is sometimes applied to the serrated forms.

Courtesy University of Missouri

FIG. 37—Meserve or Dalton Points from Missouri.

The full archaeological significance of Meserve points is not known. In some cases they are found alone and in others they are found in association with Plainviews. At Graham Cave, Missouri, (discussed on page 64) points attributed to the Dalton (Meserve) category were found in a level dated at some 8,800 to 9,700 years ago. At the Red Smoke Site, (discussed on page 117) were found specimens which appear to be Plainviews reworked in such a way as to give the appearance of Meserve points. William Mulloy has suggested that these may be broken Plainview points rechipped without being removed from the shaft. The presence of the shaft would make it more practical to turn the point over than to reverse it.

Finds in North Central Texas

The study of finds of early cultural remains in north central Texas has been greatly confused because of terminological differences between workers in the field. In some cases archaeologists have assigned identical names to different forms; in others they have used different names for identical forms. The results of much basic research have not been published. In addition, there is a variety of opinions not only regarding the ages of certain key formations, but also the names applied to them.

In 1929 Cyrus N. Ray first found worked flints in the Abilene region at such depths as to suggest the possibility of considerable age. Following this discovery further work was done by Ray (1930-1948), E. B. Sayles (1935), Harold S. Gladwin (1937), and others. More recently other archaeologists, notably Joe Ben Wheat (1940), J. Charles Kelley (1947) and Thomas N. Campbell (1948) have obtained new data through further work in the area. Alex D. Krieger (1946) has written of the culture and chronology of northern Texas, and Robert L. Stephenson (1950) has presented a brief summary of archaeological sequences in Texas. Dee Ann Suhm and Alex D. Krieger (1954) with the collaboration of Edward B. Jelks, have produced "An Introductory Handbook of Texas Archaeology."

In order to understand some of the problems involved it is necessary to know something of the geological formations in which finds have been made. The geology of the Abilene area was first studied and reported on by M. M. Leighton who distinguished two formations of river alluvium separated by a disconformity which indicated a long period of erosion. The lower was named the Durst Silts and the upper the Elm Creek Silts. Leighton tentatively attributed the Durst Silts to the Illinoian glaciation which preceded the Wisconsin, and the Elm Creek Silts he assigned to the Wisconsin or the early Recent. On the basis of all other evidence, the proposed date for the Durst Silts appeared excessive and was not accepted by archaeologists. It has been generally believed that, as Ernst Antevs (1948) suggested, the period of erosion of the lower alluvium correlates with the Altithermal. Now, however, there is evidence from the Scharbauer Site near Midland, Texas, (discussed on page 241) that suggests there was a still earlier drought. Even if this should prove to be a widespread manifestation, and the disconformity should correlate with this, the underlying silts would still be attributed to the Wisconsin rather than the Illinoian. It will be impossible to determine the age of the disconformity and the silts until further work is done.

In the Durst Silts artifacts and extinct animal remains, including mammoth, have been found. Some extremely crude specimens, suggestive of hand axes, were called Durst Eoliths (Gladwin, 1937). Most archaeologists do not believe these represent a very primitive form of implement, but rather that they are unfinished artifacts and reject material. The deposits on Lone Wolf Creek near Colorado City, Texas, (discussed on page 110) which produced points of the types now called Plainview and Milnesand, are tentatively considered Durst Silts. In the Abilene region Ray (1940) found specimens that resemble Plainview and Meserve points in sites in the Durst Silts. These deposits may represent a long time interval, and artifacts and bones found within them could be of different ages. It is also possible, as W. W. Crook Jr. (1955) has suggested, that mistakes have been made in correlating deposits that are lithologically dissimilar.

Ray (1934) has also described other artifacts which he calls Abilene points. These are roughly leaf-shaped, thick, crudely flaked by percussion, and about two or three inches long. In some examples flakes have been removed from one side, resulting in a stem beveled to the right. There is some controversy regarding the provenience of these points and the validity of the type. Ray believes them to be of Wisconsin age. Kelley (1947) has suggested that the age of Ray's specimens may not be greater than that of the erosional period indicated by the disconformity between the two silt units. The evidence is not conclusive and even the age of the disconformity is still in question. Stephenson (1950) and Suhm and Krieger (1954) do not include Abilene points in their lists of types. In view of the unsatisfactory nature of the data, this seems the best solution.

Ray and Sayles found evidence of a complex which they originally called by different names but which they later agreed to designate the Clear Fork (Ray and Sayles, 1941). The most distinctive artifacts in this complex are chipped implements that are called gouges although it is not certain what their function may have been. These are triangular to ovoid objects with the larger end shaped to form a cutting edge which is usually concave but may be convex; the smaller end comes to a point or a chisel edge. There were also projectile points. Some are stemmed and have somewhat beveled blades, other are stemless triangular forms. Ray (1948) suggested that they might be as much as 20,000 years old. Most archaeologists now believe that the Clear Fork Complex belongs to the Archaic Stage and that it is a local manifestation of the Edwards Plateau Aspect. Some feel that similar artifacts may have continued to be made in a later period when pottery was being produced (Krieger, 1946; Kelley, 1947). However, Kelley found Clear Fork specimens deeply buried in a forty foot terrace near Austin, and in a number of localities they have been found with lanceolate points reminiscent of Paleo-Indian types. It has been suggested that this and other complexes of the Edwards Plateau Aspect may have persisted over a very long period of time, perhaps having begun as much as 6,000 years ago.

The Red Smoke Site

In the area some eight miles from Cambridge, Nebraska, which is now flooded by the Medicine Creek Reservoir, a number of important early sites were found. Before they were covered by water they were excavated by the University of Nebraska State Museum. One of these is the Red Smoke Site which lies on the north side of Lime Creek, a small western tributary of Medicine Creek. It was tested in 1947 by C. Bertrand Schultz and Weldon Frankforter (1948). E. Mott Davis (1953) undertook more intensive excavations during the seasons from 1949 through 1952.

Eight cultural zones were recognized. The four lowest produced bone scraps, hearth areas, scraping, chopping, and cutting tools, and one whole and two fragmentary projectile points. These are lanceolate concave-based forms. The bases, found in Zone III, the third from the bottom, could probably be classified as Plainviews, but the complete specimen found in Zone IV is narrower and thicker than the usual Plainview type. Davis equates the material from the latter zone to the Frontier Complex discussed on page 137.

The fifth zone from the bottom was the richest at this site. It yielded more than 500 identifiable artifacts, many flint chips, and fragmentary bison bones. Concentrations of charcoal in bowl-shaped depressions probably represent hearths. Of the greatest diagnostic significance were twenty-six whole or fragmentary specimens which have been classified as Plainviews, and two which have the appearance of Meserve points. Davis regards them as reworked Plainviews. He thinks they were used for scraping or boring rather than as weapon tips. Most of the fragments represent the basal portions of points, which suggests that this was not a kill site but a workshop or campsite to which shafts with broken points were brought for refitting. Associated artifacts included scrapers and bifacial chopping and cutting tools.

Cultural evidence from the three uppermost zones, which were separated from the fifth by an unconformity and which must be of more recent age, was scattered and discontinuous. These zones contained ochre stains and grinding stones, which are very rare in the lower horizons, and a stemmed point, a form which was not represented below. A hearth in the uppermost zone contained charcoal. Two samples produced dates averaging 8,862 ± 230 years ago (Libby, 1955). Specimens from the underlying zones must be still older.

SCOTTSBLUFF AND EDEN POINTS

The Scottsbluff Bison Quarry

Points that were fairly wide relative to their length, had parallel-sided or somewhat triangular blades, were lenticular in cross-section, and bore horizontal flake scars which were usually essentially parallel, were found in Yuma County blow-outs when the area was first investigated. However, the first point of this type was not found in a site until 1932. In that year C. Bertrand Schultz and E. H. Barbour excavated a site near Scottsbluff, Nebraska, which contained such specimens (Barbour and Schultz, 1932; Schultz and Eiseley, 1935). It is this site which has given the type its name. Bison bones were found imbedded in a gravel deposit two to four feet thick. The gravels were overlain by silts and sands, which in turn were overlain by loess deposits. Schultz regards the bison as an extinct form, possibly *occidentalis.*

Associated with the bones were eight artifacts. One was a plano-convex end scraper and three were modified flakes that have no diagnostic value; but there were also three fragmentary points and one complete specimen. The latter is the one which has provided the name for the Scottsbluff type. There is another specimen, with only the tip missing, which resembles the former but has a more triangular blade, a more deeply inset stem, and is thinner. Another point, which lacks only a small portion of the base, is a lanceolate form with somewhat convex sides, and can be classified as a Plainview. The flaking is essentially oblique. The fourth point lacks the basal portion and cannot be identified.

Unfortunately, the exact provenience of these specimens is not known, and it is not certain that the stemmed points and the Plainview point are of the same age. At the Lime Creek Site, to be discussed next, a Plainview was found in a higher level than a Scottsbluff, which shows that at that site, at least, the Plainview was younger.

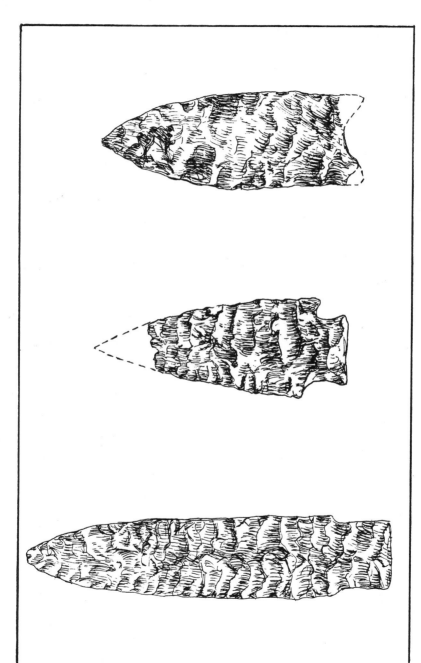

FIG. 38—Artifacts from the Scottsbluff Bison Quarry, Nebraska. (After Barbour and Schultz, 1932.)

The Lime Creek Site

An important site in the Medicine Creek Dam area was Ft 41, or the Lime Creek Site, which lay one-third of a mile east of the Red Smoke Site. It was first investigated by C. Bertrand Schultz in 1947 (Schultz and Frankforter, 1948). Further excavations were carried on by E. Mott Davis in 1949 and 1950 (Davis, 1953, 1954). The site was inundated in 1950.

The Lime Creek Site lay on a level exposed by floods, in the base of a high terrace, known as Terrace 2A, in the Republican River drainage. Three occupation zones were found. The lowest, called Zone I, lay forty-seven and a half feet below the surface. One hundred fifty-seven artifacts were found in this zone. Most of them were large implements ranging in length from four to seven inches. They were flaked on both sides, roughly parallel-sided, and most bases were straight although some were slightly convex. These could have served as knives or choppers. Davis has suggested that possibly they were wood-working tools. The presence of two grooved abrading stones indicates that shafts were prepared here. The possibility that the large bifacially flaked objects are blanks might also be considered. Near the site are outcrops of jasper, and it is quite likely that people were attracted to the locality because of the presence of this material. Some preliminary shaping of the stone could have been done at the site and then the blanks taken elsewhere for final processing. The presence of numerous chips, hammerstones, and a flaking tool made of antler, suggests that stoneworking was an important activity. The fact that only a small number of scrapers was found, and that drills and awls were absent, would suggest that little emphasis was placed on the preparation of hides.

One almost complete point and four fragmentary specimens were found. Two of the fragments have no diagnostic value. The almost complete point and two of the fragments have fine transverse flaking. The former, which lacks only a tiny portion of the base, is a good example of the Scottsbluff type, although the stem insets are not so pronounced as in the case of specimens from the type station and some other sites. It is basally ground. The fragmentary pieces with the same type of flaking have essentially the same outline but they are not shouldered. Apart from the fact that they lack basal grinding, they closely resemble Milnesand points discussed on page 111.

Carbon 14 dates averaging 9,524 ± 450 years ago were obtained at the University of Chicago Laboratory from charred logs found in clay which underlies Zone I (Libby, 1955). Schultz, however, believes that the carbonaceous clay and silt of Zone I represents the earlier fill of Terrace 2A which he regards as of Two Creeks age. This pre-Mankato stage has elsewhere been dated by the radiocarbon method at a little over 11,000 years ago. Many archaeologists, including the writer, believe that Zone I at Lime Creek is post-Mankato rather than pre-Mankato in age.

Courtesy University of Nebraska State Museum

FIG. 39—Projectile point and fragment from Zone I at the Lime Creek Site, Nebraska. Left, Scottsbluff point, right, specimen which resembles a Milnesand point, but lacks basal grinding.

The next occupation zone, No. II, was encountered two to three feet higher in the formation. Only a small area was investigated, and few artifacts were recovered. None has any diagnostic value.

Zone III lay eight feet above Zone I. It contained two hearths, various bone fragments, flint chips, and thirty-six artifacts. Most of the artifacts were cutting and chopping tools that have little diagnostic value, but two lanceolate projectile points were found. One has a concave base and resembles a Plainview; the other has a straight base and resembles a Milnesand point. Both, however, lack the basal grinding which is normally found on these types. A mid-section of a point which has parallel oblique flaking and is unifacially beveled was also found in this horizon. Other artifacts included a tip fragment, which might have been part of a drill or point, and several asymmetrical specimens that were probably knives.

Bison bones were found in all three zones, and it seems probable that these animals supplied much of the food for those who camped here. However, the discovery, in Zone I, of a sandstone object with two flat faces, which could have served as a mano, might indicate some dependence on seeds. No positive identification of the bison bones has been made, but they seem to resemble those of an extinct form, *Bison antiquus,* rather than those of modern buffalo.

The MacHaffie Site

At the MacHaffie Site near Helena, Montana, described on page 41, was found an occupation level that contained essentially the same assemblage as did Zone I at Lime Creek (Forbis and Sperry, 1952). In a gray clay, which overlay the black soil level that contained Folsom points, were found well-flaked Scottsbluff points, square-based unstemmed forms with marked basal grinding, and more crudely flaked lanceolate specimens. Associated with them were large bifacial tools, like those commonly found in the lower level at Lime Creek, and various cutting, scraping, chopping, and abrading tools. Faunal remains included bones of bison, too fragmentary for species identification, and bones of antelope, rabbit, and ground squirrel.

Scottsbluff Points at the San Jon Site

The geology at the San Jon Site was studied by Sheldon Judson (1953). Above the horizon which yielded the single square-based point, discussed on page 113, lay an alluvial deposit. There was a marked disconformity between the two beds, which suggests that a long period of erosion preceded the deposition of the upper bed. Judson correlated this with the Altithermal or Thermal Maximum period, which would mean a post-Altithermal age for the alluvial deposit. This would accord with the faunal evidence, for the bison bones recovered were of the modern species, *Bison bison.* Difficulties arise, however, because of the reported presence of Scottsbluff points in this horizon. Elsewhere evidence has suggested an age of some 7,000 to 9,000 years for such points, and it seems highly unlikely that the type would persist over such a very long period of time. Unfortunately, the site has not been fully reported upon; there is no way of knowing how many points were found, how many were of the Scottsbluff type, nor exactly where they lay in the deposit. If Judson is correct in attributing this deposit to the Medithermal, the Scottsbluff points are almost certainly intrusive. Perhaps they were washed in as the alluvium was deposited, or perhaps they were brought in by later people. There is a possibility, however, that the disconformity may date from an earlier dry period for which evidence has been found at a site near Midland, Texas, discussed on page 241. Points which resemble more recent forms from Texas were found somewhat higher in the San Jon desposits.

Miscellaneous Finds of Scottsbluff Points

Many Scottsbluff points have been found on the surface in northwestern Louisiana and eastern Texas. R. K. Harris (Personal communication) has reported that, in 1924, H. H. Allen found a cache of ten or eleven Scottsbluff points, all made of the same light flint, near Okolana, Arkansas. Recently, W. W. Crook, Jr. and R. K. Harris (1955) reported the finding of a Scottsbluff point *in situ* at the Obscher Site near Dallas, Texas. Another Scottsbluff was in probable, but not certain, association. This site also contained artifacts of the Carrollton Focus, which is of the Archaic Stage. Quite possibly this specimen was picked up and brought in by Archaic people and the association is a fortuitous one. However, several sites of the Carrollton Focus have contained Plainview points. Perhaps here, as in Graham Cave, there is some overlapping of the Paleo-Indian and Archaic horizons.

Scottsbluff points have also been found farther north. One specimen was received at the Washington State Museum in 1925 with the information that it came from "western Washington or British Columbia" (Osborne, 1956). Another was found in a collection from the East Kootenay region of British Columbia (Duff and Borden, 1954). It is thought to have come from the Lake Windimere District. More detailed information regarding provenience would be desirable, but it seems entirely probable that these specimens came from the regions indicated, for many such points have been found in the provinces of Alberta and Saskatchewan. The specimens from the Prairie Provinces have been found frequently associated with Eden points and are considered part of the Cody Complex. They are discussed on page 132. A fragmentary point that resembles a Scottsbluff was found at the George Lake Site discussed on page 205. A Scottsbluff-like point was found in Alaska associated with material of the Denbigh Flint Complex discussed on page 208.

Eden Points

There is another type of projectile point that has some of the same characteristics as the Scottsbluff and which has been found associated with it in a number of sites. This is the Eden point. It is much narrower in relation to its length than the Scottsbluff and has a less strongly indented stem. It is horizontally flaked, but the flaking, although sometimes of the transverse type, is more frequently of the collateral type which produces a diamond-shaped cross-section. Edens have a more limited distribution than Scottsbluffs, their range apparently being limited to the High Plains and areas to the north. The writer has seen one example found on the outskirts of Peace River, Alberta. Another specimen, now in the collection of Joseph Cramer (Personal communication) was found by Oscar Lewis while doing reconnaissance along the Alaskan Highway. One fragment was found near Fairbanks, Alaska, in frozen muck deposits which contained bones of extinct animals (Hibben, 1943).

The Finley Site*

The points now known as Edens were first found in Yuma County blow-outs during the 1930's, but none was found *in situ* until the spring of 1940 when Harold J. Cook spent several days digging in a site discovered by O. M. Finley near the town of Eden, Wyoming. This site was named in honor of Finley. Later in the summer more intensive excavations were undertaken on behalf of the University of Pennsylvania Museum by a party under the direction of Linton Satterthwaite, Jr. (Howard, Satterthwaite, and Bache, 1941; Howard, 1943). Work was resumed the following year under the joint sponsorship of the University of Pennsylvania Museum and the Nebraska State Museum by a group headed by Edgar B. Howard.

Twenty-four projectile points were found, sixteen of them *in situ*. Some of these specimens and the associated artifacts are still in the possession of Cook and Finley, and have not been available for examination by the writer. She has, however, seen the actual specimens or

---

*The University of Pennsylvania Museum will publish an outstanding report on this site which provides much new data. The monograph, prepared by Linton Satterthwaite, Jr., is now in press.

FIG. 40—Projectile points from the Finley Site, Wyoming. Top row, Eden points, Nos. 1 and 2 collateral flaking, No. 3 transverse flaking. Center row, Scottsbluff points, Type I. Lower row, Scottsbluff points, Type II. Type definitions page 267.

adequate photographs in the case of eleven specimens, and has utilized Dr. Satterthwaite's field notes in attempting to classify the remaining artifacts. She would classify six as Scottsbluffs (similar to the narrowest stemmed point found at the type station), five as Edens with collateral flaking, and three as Edens with transverse flaking. Two points were broader and thinner, and the blades were more triangular and the stems more deeply indented than those usually classified as Scottsbluffs. These resemble the broadest stemmed point found at the Scottsbluff Bison Quarry. There was also a larger, thicker artifact which resembled these specimens but probably did not serve as a projectile point.

A great many bison bones were found with the artifacts. These bones have not been specifically identified, but what makes them of particular interest is a certain marked selectivity. They consist almost entirely of lower limb bones, and there is a strong preponderance of foot bones. Most of these bones appear to have been intentionally split or broken, but there is no evidence of workmanship. Quite a number of bison teeth were also found.

The artifacts and associated bison bones lay under a layer of wind-blown dune sand in a pink clayey sand horizon which overlies a stratum of greenish sand, fine-grained toward the bottom and coarser toward the top. The first geological interpretation of the site was undertaken by John T. Hack (1943). His general approach was to correlate the deposition of the culture layer with the cutting and filling of gravel terraces in the Eden Valley, and then try to correlate these with the glacial chronology of the Wind River Mountains. The culture layer was obviously more recent than the terrace on which it lay. Hack believed that this terrace, which he called the Farson, was of post-Mankato age and was more recent than the one on which the Lindenmeier Site lay. He suggested that the Finley Site was younger than Lindenmeier. This is in accord with other evidence, for Roberts (Johnson, Editor, 1951) reports finding Eden points stratigraphically higher than Folsoms at the latter site, but there is some disagreement on the part of geologists as to the age of the Farson terrace.

Hack stressed the need for further studies, and when other duties prevented him from continuing his work in this area, John H. Moss (1951, 1952) undertook to complete the geological interpretation. The gravels which underlay the artifact-bearing sand he attributed to the Mankato. Under the upper sand he found a layer of caliche, which indicated a long and intense period of aridity. This he equated with the warm Altithermal period generally believed to have lasted from about 7,000 to 4,000 years ago. On this basis the date for the archaeological level would be expected to fall between the terminal date for the Mankato and the beginning date of the Altithermal. The occupation of the site must have occurred during a fairly moist period, since there would have had to be sufficient grass to nourish the herds of bison on which the early hunters depended. Moss feels that the period of occupation correlates with a minor post-Mankato advance represented by the Temple Lake Moraine in the Wind River Mountains. He has suggested that the date of occupation would fall between 7,000 and 9,000 years ago. Such a date would accord with evidence from other sites and is probably of the right order of magnitude. Some geologists, however, question the accuracy of Moss's correlations, for they regard the Temple Lake stage as of post-Altithermal age.

The Horner Site

Another Wyoming site which yielded Edens, Scottsbluffs, and similar types, provided information about the other artifacts that were used by the makers of these points. It also contained material suitable for radiocarbon dating. This is the Horner Site, which was discovered by Jimmy Allen of Cody. It was named after Pearl Horner, the owner of the land. The site lies on a 150-foot terrace near the confluence of Sage Creek and the Shoshone River, four miles northeast of the town of Cody. Excavations on behalf of Princeton University were begun in 1949 and continued in 1950 under the direction of Glenn L. Jepsen. In 1952 a cooperative project with the Smithsonian Institution was begun with Waldo Wedel supervising the archaeological aspects of the work. Unfortunately, no detailed report has yet been published, but two brief accounts have provided some interesting data (Jepsen, 1951, 1953 a and b).

The site, which is a large one covering several thousand square feet, was a butchering ground for bison and possibly also a habitation area. The poorly preserved remains of 180 bison had been found by August, 1950. There is no published report on those found since. The species has not been identified, and it is not certain that it will be possible to identify it, for the tops of the skulls were removed by the hunters in all but two instances. This can scarcely have been done simply in order to obtain the edible brains, for in that case the bony portions which were removed would have been left nearby. Perhaps the top of the skulls and horns were taken elsewhere to be used in some ceremony. Many of the long bones were broken, probably to obtain marrow. Some bones appear to have been used as cutting or scraping tools. Others bear marks which suggest intentional scratching or incising.

The ages of the bison whose teeth were found indicate that they were all killed in the autumn or early winter. Perhaps all of them were killed during one season, or perhaps people returned to the site each year at approximately the same time. Nearby hot springs, which are now extinct, may have been active during the period of occupation and could have served to attract people to the area during this season.

The 210 artifacts recovered included some of the most magnificent specimens of Scottsbluff and Eden points that have been found. The men who made them were truly great craftsmen. Other projectile points of new but similar forms were also found, but they have not yet been described. Of the utmost importance was the discovery of other tools and implements as well as weapon tips. These will make it possible to define the complex of which the points were a component part. The name Cody has been assigned to this complex (Jepsen, 1951).

No detailed description of the other artifacts which go to make up the Cody Complex has been published, but they include scrapers, knives, engraving tools, perforators, choppers, pounders, and rubbing stones. There is one distinctive artifact which can serve as a diagnostic for the complex even though it is unaccompanied by the characteristic projectile points. This is a form of knife which has a transverse blade and is usually stemmed on one side. It has been informally called a Cody knife.

The site has not yielded evidence of dwellings nor of prepared hearths. There are, however, some burned areas where fires had been built. Of particular interest is the finding of shallow lineally arranged pits dug into the gravel of the terrace. They are from twelve to thirty inches across at the top, narrower at the bottom, and about a foot deep. Perhaps they were used for storage.

Preliminary geological studies by Sheldon Judson and John Moss led them to propose a guess date of between 5,000 and 9,000 years ago. Carbon 14 dates obtained from charred bones averaged 6,876 $\pm$ 250 years ago. Dates from charcoal from a heavily burned area that probably represents a hearth averaged 6,920 $\pm$ 500 years ago (Libby, 1955).

The Claypool Site

A site nineteen miles south of Otis in Washington County, Colorado, named the Claypool Site after the property owner, has also

Courtesy University of Colorado Museum

FIG. 41—Cody knives from the Claypool Site, Colorado. Surface finds. Bert Mountain Collection.

yielded artifacts of the Cody Complex. It lies in a deflation basin or blow-out in which the late Perry Andersen began to find artifacts in the mid-1930's. Bert Mountain, a capable amateur archaeologist, was shown the site by Andersen, and during the following years, as the deposits eroded, he returned to the site intermittently and found artifacts on many occasions. Fortunately, he maintained a properly catalogued collection, and when the need arose to study material from the site it was easy to segregate the specimens from this site from others in his collection which came from other localities. Had these important specimens been found by a less conscientious collector, extraordinarily valuable data would have been lost.

In 1953 Mountain brought this site to the attention of Herbert Dick who spent two months excavating the site for the University of Colorado Museum. He found eighteen artifacts *in situ*. Twelve of these were projectile points of Eden and Scottsbluff types or variants of these forms. Also found in place were a point blank, two scrapers, and three pieces of sandstone with grooves that were probably used as shaft smoothers. A Cody knife was found on the surface before excavations were started. Specimens found on the surface by Mountain include eleven projectile points that could be classified as Scottsbluffs, seven that could be classified as Edens, and ten Cody knives. Some of the latter lack stems or barbs but have transverse blades. The same locality produced a Clovis point and two Plainviews, but, since they were surface finds, there is no way of determining their stratigraphic relationship with the other material.

Some 243 artifacts from the site have been made available to Dick for study, thanks to the cooperation of Mountain and of Harold Andersen who has inherited the collection of his father, Perry Andersen. No description of the artifacts has yet been published; but when the studies are completed, knowledge of the Cody Complex will doubtless be materially increased.

The Claypool Site is doubly important because of the geological studies undertaken by Harold E. Malde of the U. S. Geological Survey. Much of the merit of this fine report, which has not yet been published, is due to the fact that it contains excellent descriptions of the deposits, which will provide invaluable comparative data for geologists investigating other sites. Also, Malde has not emphasized chronologic data at the expense of information pertaining to climate and environmental conditions that undoubtedly had a marked effect on the lives of the inhabitants of the site.

FIG. 42—Artifacts from the Claypool Site, Colorado. Surface finds. Bert Mountain Collection.

Courtesy University of Colorado Museum

The site lies in a deflation basin formed in a sandy plain between dunal ridges. The blow-out has eroded down through a succession of beds. The artifacts occurred in a massive sand deposit with a well zoned soil profile in the top few feet. It lies unconformably on a fossiliferous marl bed which is at the top of a bedded sand deposit. Mammoth remains and freshwater mollusks have been found in the marl. The fauna indicates pronounced wetness which produced boggy conditions and local ponding. Malde believes this deposit is of pre-Wisconsin age. Deposits lithologically similar to the underlying sand have elsewhere been attributed to the Kansan glacial age, and certain mollusks found in the marl apparently became extinct then.

No artifacts were found in the marl at the Claypool Site, but the accuracy of this correlation is of the utmost importance because of other reported discoveries in Yuma County, which adjoins Washington County. Harold Cook (1927) reported finding a projectile point in a deposit that probably represents the same marl. Paul Gebhard has described a similar marl and basal sand in the same stratigraphic position in Yuma County. He stated that "Yuma points and points typologically related to Yuma points were found in and upon the marl" (Gebhard, 1949, p. 136). He also states that one "Folsomoid point" was found upon the basal sand that underlay the marl. However, if Malde is correct in assigning the marl and basal sand to the Kansan stage, these artifacts must have been intrusive. They could, perhaps, have been trampled into the marl during a later period of occupation.

The artifact-bearing sand at the Claypool Site was deposited by wind. It ranges in thickness from three to at least eight feet. Some sand had accumulated before the occupation began, and it continued to accumulate during the period of occupation. The sand is weathered. This weathering, which occurred after the sand was deposited, may correlate with a soil in Nebraska that yielded a Carbon 14 date of 4,150 ± 350 years ago. Malde believes that the site was occupied during a time, prior to the beginning of the Altithermal, when a cool dry climate prevailed, and that the date of occupation would fall between 9,000 and 7,000 years ago.

Finds in Alberta and Saskatchewan, Canada

As early as 1936 the basic elements of what is now called the Cody Complex had been recognized in southern Alberta. During the drought years of the 1930's Russell A. Johnston assembled a large collection of artifacts from blownout areas in the Little Gem region

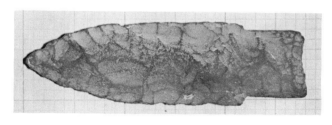

FIG. 43—Artifacts found near Cereal, Alberta, Canada. Russell A. Johnston Collection. No. 1, Fragmentary Eden point. No. 2, Scottsbluff point, Type I. No. 3 Scottsbluff point, Type II (Type Definitions page 267). No. 4, Cody Knife. No. 5, Alberta point.

north of Cereal. Scottsbluff and Eden points, and the distinctive implements now called Cody knives, occurred so consistently together in
certain localities that Johnston was convinced they were made by the
same people and belonged to the same complex to which he applied
the name Little Gem. He made every effort to interest archaeologists
in his discoveries, but, unfortunately, funds were not available and no
excavations could be undertaken at that time. Now archaeological
work is being sponsored in western Canada by the Glenbow Foundation of Calgary, and it is hoped that some excavating can be undertaken in these sites. Much of the vital evidence has been destroyed by
wind erosion, but, with luck, artifact-bearing remnants of the deposits
from which Johnston's artifacts came may be uncovered.

A study of Johnston's meticulously documented collection suggests
various interesting possibilities. The localities that produced Scottsbluff and Eden points also yielded points strongly reminiscent of Lake
Mohave points (discussed on page 161), and others with more marked
stems and rounded shoulders. Since these are blow-out sites, it is possible that artifacts which had eroded from more than one horizon may
be represented. It is also possible, however, that all belong to the same
complex.

In Johnston's collection, and in collections made in the vicinity
of Red Deer by Hugh Bower, and near Edmonton by James MacGregor,
are found points of a distinctive type. They are commonly found in
sites that yield Scottsbluff points, and they resemble them sufficiently
that it seems probable there is some close relationship. They differ,
however, in a number of respects. They are larger, the stem is longer,
the base is slightly convex, and the tip is somewhat blunted. It is
suggested that they be called Alberta points. (Fig. 44.)

Artifacts which duplicate these and specimens from Cody Complex
sites have also been found in collections from Saskatchewan. There
are many examples in the Kenneth Jones collection from Mortlach.
Both Eden and Scottsbluff points were found northwest of Silton by
Albert Swanston. Five Cody knives and a somewhat similar specimen
with a drill-like tip are represented in the W. J. Orchard collection
from Saskatchewan. This collection also contains knives with similar
transverse blades but with notches at the base. These probably are
of a later age, for similar specimens in the Johnston collection come
from sites which Johnston regards as more recent and which did not
contain any specimens suggestive of the Cody Complex.

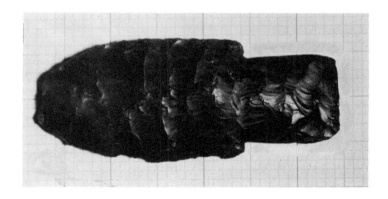

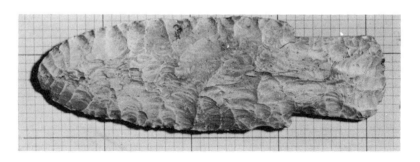

FIG. 44—Alberta points. No. 1 James MacGregor Collection. No. 2 Hugh Bower Collection. No. 3 E. L. Smith Collection.

Cody Points. A Proposed Designation

There is evidence from a number of sites that, in the western plains of the United States and Canada, both Scottsbluff and Eden points were used by the same people. Furthermore, there are strong resemblances between them, and it is not always certain in which category a given specimen should be placed, although in any series there will be points so markedly different that there can be no confusion. It seems desirable to have one overall term that can be applied to this entire intergrading range of points extending from the narrowest Edens through intermediate types to Scottsbluffs and the broader thinner points with triangular blades. Essentially, it is the need for such a general term that has been largely responsible for the survival of the term "Yuma." Since it is at the Horner Site near Cody, Wyoming, that the greatest number of such points have been found *in situ*, it seems best to utilize the name of the complex found there and to propose that the term Cody points be applied to both Eden and Scottsbluff points and to the other points of the complex.

It might appear that the term Cody points should be used exclusively and that the terms Eden and Scottsbluff should be dropped altogether. This, however, would be unwise, for distinct types are represented, and distributional and typological studies suggest that in some cases these differences may be of chronological significance. Although in some areas Edens and Scottsbluffs were used by the same people, there appear to have been some groups that used only the Scottsbluff type. This type is more widely distributed, for examples have been found in many parts of North America, while Edens have been largely limited to the northern and central Plains. Sites have been found that contain only Scottsbluffs, but none has been found that contains only Edens. Furthermore, the Scottsbluff is a less highly specialized type of artifact. It seem probable that Edens are a specialization derived from the Scottsbluff.

It is possible that the Scottsbluff type may be a refinement of a still less specialized form. At the site of Santa Isabel Iztapan, in the Valley of Mexico, discussed on page 91, a point which resembles a Scottsbluff, but appears to be more amorphous and of a less highly evolved type, was found in association with articulated mammoth remains. The bones and artifacts lay in the Upper Becerra formation. Peat from this formation in another area yielded a Carbon 14 date of 11,003 ± 500 years ago, and a wood sample was dated in excess of 16,000 years ago by the same method (Libby, 1955).

Some provision should also be made for designating the thin triangular-bladed points with pronounced shoulders which are part of the same complex as Scottsbluffs and Edens. These have sometimes been referred to as Scottsbluff variants, but the differences are sufficiently marked that it seems desirable that there be some specific designation for this particular variation in order to facilitate distributional studies. Little is known of the distribution of these points, largely, perhaps, because they have been lumped with the narrower, thicker type. Such a specimen was first found at the Scottsbluff Bison Quarry, and this should constitute the type station, but two subtypes should be recognized. It is proposed that specimens resembling Point 1, Fig. 38, be assigned to Scottsbluff Type I, and those resembling Point 2, Fig. 38, to Scottsbluff Type II.

There are also two variants of Eden points, but they differ only as regards flaking techniques. Such differences do not seem sufficiently important to warrant the establishment of subtypes, but it may sometimes be useful to add the term collateral or transverse to the name to indicate the type of flaking.

The Frontier Complex

An interesting assemblage of artifacts, which differs from those found at the Red Smoke and Lime Creek sites, was found at another now inundated site on Medicine Creek in Frontier County, Nebraska. It is known as the Allen Site or Ft 50. The complex found here has been called the Frontier by Preston Holder and Joyce Wike (1949), who conducted the excavations. No single trait provides a diagnostic for the complex, but the general pattern is distinctive.

Cultural debris was found in a band between two and a half and three feet thick, which occurred some twenty feet below the surface in terrace fill. Within this band two occupation levels could be distinguished, but there was no evidence of any marked differences between the two. They both contained artifacts and workshop debris, fragments of hematite, animal bones, and remains of campfires. Chipped stone artifacts were rather crudely flaked. Projectile points have thinned concave bases. A few are small, about an inch and a half in length, but others are almost three inches long. The smaller specimens are more or less leaf-shaped. In the case of the larger specimens, the sides are essentially parallel although the basal portion is slightly contracted. A number of scrapers were found. They were more common in the lower level. The most characteristic form is basically trapezoidal in outline with flakes removed from both faces to form the working edges. Fairly large knives and expanded-base drills were also found.

Ground stone implements consisted of a few fragments of abrading stone, possibly used to hone awls, and a grooved ball of Niobrara chalk which may have been used as a bolas weight. It resembles specimens found in Manzano and Deadman caves. Similar objects have sometimes been identified as net sinkers, but it seems unlikely that the specimen found at the Allen Site could have served such a purpose since it was made of a material which becomes soft when wet.

Bone was used to produce needles, awls, and fishhooks. Many broken but unworked animal bones were also found. There was a greater concentration of them in the lower level. Few bison bones were found in the upper level although they were present in large numbers in the lower one.

A mixture of soils from both occupation zones was tested by the radiocarbon method at the University of Chicago and produced a date of 5,256 ± 350 years ago. It seemed probable that there could have been some contamination, and charcoal from the lower occupation level was tested. It was dated at 8,274 ± 500 years ago. Other charcoal provided a date of 10,493 ± 1,500 years ago. In the report on this sample (Johnson, Editor, 1951, page 14) it is stated that it came from the same feature as the one dated at 8,274 ± 500, but that it was obtained at a later date and was more carefully collected. In another section of the same publication (page 21) however, Frank H. H. Roberts, Jr., states that the sample dated in excess of 10,000 years came from below the occupation zone. If this is the case, this sample does not provide a date for the cultural material. The status of this sample is not at all clear. E. Mott Davis has suggested that the material found in the fourth zone from the bottom at the Red Smoke Site (see page 117) may equate with the Frontier Complex.

Angostura Points

Two sites that lie forty miles from each other, one in South Dakota and the other in Wyoming, have produced well-flaked points which have certain similarities. The Ray Long Site is located thirteen miles south of Hot Springs, South Dakota. It was excavated by archaeologists of the Missouri Basin Project of the Smithsonian Institution before it was destroyed by the filling of the Angostura Reservoir. The first work, begun in 1948, was done by Jack T. Hughes, who has published a preliminary report on the site (Hughes, 1949). Later excavations were under the direction of Richard P. Wheeler, who has prepared a detailed report which is awaiting publication.

An occupation horizon was found five to seven feet below the surface in a stream terrace. Unprepared hearths and a variety of artifacts were found. The latter include various cutting, scraping, and perforating tools, and some distinctive projectile tips. These are long,

5 CM

Courtesy Smithsonian Institution

FIG. 45—Angostura Point. University of Nebraska State Museum Collection.

slender, and lanceolate, and taper to a narrow base which may be straight or concave. The points are quite thin. The flaking is fine, and the flake scars, which are parallel, are usually directed obliquely across the face of the blade. In a few cases the flaking is horizontal. There is some basal thinning and basal grinding. The points range in length between two and one half and three and one quarter inches. Four bases and three tips were recovered through excavation. Hughes gave the site name to these points, but this has resulted in a certain amount of confusion since many people have felt that the word "Long" referred to the length of the points. Wheeler (1954) has proposed that these be re-named Angostura points. This seems a better term.

Two other types of points were found at the Ray Long Site, but they were surface finds, so it is not certain that they are part of the same complex. One looks like a crude Plainview, while the other is a very short point with a deeply concave base and some serrations along the blade. Of particular importance is the occurrence of grinding stones, which would suggest a dependence on plant foods at this site. Small handstones with smoothed surfaces were found, and at least one thin slab with an oval depression which must represent a nether milling stone.

The site has not lent itself well to geological dating, for the bench on which it was found is possibly a meander bench without chronological significance, rather than a true terrace. No bones were found, probably due to soil conditions, so there is no way of knowing if any of the animals that were hunted are now extinct. Three Carbon 14 samples were run at the University of Chicago. One yielded a date of 7,715 $\pm$ 740 years ago, and another 7,073 $\pm$ 300 years ago (Libby, 1955). These samples were taken from an area which had not yielded any of the diagnostic points, but it was thought that the section from which the samples came could be equated with that which produced the artifacts. A composite sample made up of hundreds of tiny pieces of charcoal taken from the zone in which Angostura points were found *in situ* gave a date of 9,380 $\pm$ 500 (Crane, 1956).

Points with similar shapes have been found widely distributed from Alaska to Mexico. Many have been found in Texas. Some archaeologists call all points with somewhat similar shapes Angostura points. This term is rapidly, and most unfortunately, replacing Yuma as a name to be applied indiscriminately to all lanceolate points. The writer feels that until more information is available the term should be applied only to points that have the same shape and general thickness and the parallel flaking that characterizes those from the type station.

Specimens found in a site on the west end of Great Bear Lake in the Northwest Territories by Richard MacNeish (1956a), and called Angostura points by him, do not in the writer's opinion, closely resemble those found at the Ray Long Site. They are thicker, more crudely flaked, and less symmetrical. The Great Bear Lake specimens occurred in a stratum that lay above one that contained the Plainview points discussed on page 109. It was dated at 4,600 ± 230 years ago at the University of Saskatchewan Laboratory. Specimens found by MacNeish at the Engigstciak Site on the Firth River (discussed on page 216) and those found by Larsen at the Trail Creek Site (discussed on page 212) appear to more nearly approximate the Angostura type.

Agate Basin Points

Points with forms similar to the Angostura type were found in a site between New Castle and Lusk in eastern Wyoming. Not much is known of this site, since only a very brief account has been published by Frank H. H. Roberts, Jr., (1943) who investigated it. It was a site where bison were killed. It has been stated that they were not of an extinct type, but were of the present-day species, *Bison bison*. However, no detailed study of the material was made before the bones were discarded, and it is not impossible that they were incorrectly identified. Thirty-two points were found by Roberts, and over thirty-eight by collectors. These points are long and slender with parallel or slightly convex sides. They have basal grinding. The general shape of some is much like that of Angostura points, but there are various differences between the two types. Most of the Agate Basin points are larger, and the bases are straight or convex; the flaking is always of the horizontal type; there is a finer marginal retouch, and basal thinning is usually absent. Some of the Agate Basin points are doubly pointed like the laurel-leaf forms discussed on page 99. What appears, on the basis of surface evidence, to be an extensive Agate Basin Site has recently been discovered near Moose Jaw, Saskatchewan. (Robert W. Nero, Personal Communication).

The Cumro Site

Until the discovery of the Ray Long Site, points with oblique parallel flaking had been found in very few excavated sites, although

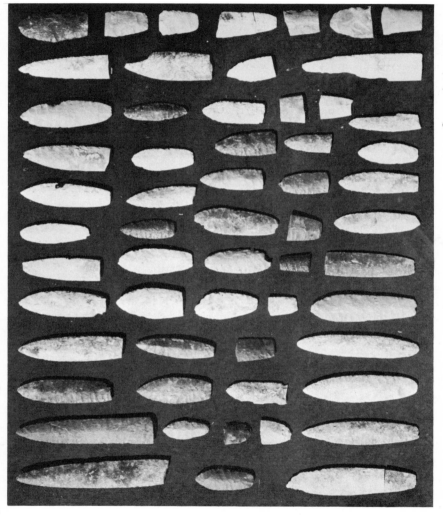

Fig. 46—Agate Basin Points.

this type of flaking was represented on points of various shapes in surface collections. One such specimen was found in a bank face near Cumro, Nebraska, which also yielded bones of extinct bison (Schultz, 1932). It was removed before the animal bones were, however, and when the bones were excavated no further artifacts were uncovered.

The Browns Valley Site

Points with oblique parallel flaking were found in association with a human skeleton near Browns Valley, Minnesota, in 1933. This discovery was reported on by A. E. Jenks (1937). William K. Jensen found fragments of human bones and a parallel flaked point with a concave base in a load of gravel brought from the Browns Valley Municipal Gravel Pit. He immediately went to the gravel pit where he found one point in a wagon that had just been loaded, and another point, some skull, jaw, and long bone fragments at the spot from which the gravel had been removed.

Examination revealed a burial pit, apparently lined with red ochre, in the face of the gravel, below undisturbed dark humus. It appeared probable that the bones and artifacts previously recovered had fallen from this pit. A large bifacially flaked object that was slightly asymmetrical, and a flat stone six inches thick and ten inches in diameter, possibly placed on the body, were found in the grave. Later sifting of the gravel from which the bones had been taken yielded other bone fragments, teeth, another asymmetrical chipped artifact, and two small pieces of sandstone that appeared to have been rubbed. In the summer of 1934 the site was visited by Jenks and an archaeological field party from the University of Minnesota. They re-dug the gravel near the burial and found seventeen additional bone fragments, some of which had contacts that could be fitted to bones previously obtained, and an obliquely flaked point very similar to the first. (Fig. 71, p. 268.)

The first and the last points found are the type specimens for what is now called the Browns Valley type. They are lanceolate forms slightly more than three inches long, with a maximum width at the mid-section of about one and a quarter inches. They are characterized by fine parallel flakes directed obliquely across the face of the point. Bases are concave and cross-sections are lenticular. There is some basal thinning produced by the removal of small vertical flakes, and some grinding of the basal edges. The other two points had essentially horizontal flaking. One had a straight base. The other chipped specimens were somewhat asymmetrical in outline and probably served as knives rather than as projectile points. The flaking was less regular.

There were also two small pieces of sandstone that may have served as abraders.

Geological evidence, as interpreted by Frank Leverett and Frederick W. Sardeson (1932), indicated that the gravel ridge in which the burial was found had been formed as a gravel bar by water flowing from Glacial Lake Agassiz through an ancient river. The period when water flowed through this river channel was correlated with a beach level known as the Tintah. Leverett and Sardeson, who considered Lake Agassiz to mark the retreat of the Mankato ice, gave a date of 18,000 years ago for the beginning of the lake. They dated the beginning of the Tintah stage at about 12,000 years ago, and the end at between 8,000 and 9,000 years ago. Since the skeleton and the artifacts were intrusive into the gravels, they could not be of the same age as the deposits; but the fact that the top of the burial was level with the gravel, and the absence of humus in the burial pit, suggested to Jenks that it was dug soon after the formation of the gravel ridge, before vegetation was abundant.

Most geologists, on the basis of radiocarbon dates, now accept a date in the vicinity of 11,000 years ago for the Mankato. On this basis, more recent dates would be suggested for the formation of the lake and the subsequent stages, if the Leverett and Sardeson correlation is correct. However, some Carbon 14 dates suggest that the lake began to form before the last major advance of the ice (Wright and Rubin, 1956). If this were the case, the earlier dates suggested for the Tintah stage would not be far from the right order of magnitude in the opinion of most geologists.

Actually, we are not certain of the age of the deposits in which the Browns Valley material was found, and we cannot assign a date to the skeleton and the artifacts found in the intrusive burial pit. However, the form and the flaking of the points is unlike that of recent points found in the area, and the discovery of very similar points in a site in Wyoming, dated at almost 8,000 years, does suggest some antiquity.

The Jimmy Allen Site

The Wyoming site which contained artifacts reminiscent of the Browns Valley specimens, was found by Jimmy Allen, who also discovered the Horner Site. It was named in his honor. The site was excavated by William Mulloy (Personal communication).

The Jimmy Allen Site lies on the north flank of a boulder ridge about sixteen miles south of Laramie. It is at the foot of an area where the slope is greater than usual and could, perhaps, represent a bison trap. Scattered bison bones, artifacts, and flakes were found over a forty-foot-square area. One point and some bone fragments were found on the surface; the remainder of the material was recovered through excavation. The bones have been identified as those of an extinct form, *Bison occidentalis*.

Fig. 47—Artifacts from the Jimmy Allen Site, Wyoming. Note variation of color on the center point. Opposite sides of matching fragments were exposed to weathering.

Thirty fragmentary projectile points were recovered. Some were almost complete while others were represented by tiny fragments. Most were made from quartzite, a material that is normally thought to be very difficult to flake; but these specimens are extremely well flaked. They bear slender flake scars going obliquely across the face of the point and lying parallel to each other. A superficial examination suggests that the flake scars extend from edge to edge. Closer examination reveals that narrow flakes were removed from both edges, but they were joined so smoothly that they give an impression of a continuous scar.

All of the points are of essentially the same shape, unnotched lanceolate forms with concave bases and rounded corners. They are quite thin and lenticular in cross-section. The sides are more nearly parallel than are those of the Browns Valley specimens, and the bases are more markedly concave. Bases and lower edges were ground. In some cases this produced a barely perceptible constriction of the lower third of the point. Most of the points appear to have been between three and four and a half inches long and about an inch wide. One point, although similar to the rest of the group in appearance, is much smaller with a probable length of no more than one and a half inches. J. M. Shippee (1950) has reported that a point that is almost an exact duplicate of some of the larger specimens was found a few miles from Kansas City, Missouri.

Associated with the points at the Jimmy Allen Site were plano-convex scrapers. Most of these were end scrapers of the snub-nosed variety, but some were side scrapers. Their presence suggests that at least some preliminary hide working may have been done here, although a kill site rather than a habitation site appears to be represented. No tail bones were recovered, which suggests that the hides were removed and taken elsewhere.

The site did not lend itself to geological studies. The bones and artifacts were covered by a thin layer of blown sand. Some of the materials that are susceptible to patination show the effects of a long period of exposure, and it seems probable that the artifacts and bones lay on the surface for some time before the sand covering developed. Charred bison bones, dated at the University of Michigan, produced a Carbon 14 date of 7,900 ± 200 years ago.

Nebo Hill Points

On high terraces in western Missouri, within a few miles of Kansas City, surface sites have been found by J. M. Shippee (1948 and Personal communication) which have produced various styles of well-flaked lanceolate points. Those which Shippee regards as diagnostic for a complex, to which he has given the name Nebo Hill, constitute sixty percent of the total number found. They are long, narrow, and thick, and have straight bases. They range in length from three to six inches, with an average length of four and a half inches. The broadest and thickest portion is above the mid-section. They lack basal thinning and basal grinding. Certain of the other lanceolate points sometimes found on the same sites are broadest and thickest below the mid-section, some have convex or concave bases, some are thinner, and a few exhibit basal grinding and basal thinning.

Nebo Hill points resemble those of the Guilford Complex (discussed on page 74) which is believed to be more than 6,000 years old. Grooved axes are found on Nebo Hill sites. Since these are surface finds, however, there is no proof that they are of the same age as the points.

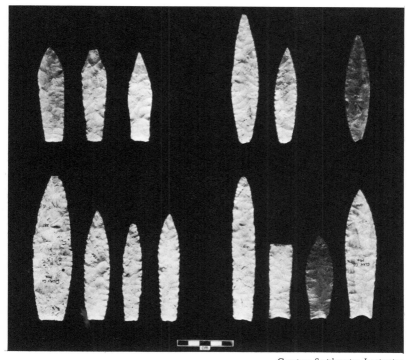

Courtesy Smithsonian Institution

FIG. 48—Lanceolate points found on High Terraces in western Missouri. Nos. 1, 2, 3, 9, 10, are typical Nebo Hill points. Thousands of specimens that resemble Point No. 7 have been found near Sedalia, Missouri.

The Modoc Rock Shelter

Excavations were carried on during 1952 and 1953 in a rock shelter with a deep midden deposit, that lies between the villages of Modoc and Prairie du Rocher in Randolph County, Illinois. Melvin L. Fowler and Howard Winters (1956) have reported on this site. The former was in charge during the first year, and the latter during the second season. The site is now called the Modoc Rock Shelter, although in

Carbon 14 lists it has been referred to as the Barbeau Creek Rock Shelter (Libby, 1955). Five zones containing occupation debris were recognized. The material from the three middle zones, which extend from a depth of five feet to twenty-one and a half feet, is attributed to the Archaic Stage.

One Carbon 14 date for material from Zone I, which extended from twenty-one and a half feet to twenty-six and a half feet below the surface, was 9,101 ± 440 years ago, and the other 10,651 ± 650 years ago. Dates from Zone II ranged from 8,546 ± 380 years ago to 11,200 ± 800 years ago. Two of these dates exceeded in age those from the lower, and older, zone. For reasons that are not clear, Fowler and Winters have taken the two dates that are consistent with each other and with the stratigraphic position and averaged those to obtain a date of 7,273 ± 488 years ago for the lower portion of Zone II. It seems a questionable procedure to reject the dates that are inconsistent with the stratigraphic picture but to rely on those that seem more suitable.

In the lower portion of Zone I was found a side-notched bunt or scraper, a small pointed bone tool, a scraper, and many flakes. A band of water-deposited clay that lay above contained a polished bone rod, a perforated pebble that probably served as a pendant, a scraper, and some flakes. Fowler is of the opinion that these should be attributed to Zone I, while Winters believes that they belong to the Zone II assemblage. A projectile point with a contracting stem was found in loose dirt in the bottom of the excavation. It could have come from Zone I or from a higher level. This point was compared with the Gypsum Cave type (discussed on page 158) and was said to be similar but not identical. The writer fails to see any close resemblance. The Modoc Rock Shelter point has a large, broad, straight-based stem, while the Gypsum Cave specimens have small convex stems. The blades of the points are similar, but so are those of almost all stemmed points.

Zones II, III, IV contained projectile points of types commonly found in Archaic sites. Side-notched forms predominated. There was a variety of stone and bone implements. Some of the stone tools were polished. A copper awl was found in Zone IV. Zone V contained pottery.

Russell Cave

A large, relatively dry cavern, called Russell Cave, which lies near Bridgeport in northeastern Alabama, has been excavated under the direction of Carl F. Miller (1956). It has yielded evidence of intermittent occupation beginning about 8,000 years ago and continuing until about 1650 A. D. The excavators had gone through some fourteen feet of stratified occupational debris, but bedrock had not been reached when the first report was published. Estimates based on the floor level of a nearby cave suggested that there might be some twelve feet of deposit below the level reached through excavation. As yet, only a popularized account of the discoveries has appeared and no details are available. One plate suggests that the projectile points found in the lowest level, for which a date of 8,160 ± 300 years ago was obtained by the radiocarbon method, are lanceolate specimens with a slight basal constriction, and triangular forms. In the next level were similar points as well as some stemmed and notched forms. These are all attributed to the Archaic. In higher levels were found Woodland and Mississippian artifacts.

The Eva Site

An antler sample from the Eva Site, an Archaic site in Humphrey County, Tennessee, produced a date of 7,150 ± 500 years ago when assayed at the University of Michigan Laboratory (Crane, 1956). Five stratigraphic divisions were recognized at this site, which was excavated by T. M. N. Lewis and Madeline Kneberg (1947 and Personal communication). The earliest occupation, represented in Stratum 5, was on an old land surface. The antler which provided the Carbon 14 date came from Stratum 4. Lewis and Kneberg believe the site was occupied for a considerable time before Stratum 4 accumulated.

In a forthcoming publication Lewis and Kneberg propose to divide the Eva Focus, described by Kneberg (1952), into six phases. The earliest of these is the Eva Phase represented in the stratum that produced the sample for radiocarbon dating. A list of culture traits of this phase has been published by Kneberg (1954). Mussels were the dietary staple of the Eva people. The dead were buried in a fully flexed position. Dogs as well as people were buried. Stone projectile points were usually corner-notched or basally-notched, more rarely side-notched or stemmed. Many snub-nosed end scrapers were made, a few were stemmed. Long drills were common tools. Polished stone atlatl weights were used. Antler provided the material for some projectile points, scrapers, and shaft wrenches; needles were made of bone. Pigments were derived from red and yellow ochre.

The Old Copper Assemblage

In Wisconsin and adjacent parts of the Upper Great Lakes area in the United States and Canada have been found heavy copper weapons and tools which have been referred to a complex called the Old Copper Culture or Assemblage (McKern, 1942; Quimby, 1952; Wittry and Ritzenthaler, 1956). Among the well-made copper artifacts recovered were large spear or lance points, some of which were socketed, knives that bore some resemblance to certain Eskimo forms, gouges, adzes, axes, chisels, harpoon heads, awls, and ornaments. In Wisconsin copper was available in the form of nuggets in the glacial drift; it could also have been quarried from the trap rocks of Isle Royale and the Keweenaw Peninsula. It was difficult for archaeologists to believe that so well-developed a metal industry could be very early; yet the discovery of a typical Old Copper gouge in an Archaic (Laurentian) site in New York, and the absence of Old Copper artifacts in sites of later periods, suggested that it must be fairly old. The deep acid erosion and dense patination which often characterized the specimens also suggested antiquity.

Radiocarbon dates from the Oconto Site in Wisconsin, obtained at the University of Chicago, have provided further evidence of age. One wood sample from a crematorium produced a date of 5,600 ± 600 years ago, and another collected from two other locations in the site was dated at 7,150 ± 600 years ago (Libby, 1955). Wittry and Ritzenthaler (1956) have suggested that the sample that produced the more recent date may have been subjected to root contamination and the older date may be the more reliable. These dates tend to strengthen the case for a possible association of Old Copper artifacts and extinct animal remains discussed by George Quimby (1954b).

In the Thunder Bay area of Ontario T. L. Tanton (1931) found a copper spear point and some mammal bones lying on a blue clay deposit covered by some forty feet of cross-bedded sand. Some of the bones appeared to be those of bison and others of horse. Tanton regarded the bones as modern but was puzzled by their occurrence at such depth. It does seem possible that, as Quimby has suggested, the deposits could be of Altithermal age and the horse bones might be those of the extinct native type rather than the modern variety first imported by the Spaniards. The bison bones could also be those of a fossil type. Farther west horses are thought to have become extinct at a somewhat earlier time, but they might have survived later in an area such as this where conditions would not have been so arid.

The excavation of two sites has contributed a great deal to the knowledge of the Old Copper Complex which, prior to 1945, had been

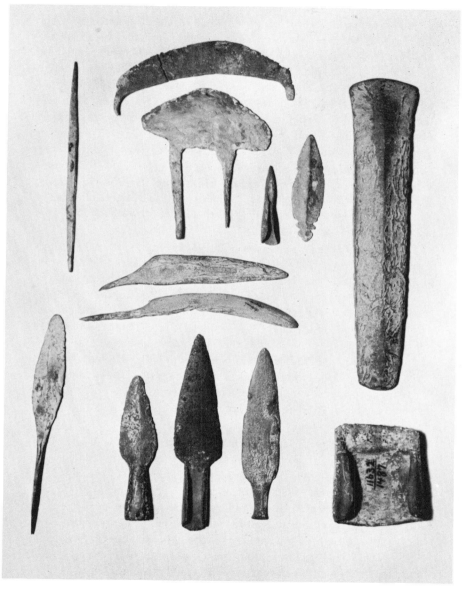

FIG. 49—Copper Implements of the Old Copper Culture.

known largely through surface finds and poorly documented discoveries of caches or burials which contained some of the distinctive artifacts. The Osceola Site, near Potosi, Wisconsin, was the first to be excavated (Ritzenthaler and Scholz, 1946). It was a large cemetery, containing an estimated 500 burials, which was partially destroyed by the action of the waters of the Mississippi River. Excavation revealed the presence of bundle reburials (bones buried in a bundle after the flesh had decomposed) and partial cremations. The bones were very poorly preserved. Chipped and ground stone implements as well as copper specimens were found. The former included long, well-flaked, side-notched projectile points with concave or straight bases, "T" shaped drills, and side-notched end scrapers which may have been produced by reworking projectile points. Ground and polished bannerstones, small grinding stones, smoothed through use, and hammerstones were also recovered.

The Oconto Site (Ritzenthaler and Wittry, 1952) was also primarily a cemetery, but it yielded some possible evidence of occupation in the form of scattered post holes which may indicate the presence of structures. The operations of a gravel company destroyed a large portion of the site. The dead were disposed of by means of cremation and inhumation. Some individuals had been buried while the flesh remained on the bones; some were in an extended position and others were partially or fully flexed. Other graves contained bundle reburials. Associated with the burials were copper awls, projectile points and ornaments, a few chipped stone implements, a carved whistle made from a swan humerus, worked antler, and perforated shells used to form a bracelet.

Similarities have been noted between artifacts of the Dorset Culture, an Eskimo culture of the central and eastern Arctic, and the Old Copper Culture of Wisconsin and certain Archaic cultures of New York State (Strong, 1930; McKern, 1942; de Laguna, 1946). It seemed probable that these resemblances were due to a north to south diffusion of certain elements. More recently it has come to appear more likely that diffusion may have been in the opposite direction (Ritchie, 1951; Hoffman, 1952) and that some of these traits have greater antiquity in the Great Lakes area (Wittry and Ritzenthaler, 1956).*

---

*Elmer Harp, Jr. (Editor, 1957, p. 437), has quoted a statement of Albert C. Spaulding's suggesting that "The Old Copper, together with the related Laurentian and Red Paint Cultures, is a representative of an ancient boreal forest culture type which formed at least a part of the ancestry of Eskimo Culture." Spaulding found the skeletons of two large dogs, presumably having Arctic affinities, and a shaft wrench made of the antler of Barren Ground caribou, associated with an Old Copper burial in Menominee, Michigan.

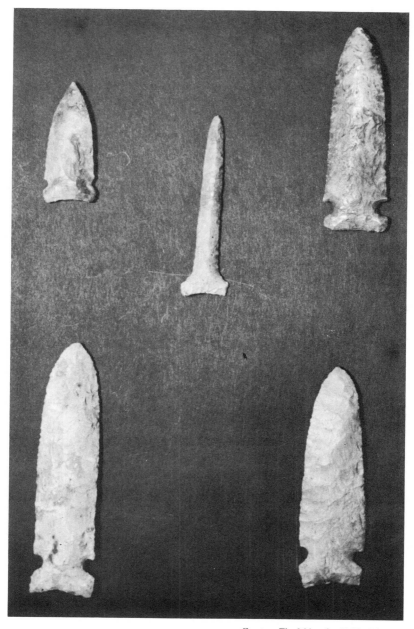

FIG. 50—Chipped stone implements of the Old Copper Culture.

FIG. 51—Concretion carved to represent a human face, found near Malakoff, Texas. (Fig. 47, p. 101, Sellards 1952.)

The Malakoff Heads

Mention should be made of a discovery that cannot be attributed to any lithic tradition, but that warrants consideration. It was reported upon by E. H. Sellards (1941, 1952). Five miles west of Malakoff, Henderson County, Texas, were found three stones carved to represent human faces. They lay in a deposit that contained the remains of a Pleistocene fauna, and there is geological evidence that suggests considerable antiquity.

The first image was found in 1929, more than sixteen feet below the surface in a gravel pit. It was a sandstone concretion on which were carved depressions representing eyes, ears, nose, and mouth. Bore holes were used to depict teeth. It was about sixteen inches long, thirteen or fourteen inches wide, and weighed ninety-eight and three-eighths pounds. When a new pit was opened a thousand feet away in 1935, a second image was found. It was formed from a somewhat smaller concretion that weighed sixty-three and one-quarter pounds. In 1940 a third carved concretion was found in the same pit that had produced the first. It lay twenty-two feet below the surface. This was the largest of the three, with a length of twenty inches and a weight of one hundred thirty-five pounds. The carving was less clear, and the holes and cuts could have been produced by the sharpening of implements. There is a possibility that two faces are represented, one perhaps non-human.

Various extinct species including mammoth, horse, large bison, and camelops, were found in pits dug in the deposit. At times in the past the river valley was lowered and a succession of terraces was formed. The images came from the oldest valley. Sellards, who places the end of the Pleistocene at the time of the disappearance of most of the large mammalian species, states that this valley was formed much before the close of the Pleistocene period.

THE PALEO-WESTERN TRADITION

Recent discoveries have provided further information about the way of life of the early peoples who lived in the area west of the Rocky Mountains. New dates, obtained by the radiocarbon method, suggest that this part of the continent was occupied at an earlier date than had been previously accepted. Studies of climatic changes have been important in this area. It has been generally believed that in California and the Great Basin the belts of pressure and precipitation were forced south of their present positions by the presence of large ice sheets in other areas, and that, in this region, pluvial periods during which lakes reached high levels were contemporaneous with glacial substages. It is now felt that the history of pluvial periods in the area is more complicated than was first thought. After the last pluvial maximum the lakes were reduced in size and ultimately some disappeared entirely.

FIG. 52—Ground Sloth. Detail from mural by Mary Chilton Gray, Fossil Mammal Hall, Denver Museum of Natural History.

During the Altithermal or Long Drought stage that lasted from about 7,000 to 4,000 years ago, most of the western basins were dry (Antevs, 1948).

Gypsum Cave

The first site to be discussed lacks many of the characteristics of the Paleo-western tradition, but it has provided a named type of projectile point that is of importance in any discussion of the western area during Paleo-Indian times. In 1930 a field party from the Southwest Museum, under the direction of M. R. Harrington, investigated a site known as Gypsum Cave, which contained evidence of the association of man and the now extinct ground sloth, a llama-like camel, and, possibly, horse (Harrington, 1933). Gypsum Cave is a large limestone cavern, 300 feet long and 120 feet at its widest point, with five connecting chambers. It lies approximately sixteen miles east of Las Vegas, Nevada.

The story of this discovery is an excellent illustration of the detective methods used by archaeologists. Harrington first visited the cave in 1929 and observed that on the floor was a layer of dung differing in many respects from that which might have been produced by any animal living in America during historic times. The fibrous nature of the dung indicated that the animal must have been a vegetarian. The position of the cave made it obvious that the animal must have been capable of crawling into holes. Harrington believed that the only animal fulfilling all these requirements was the giant ground sloth, *Nototherium shastense*. Later excavations, which revealed not only the skeletal remains of ground sloth but also well-preserved claws and hairs, proved the assumption to have been well founded.

On the surface above the sloth dung layer Harrington found Basketmaker, prehistoric Pueblo, and recent Indian artifacts which are probably Paiute. In and below this stratum were found man-made objects and the bones of sloth, camel, and horse. The protection provided by the cave led to the preservation of wood and other normally perishable materials.

Harrington states that fragments of cane, burnt at one end, apparently the remains of a torch, and the bones of a baby sloth were found under an undisturbed layer of dung over which gypsum had formed; and pieces of painted dart shafts were found underlying mixed dung and sloth hair. A fragment of a polished wooden dart shaft and a dart point were found imbedded in sloth dung. Above the dart point was a rock-fall on top of which was found a sloth skull. Still another dart point was uncovered in partially consolidated gypsum with burnt sloth dung lying above and below it. Above this point, and only a few feet away, was found a camel bone. The remains of campfires lay eight feet below the surface, under a sloth dung layer. Still further evidence was afforded by the finding of sloth bones apparently cut or scraped by a stone knife while still green.

The stone dart points are of a distinctive form to which the name Gypsum Cave point is now applied. They are lozenge- or diamond-shaped, about two inches in length, with small tapering stems. Pitch, evidently used in hafting, still clings to the stems of some specimens. The painted dart shafts differ from Basketmaker shafts in that they are more crudely made, yet more highly decorated.

In addition to the finds already mentioned, other dart points of the same characteristic form were found in the cave, but they were not found in direct association with extinct animal remains. One other interesting specimen was brought to light, but the conditions under which it was found make it impossible to include it in the Gypsum Cave complex with any degree of certainty. It is an unusual piece of basketry, with a weave resembling lattice or tee-weave, found in a pack rat nest. Although it cannot be proved, it appears probable that it belongs to the older complex for several reasons: first, the crevice in which the pack rat's nest was built had been sealed by the growth of stalagmites which are not believed to have formed for a considerable period of time; and, second, the basketry is different from that which characterizes the Basketmaker complex as it is now known. Furthermore, evidence from other sites in the Great Basin indicates that basket-making was well-developed at an early period.

Again the question of dating arises. The association of artifacts with the type of extinct fauna represented was not regarded as sufficient, for some students of the subject have felt that the ground sloth persisted into much more recent times than other Pleistocene forms. There is no proof, however; and work in recent deposits in the Rocky Mountain area by Charles B. Hunt (1953) serves to indicate that this was probably not the case.

An effort was made to determine the climatic conditions under which the Gypsum Cave deposits were formed, and to correlate them with pluvial phenomena. The layers underlying the deposits containing faunal and cultural remains were deposited by water. Water deposits in a high cave in a now extremely arid region must have been

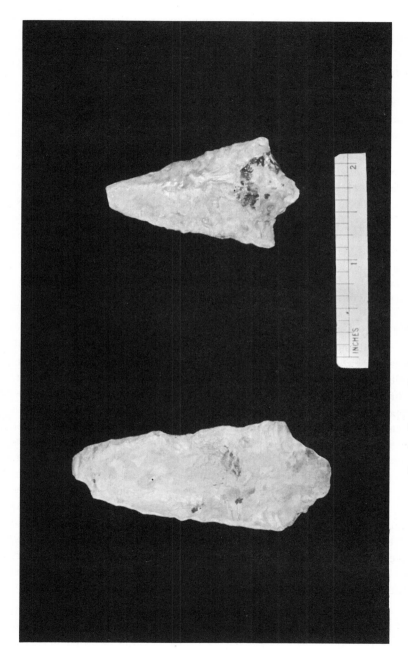

FIG. 53—Gypsum Cave points from Gypsum Cave, Nevada.

laid down under different climatic conditions from those that now prevail. The sloth level proper shows indications of having been formed during a somewhat drier period than the lower layer, but under more moist conditions than those of the present day. This is indicated by the formation of stalagmites during the period of occupation. Also, some of the sloth dung found in the cave contained vegetation of a type now found only at a considerably higher elevation, and this, too, is thought to reflect a moister climate.

Ernst Antevs (1952) attributed the water laid deposits to the Provo Pluvial and the period of occupation to the Anathermal. He dates the Gypsum Cave occupation at between 7,500 and 9,500 years ago. Radiocarbon dates from dung collected six feet four inches below the surface averaged 10,455 ± 340 years old. Dung samples collected two feet six inches below the surface averaged 8,527 ± 250 years ago (Libby, 1955). Wherever possible, it is desirable to obtain dates directly from artifacts. One of the dart shafts from the cave should be tested. This would eliminate any uncertainty regarding the contemporaneity of the dart shaft and the sloth dung.

Manzano Cave

Manzano Cave, which lies in the Manzano Mountain region of New Mexico south of Sandia, has yielded interesting data; but, unfortunately, the geological evidence does not lend itself to exact dating. Three projectile points were found here which resemble Gypsum Cave types, although they are somewhat smaller and broader and have more clearly defined stems and shoulders. They were found in a level that overlay a cemented layer which may correlate with the calcium carbonate that covered all the lower levels in Sandia Cave (Hibben, 1941). Bones found in the cave debris were those of extinct camel and sloth. In a lower level a Sandia point was reported found under a lens of yellow ochre by a guano digger. The evidence is not conclusive, but it would suggest that people who made projectile points similar to those of the inhabitants of Gypsum Cave, and who hunted the same animals, lived in the Manzano area in more recent times than did the makers of Folsom and Sandia points. A point of the Gypsum Cave type was found above the Folsom layer at the Lindenmeier Site (Roberts, 1940).

Darts propelled by atlatls may not have been the only weapons of the people who lived in Manzano Cave. On the same level as the projectile points were found five stone balls. Four were encircled by grooves, and it is thought that they may be weights which were tied with thongs, forming a bolas. This is a weapon still used by South American Indians who throw the weighted cords around the legs of game animals they wish to capture. Three of the Manzano specimens lay together and may represent a set.

The Lake Mohave Finds

An interesting artifact assemblage was found on fossil beaches and terraces of former Lake Mohave by Elizabeth W. Crozer Campbell and the late William H. Campbell (1937). Many artifacts were found on the surface, and a few flaked flint objects were found from six to fifty-four inches below the surface. The area in which the sites occur lies in the Mohave Desert in southeastern California, 140 miles northeast of Los Angeles.

Courtesy The Southwest Museum

FIG. 54—Points from Lake Mohave. Left, Lake Mohave type. Right, Silver Lake type.

At the present time the region is one of barren, forbidding clay flats broken only at intervals by the gray, stunted vegetation of the desert. There is a great trough with two shallow basins, known as playas, separated from each other by a narrow divide. Soda Playa lies to the south, and the smaller Silver Playa to the north. The basins are only the remnants of a large lake, Lake Mohave. By checking the many shore features which still remain, it has been estimated that Lake Mohave was more than twenty-three miles long, from three to six miles wide, and ranged in depth from twenty to forty feet. The shore lines are so well marked as to indicate that Lake Mohave must have been a perennial rather than a modern ephemeral lake. Ernst Antevs (1952) attributes it to the last great pluvial, the Provo.

The artifacts, which show a wide range, were studied and described by the late Charles Amsden (1937). They are exclusively of stone. Projectile points are of two types. The first, to which the name Lake Mohave has been given, consists of points almost leaf-shaped in form, but with long tapering stems, very slightly shouldered, and somewhat rounded at the base. They range in length from one and three-quarters to three inches. Some are flaked entirely by the percussion method, some have a pressure retouch. The second is the Silver Lake point. These points resemble the Lake Mohave type, but in general they are somewhat shorter and have more definite shouldering and less basal tapering. For the most part, they show percussion flaking, although a few examples exhibit a pressure retouch. They are not highly stabilized types, which reduces their value as index fossils.

The same sites also yielded leaf-shaped specimens, some as much as four inches long. These somewhat resemble the Lake Mohave points but usually lack the slight shouldering that characterizes the latter. The tips are thinner and more carefully shaped than the butts, and it seems possible they were hafted. It is impossible to be sure of their function. They might have been used as knives, or, as Amsden suggested, they could, perhaps, have been used as tips for lances or hand-spears. They could even have been used with atlatls in the hunting of large game.

Associated artifacts included crude choppers; various keeled or domed scrapers, some of which are called scraper-planes; end and side scrapers; scrapers with small, sharp points, called gravers; biface oval knives; large flake knives; crescentic implements; drills, and perforators. A small number of smoothed stones was also found. A few appear to have been deliberately shaped, but most seem to have been utilized without modification. Some specimens with battered ends are thought to have served as hammerstones, and there are a few worn pieces which might have been manos. Nothing was found that could be identified as a metate or milling stone.

As in all surface finds, the lack of stratigraphic evidence makes it impossible to determine with any degree of accuracy how many complexes may be represented in the Lake Mohave sites. In a basically arid region the presence of water may attract many different peoples. In addition to the Lake Mohave and Silver Lake points found during the original survey, there were Pinto-like forms, discussed in the following section, and a few specimens somewhat reminiscent of Plainviews. At a later date, the base of a fluted point was discovered.

Ernst Antevs (1952), who attributes Lake Mohave to the Provo Pluvial, believes that the artifacts found there derive from the last stage of the pluvial, from about 9,000 years ago. There is some ten feet of variation in occupation levels, but he feels that materials found at low overflow levels were left there during seasonal low water stages. Robert F. Heizer (Personal communication), however, notes that the specimens do not show evidence of submergence or water wear. Similar materials found on Owens Lake, California, Antevs attributes to the Anathermal with an age in excess of 7,000 years ago.

Malcolm J. Rogers (1939) has interpreted the evidence in another way. He has described a comparable complex from the north central part of San Bernadino County, California, which he called the Playa Industry, and a western coastal branch, which he named the San Dieguito. He placed the earliest horizons of these complexes in the period between 2,000 and 1,000 B. C. A. E. Treganza (1947), who found San Dieguito remains about the margins of extinct lakes and on elevated terraces in Baja California, however, felt that the complex was far more ancient.

One of Rogers' arguments for the recency of the Lake Mohave material was based on his discovery of a large site on a bar across the outlet channel, which he believed could not have been occupied during the period of overflow. Later work by the late George Brainerd (1953), however, indicated that the bar did not actually block the old outlet, and the period of occupation did not necessarily postdate the period during which the lake overflowed. He found that artifacts occurred almost exclusively on beaches, and he came to the conclusion that the artifacts were laid down during the life of the lake. The writer believes that the period of occupation may fall in the Anathermal period, but the evidence is not conclusive.

It is possible that, at the present time, Rogers is no longer completely convinced of the recency of the Lake Mohave and the similar Playa and San Dieguito industries; and his estimated dates may not now be so greatly at variance with those suggested by others. In charts published by Haury (1950, Figs. 116, 117, pp. 534, 535), which Rogers assisted in compiling, the earliest San Dieguito material is placed below 7,000 B.C. Rogers has not published any new estimates, however, and it is impossible to be sure what his present opinion may be.

The Malpais Industry

Malcolm Rogers (1939) also postulated the existence of an industry earlier than the Playa and the San Dieguito, to which he gave the name Malpais. Sites attributed to this industry were found in a large area along the lower Colorado River and in adjacent desert regions. Objects of flaked stone assigned to this complex were scarce and extremely crude. They consisted primarily of simple choppers and flakes. Other traits attributed to the Malpais Industry were circular clearings, occasionally surrounded by low walls, thought to represent house sites, and geometric and life form designs constructed on level surfaces by raking and scraping gravel into lines and piles or by the removal of sections of the underlying black surface cobbles. The complex is not clearly defined, and it is not accepted by many archaeologists. More than one complex may be represented in the lithic collection, and the gravel petroglyphs are generally thought to be late.

Potter Creek, California

Bone splinters were found in association with a Pleistocene fauna by palaeontologists working in Potter Creek Cave, California in 1904. Alex D. Krieger (1953) has examined these specimens and is convinced that some were beveled and perforated by man. Robert F. Heizer and Frederick Johnson (Personal communications) who have also seen these splinters are equally convinced that they are not the products of human workmanship. The writer has not seen this material and is not in a position to judge whether these should be classified as artifacts.

The Farmington Complex

An artifact assemblage found along Hood Creek, near Farmington, California, has been described by A. E. Treganza and R. F. Heizer (1953). Crudely flaked stones, largely workshop refuse, were found *in situ* in consolidated, buried auriferous gravels. The term "auriferous" is applied to gravels that lie within the geographic province of the old hardrock and placer diggings of the Mother Lode area. The artifact-bearing stratum rests unconformably on Miocene tuff. It is overlain by fine compacted sediments. Much similar chipped stone material, believed to have been derived from the gravels, has been found on the surface in some forty streambed stations in two other localities. Treganza and Heizer originally assigned the gravels to the Anathermal period and dated the artifacts at between 9,000 and 7,000 years ago. In 1957, however, they will publish a more detailed report which will tell of further excavations undertaken in 1952, and which will contain a section by Ernst Antevs who believes that the artifacts date from the Altithermal and are somewhere between 4,500 and 7,000 years old (Heizer, Personal communication).

The Pinto Basin Finds

In 1934, Elizabeth and William Campbell (1935) discovered a series of campsites containing numerous stone projectile points and other implements in a large desert drainage system, known as the Pinto Basin, which lies in the north central part of Riverside County, California. All finds were from the surface, and there was no direct connection with extinct animal remains. However, on the basis of archaeological and geological evidence, it was postulated that an ancient complex was represented.

Charles A. Amsden (1935) described the artifacts. Projectile points, thought to represent dart tips, were of two main types. One of these provided the most distinctive feature of the complex, and the name Pinto point was assigned to it. Typical examples are thick, about an inch and a half long, and are characterized by narrow shoulders and concave bases. Many specimens are serrated. As a rule they were flaked by percussion, but occasional examples show a pressure retouch.

The second type was represented by only a few specimens. This group consists of leaf-shaped forms shaped by percussion. They are not sufficiently distinctive to be of much diagnostic value. Since there is no stratification, there is no proof that they were associated with the Pinto type, but Amsden suggested that the fact that the associated implements were similar in form and, to a great extent, non-competitive in function, would indicate the presence of a single complex.

The associated flaked implements consisted of two varieties of keeled scrapers; retouched flakes, probably prepared to provide cutting edges, usually chipped only along one edge but occasionally retouched on opposite faces of alternate edges; concave scrapers; and long oval knives flaked all over on both faces. A few of the keeled scrapers showed some pressure retouch, but the bulk of the artifacts were made by the percussion method.

Grinding stones were also found in the Pinto campsites. The investigators admitted it could not be stated with certainty that they were associated with the flaked implements. They felt there was no proof they were not, however, and that it was at least possible that the early inhabitants of the Pinto Basin were seed gatherers. They believed the few pottery specimens found were of later origin and did not belong to the same complex as did most of the stone artifacts.

Courtesy The Southwest Museum

FIG. 55—Pinto Basin Points from the Type Locality.

Palaeontological evidence provided no proof of age, for there was no clear association with fossil bones. Horse and camel bones were commonly found on the campsites, but they were not in position. Where they were found *in situ* they appeared to be weathering out of a lower level. The Campbells noted, however, that some of the bones looked as if they might have been split by man, and that, at least on the basis of the preliminary survey, it appeared the bones were not found on the surface beyond the area of occupation. In Ventana Cave similar artifacts were found associated with modern fauna.

Geological evidence provided the most important clues as to possible age. At the present time the Pinto Basin is an extremely arid desert valley where, due to lack of water, there is little possibility of maintaining human life except at rare intervals. There are no water holes or springs in the vicinity which supply potable water. The small wash, known as the Pinto Wash, which runs through the Basin has been known to be wet only three times during a three-year period. The numerous campsites found by the Campbells suggest that at the time this region was inhabited there must have been far more water available than at the present time. Evidence that such was indeed the case has been found by David Scharf, who reported on the geology. Along the middle four miles of the Pinto Wash, and above the banks of the wash proper, is a bench which extends back to a second set of banks reaching to the floor of the present basin. At the upper end the outer banks are almost a mile apart. Such a channel could have been formed only by water. It appears probable that the upper end was once filled by a shallow body of water, lake-like in character, and that at the lower end it narrowed to a shallow stream with a low gradient. The ancient campsites are found along the upper banks following the course of this wide channel.

To account for such a body of water in a now extremely arid region it is necessary to postulate a wetter climate at some time in the past. It was suggested that it was probably during the Provo Pluvial period that the greatest amount of water was present. There is some evidence that the broad channel along which the Pinto campsites were found was only a remnant of a still larger body of water. Therefore, it seems unlikely that the time of the former Pinto River can be that of the pluvial maximum. However, since a great amount of water would be necessary to maintain such a stream, it does not seem probable that the period during which this river existed can have been very remote from the period of maximum moisture.

In Owens Basin the Campbells found Pinto artifacts on high beaches which must be old. Ernst Antevs (1952) thinks this Pinto occupation may date back some 7,000 to 9,000 years. However, he attributes the Pinto industry represented at the nearby Stahl Site to the last two millenia before the Christian Era and the succeeding centuries. He does not state on what evidence the latter estimate is based.

The Stahl Site

Excavations were carried on at the Stahl Site, which lies near Little Lake in Inyo County, California, during 1948, 1949, and 1951.

Mark R. Harrington, of the Southwest Museum, was in charge of the excavations (Harrington, 1948 a and b, 1951; Simpson, 1949). Artifacts were found in deposits varying in depth from two to nearly eight feet. No detailed analysis of the artifacts has been published, but it is reported that several hundred Pinto points and a smaller number of Lake Mohave and Silver Lake points were recovered. Associated with them were various kinds of scrapers, flake knives, milling stones, and manos.

The site provided evidence of house construction in the form of post holes believed to have contained supports for some type of small hut. There were seven of these house outlines. It is impossible to determine the method of construction used, but it has been suggested that willow may have been woven between poles to form wattlework walls and that rushes lying on poles may have formed the roof. Doorway openings were usually to the southeast, but one was to the northeast. There were several bowl-shaped depressions that may represent fireplaces, and an elliptical pit that may have been used for storage.

The Age of Pinto Points

There has been a great deal of controversy regarding the age of Pinto points. The first investigators accepted an early post-pluvial age for them. Ernst Antevs (1952) believes some were made in pre-Altithermal times although others are of post-Altithermal age. Frank H. H. Roberts, Jr. (1940) felt it highly probable that, although the complex was reasonably old, the stream along which the people camped resulted from a more recent period of moisture than the Provo Pluvial. Martin, Quimby, and Collier (1947) also suggested that the wet period that permitted intensive occupation of the Pinto Basin was the last time of greater moisture, dated at some 3,000 to 4,000 years ago and sometimes called the Little Pluvial. Malcolm J. Rogers (1939), who conducted investigations in the same general area on behalf of the San Diego Museum, came to the conclusion that Pinto and Gypsum Cave points were contemporaneous and partly concurrent in distribution, and proposed the use of the term Pinto-Gypsum Complex. He estimated the age at about 800 B. C. to 200 A. D.

Points resembling those found in the Pinto Basin and in Gypsum Cave continued to be made for some time after the Altithermal period, but it is possible some points of these types are of pre-Altithermal age. Furthermore, although there appears to have been some mixing in certain times and in certain areas, the presence of pure sites containing only one type or the other indicates that two separate complexes must have been represented. Apparently there was some overlap in time between Gypsum and Pinto, but the time range for both complexes is not necessarily the same. We simply do not have sufficient data.

One factor produces certain major difficulties. Almost all stemmed points with bifurcated bases are lumped together. To a great extent, so are points with triangular blades and contracting stems. The writer feels certain that, if a sufficient number of specimens could be studied, typological variations reflecting temporal and regional differences in both groups would become apparent.

Further discussion of the age of the Pinto type is impractical before discussing Bat Cave and Ventana Cave, which contained points of this type and points resembling those found in Gypsum Cave. In order to understand some of the problems involved, however, it is necessary to know something of the Cochise Culture which is also represented in these caves. This will be discussed in the following section. For further consideration of the age of Pinto points see page 180.

The Cochise Complexes

Projectile points were the most characteristic artifacts of most of the complexes previously described, but in southeastern Arizona and southwestern New Mexico has been found evidence of occupation by people who used a great many grinding stones. Although they hunted, they were largely dependent on the gathering of wild plant foods. In southeastern Arizona, where evidence of these ancient food gatherers was first found, E. B. Sayles and Ernst Antevs (1941) recognized three different stages of development which they grouped under the name Cochise Culture.

The first find was made in 1926, twelve miles northwest of Douglas in southeastern Arizona, when Byron Cummings found a mammoth skull *in situ* and below it artifacts and bones of bison and horse. From 1935 until 1940 an intensive reconnaissance survey was undertaken in southeastern Arizona and southwestern New Mexico by Sayles and other members of the staff of Gila Pueblo. Much concentrated work was done in Sulphur Spring Valley and adjacent areas which presented good opportunities for studying the geology. Many artifacts were discovered in beds exposed in the sheer walls of arroyos, and evidence was found of a pre-pottery culture with three distinct stages which extended over a long period of time.

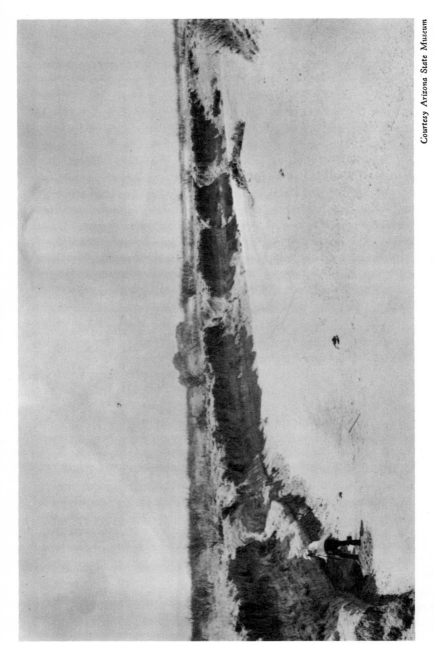

Courtesy Arizona State Museum

FIG. 56—The Double Adobe Site, Arizona. Artifacts of the Sulphur Spring Stage and bones of extinct animals were found in sands and gravels at the base of the arroyo wall.

The earliest artifacts were found at the Double Adobe Site in Sulphur Spring Valley, in old river sands and gravels overlain by clay and silts. The name Sulphur Spring stage is taken from the name of the valley. The type station is the site at which Cummings made his original discovery. Among the artifacts were some hammerstones and a few plano-convex percussion-flaked tools, probably used as scrapers, knives, and choppers. Grinding stones were the most common form of artifact. These included thin, flat, milling stones, and manos small enough to have been used with one hand. Bones of mammoth, horse, bison, dire wolf (a long extinct species), prong-horn antelope, and coyote were found with the artifacts. The fact that some of the bones were split and burned suggested that the animals had been hunted and butchered by man; but in the course of the original excavations no projectile points were found, and they were not believed to be part of the lithic industry. It seemed possible that projectile tips might have been made of wood and had not been preserved. However, in the course of later investigations by Sayles and Antevs (1955) at the Double Adobe Site, stone projectile points were found, together with the characteristic Sulphur Spring artifacts. They were relatively small. Some were leaf-shaped while others were stemmed and barbed. They were made from flakes.

The next stage is known as the Chiricahua. Material assigned to it was first obtained from erosion channels in the Sulphur Spring and San Simon valleys and from a large peat-covered midden near the mouth of Cave Creek on the west side of the Chiricahua Mountains. No sharp cultural break between this and the preceding period can be recognized. Grinding stones still predominated, but the milling stones were somewhat larger than the earlier forms and had shallow basins. There is some indication that mortars and pestles were also used. Other stone implements included hammerstones, choppers, knives, and scrapers. Plano-convex forms persisted, but there were some implements flaked on both faces. Although a few projectile points were found, it was at first thought that they were not an integral part of this stage. More recent evidence from other sites with Chiricahua material, however, indicates that points with broad lateral notches and indented bases were used in Chiricahua times.

The next stage was named the San Pedro because of the occurrence of many sites, including the type station, along the San Pedro River in Arizona. Although it appears to be possible to trace an evolutionary sequence from the Sulphur Spring stage through the Chiricahua to the

San Pedro, there is a very definite typological break between the last two. Grinding stones were less numerous. Milling stones had deep basins and handstones were larger. Mortars and pestles appeared in a fully developed form. Pressure-flaked implements became extremely common. Among them were many fairly large projectile points with broad lateral notches which produced expanding stems. Other chipped stone artifacts were both plano-convex and bifacial, and included knives, scrapers, choppers, and a great variety of hammerstones.

When the first San Pedro sites were excavated, a number of pits were found. It was thought that the small, shallow pits and hearths had been used for storage and cooking, but it was suggested that the larger pits might represent house remains. Subsequent work at Cave Creek and the San Simon Valley (Sayles, 1945) proved that houses were indeed a component of the San Pedro stage. Remains of these structures consist of shallow oval floors of hard-packed earth. The nature of the walls and roof supports is not known. Apparently the houses were entered from the side where a step in a wall led from the surface. Storage pits were dug in the floor. There were no distinct fireplaces, but some slightly defined fire areas indicate that fires were built in the structures.

The same area yielded evidence of a later stage of development. Stone artifacts and houses were like those of the San Pedro, but pottery had been added to the complex. Since the pottery was already well-developed at its first appearance, it is assumed that the trait came to the Cochise people from some other source, probably from Mexico. It is generally believed that the Cochise people were the forerunners of later agriculturists, the Mogollon and probably the Hohokam peoples.

The estimated age of the earliest Cochise stage was based on association with extinct fauna and on evidence which indicated that the Sulphur Spring deposits were laid down during a period of greater moisture presumably the Provo Pluvial. What is now a playa, dry the greater part of the year, is believed to be the remnant of a large body of water, covering approximately 120 square miles, to which the name Lake Cochise has been given. There is also evidence that Whitewater Creek, in the southern portion of the valley, which is now an ephemeral stream, had a permanent flow during this stage and that laminated clays were deposited in permanent ponds which no longer exist. Furthermore, hickory charcoal has been found in some of the sites, and trees, such as hickory, require far more moisture than is now available. On the basis of all this evidence, Antevs placed most of the beds containing artifacts of the Sulphur Spring stage of the Cochise Culture in the Pluvial. This suggested that artifacts from these levels must be at least 9,000 years old and might be considerably older. Even the maximum radiocarbon date of 7,756 ± 370 years ago, obtained from material from a Sulphur Spring site (Libby, 1955), is at variance with the faunal and geological evidence and appears to be too recent.

Some beds in which Chiricahua artifacts occur *in situ* lie above those assigned to the Sulphur Spring stage; therefore, they must be younger. There is evidence that the climate was drier at this time, so these beds have been placed in the post-Pluvial period. Antevs believes the transition from the Sulphur Spring to the Chiricahua stage took place between 6,000 and 7,000 years ago. Charcoal from a site of Chiricahua age produced a Carbon 14 date of 4,006 ± 270 years ago (Libby, 1955).

At the main San Pedro sites in Sulphur Spring Valley there is evidence of a period of erosion, caused by drought, at the beginning of the San Pedro stage. Antevs originally dated this drought at about 1,000 B. C. Now, on the basis of a radiocarbon date obtained from one of these sites, he places it at 500 B. C. (Antevs, 1955a).

The Wet Leggett Site

Chiricahua artifacts have been reported from a valley ten miles from Reserve in western New Mexico by Paul Martin, John Rinaldo, and Ernst Antevs (1949). The implements lay three to six feet below the surface, along an ancient stream bed in a hard cement-like material. They consisted of milling stones; cutting, scraping, and chopping tools; gravers, and one projectile point. The latter was a short stubby specimen with corner notches and a slightly concave base. Later excavations in the same area revealed the presence of a floor of compact clay with a surface blackened by organic refuse and bits of charcoal. It appears to be the remains of some sort of shelter. Two milling stones and a mano of Chiricahua type were found in this dwelling area (Martin and Rinaldo, 1950). The Chiricahua artifacts from the arroyo banks were dated by Antevs at between 5,000 and 3,500 years ago. Charcoal from a tributary arroyo, which contained beds that may be attributed to either the Chiricahua or the San Pedro phase, yielded a Carbon 14 date of 4,508 ± 680 years ago (Libby, 1955).

Bat Cave

In the southwestern end of the Plains of San Augustin, which lie largely between the towns of Magdalena and Datil, New Mexico, is a

large amphitheatre-like rock shelter known as Bat Cave. It was excavated for Harvard University under the direction of Herbert W. Dick
(1952). In it were found three stratified layers. The lowest, Bed I,
was entirely sterile and consisted of beach gravels thought to have been
deposited during the subsidence of pluvial Lake San Augustin. The
next level, which yielded a small number of artifacts, was composed of
dust, sand, and rock fallen from the roof. It will be referred to as
Bed II. The top layer, which produced most of the artifacts, was made
up of dust, roof debris, and decomposed organic matter. It will be
called Bed III. Ernst Antevs, the geologist who studied the deposits,
attributes Bed II to the Altithermal and Bed III to the Medithermal
period (Antevs, 1955b).

Among the great number of artifacts found in this site were over
400 projectile points. The upper third of Bed II yielded projectile
points with straight to slightly concave bases and rounded shoulders.
These have been called Bat Cave points. One similar specimen was also
found in the lower quarter of this bed. In the upper quarter of Bed II
and the lower half of Bed III were found points similar to those found
in Cochise sites of the Chiricahua stage. Overlapping these types to
some extent were artifacts, now named Augustin points by Dick, which
centered in the upper fourth of Bed II. These were pointed-base projectile tips which resembled, in a general way, those found at Gypsum
Cave and Manzano Cave, but they had a wider range of style and size.
In Bed III were found points reminiscent of Pinto Basin types. At a
higher level points like those found in the San Pedro stage of the
Cochise Culture first appeared. Above these lay other artifacts, including side-and corner-notched points and pottery. The latter, for the
most part, represented Mogollon types.

Of the utmost importance was the discovery of corn near the base
of Bed III. It is regarded as the most ancient example of maize yet
discovered. According to Paul S. Mangelsdorf and C. Earle Smith, Jr.
(1949), the botanists who studied and described it, it is also the most
primitive. It was both a pop corn and a pod corn. The ear was not
enclosed in husks. The first domestication of maize must have occurred
much farther south, quite probably in South America, but it is extreme'y
interesting to learn that it was being grown in North America at a very
early date. Prior to this discovery there had been no proof of the
practice of agriculture in the United States before the Christian Era.
Maize specimens were found throughout the upper bed at Bat Cave,
and they yielded important evidence pertaining to the evolution of corn.
There was a progressive increase in size of both cob and kernels.

Bed III was six feet thick in some sections. Dates from the lowest level should be applicable to the earliest corn and to the Chiricahua-like points. Charcoal from the sixty to sixty-six inch level gave a radiocarbon date of 5,931 ± 310 years ago; a sample from the forty-eight to sixty inch level was dated at 5,605 ± 290 years ago. Wood from this level was dated 2,862 ± 250 years ago. The difference between the first two dates and the third is large for material which should be of approximately the same age. If, as Antevs believes, intensive occupation here was not practical during the Altithermal, which ended only some 4,000 years ago, the earlier dates would appear to be excessive. The later date, on the other hand, seems too recent if Antevs is correct in saying that these deposits began to accumulate soon after the Altithermal ended and the Medithermal began. Various other Carbon 14 dates have been obtained for the higher levels, but, until the final report is published, it is impossible to evaluate them.

Surface Finds in the Plains of San Augustin

At one time the Plains of San Augustin contained several pluvial lakes. One of these was a large body of water, some thirty-four by eleven miles in extent, known as Lake San Augustin. What now remains are plains surrounded by terraces which represent old beach levels. Blow-out sites and surface sites on lake terraces in this area have been investigated by Wesley R. Hurt, Jr. and Daniel McKnight (1949).

The nature of these sites, which led to the mixing of material of markedly different ages, makes it impossible to separate the artifacts into distinct assemblages; but they are of interest because forms are represented that have been found elsewhere under circumstances indicating fairly great antiquity. Included are specimens of the Folsom type and more roughly flaked fluted forms; parallel flaked points; projectile tips similar to those found in Sandia, Gypsum, and Manzano caves and the Pinto Basin; and grinding stones reminiscent of Cochise types. They are found on the lower and middle terraces of pluvial lakes, so they cannot have been deposited when the lake waters were at their highest point. Still, the fact that they do not usually occur on the lake bottoms, as do Pueblo artifacts, indicates that during the early period of occupation most of the lakes still existed. However, there is some indication that makers of fluted points lingered in this area for some time. Evidence of their presence has been found in a lake bottom, which would indicate that the distinctive fluting technique was still employed at a time when one of the pluvial lakes was dry.

Middle Rio Grande Valley Sites

Frank C. Hibben (1951) reported on a number of sites in the Middle Rio Grande Valley that have produced artifacts similar to Cochise materials. None of these sites contained projectile points. In a gravel pit at the southern edge of Albuquerque, New Mexico, crude chopper-like artifacts, a basin-shaped milling stone, and charcoal lenses that may represent hearths, were found some twenty-two feet below the surface. Along the occupation line and below were found bones of extinct animals including mammoth, horse, and camel. There were also bison bones, but the species has not been determined.

Some twenty-five miles south of Albuquerque, at a site known as Comanche Springs, a bone bed was found eight feet below the present surface. The bones were imbedded in a blue-gray clay that resembles the diatomaceous earth in which Folsom points were found at the Blackwater No. 1 locality near Clovis, New Mexico, discussed on page 47. The two areas may have had the same general geologic history. All identifiable bones appear to be those of bison. One horn core was recovered and has been tentatively identified as that of an extinct species, *Bison antiquus*. Twenty-two roughly flaked implements that could have served as choppers or scrapers were found. Milling stones with shallow basin-shaped depressions were found under circumstances suggesting they might have been associated with the bones, but none were *in situ*.

In the drainage of the Rio Puerco, some twenty-five miles south and west of Albuquerque, was found a series of sites that contained deeply buried hearths and probable living areas. Manos and basin-shaped milling stones were associated with some of the charcoal lenses. Two milling stones were found twenty-three feet below the surface. They closely resembled Cochise specimens. Six rough chopper-like tools lay near the hearths. Due to Kirk Bryan's untimely death, studies of this portion of the Rio Puerco were not completed. However, on the basis of Bryan's (1946) work on the headwaters of the stream, Hibben suggested that the Rio Puerco hearths might be contemporaneous with the middle levels of Bat Cave (see page 174) and were probably of more recent age than the materials found at the Albuquerque Gravel Pit and at Comanche Springs.

John Campbell and Florence Hawley Ellis (1952) located and mapped many blown-out occupation sites along the Rio Grande a few miles west of Albuquerque. They contained artifacts and numerous rock-filled hearths. Most points were corner-notched forms that closely resembled those of the San Pedro phase except that they were somewhat shorter and broader. Campbell and Ellis called them Atrisco points. They assigned them to the Atrisco Focus, which they regard as the Middle Rio Grande manifestation of the San Pedro phase of the Cochise Culture.

Ventana Cave

One of the most important sites ever found in the Southwest is Ventana Cave, a large rock shelter with deep, stratified, culture-bearing deposits. This cave is in the Castle Mountains on the Papago Indian Reservation some seventy-five air-line miles south of Phoenix and west of Tucson, Arizona. Excavations were undertaken in 1941 and 1942 by the University of Arizona and the Arizona State Museum. This project was under the direction of Emil W. Haury (1950).

Ventana Cave was formed by the erosion of a mass of agglomerate at the base of a cliff. The harder basalt which lay above it did not wear away and remained to form an overhang. The protected area is one hundred eighty feet in length. It is divided into two units by a natural partition that consists of a basalt remnant. The northeastern portion is called the lower cave. The southwestern part, which is deeper and contains a spring, is known as the upper cave. It is only the latter which need concern us here, for the lower cave contained no tangible evidence of Early Man nor of extinct animals. The upper cave however, contained deep stratified deposits and has provided important information pertaining to ancient man.

The top deposit of the upper cave consists largely of trash left by man, which is called a midden. This may be divided into two zones. The higher is dry and the lower is moist, probably because of subterranean drainage from the spring. Faunal remains are all of modern form. The midden is soft, and some mixing of cultures may have occurred; but the evidence suggests a continuity of occupation with no real break or interruption during its formation until the intensive occupation ended about 1400 A. D.

Below the midden were beds formed primarily by nature. In the central part of the cave, below the midden, lay a quantity of debris derived from a talus cone outside the cave. Man probably used the cave while this talus was advancing but did not actually live in this particular section. Beneath the talus wedge lay a slightly cemented bed of reddish-brown sand, separated from the lower beds by a disconformity which must represent the lapse of a long period of time during which erosion occurred. The two lowest levels were beds cemented by calcium carbonate deposited from evaporating spring water. The upper bed consists of weathered volcanic debris which was carried into the cave by intermittent floods; the lower is a conglomerate.

In the lowest bed were found two doubtful implements. One resembles a hammerstone, the other is a basalt chip that might have been used as a scraping tool. In the volcanic zone which, in the light of geological and palaeontological evidence, appears to represent merely a later phase of the same climatic horizon, lay ninety man-made tools and the bones of animals, some of which are extinct.

Most of the artifacts recovered were very crude, probably because of the use of basalt, a material which is difficult to flake. There were two projectile points. One was leaf-shaped. The other resembled a Folsom point as to shape, but it was not fluted. Among the other artifacts were retouched flakes, probably used as knives, and end and side scrapers. Some of the latter had one concave edge. Choppers, planes, and tools with short points, presumably used for scratching hard surfaces such as bone, were also found. Manos and hammerstones were each represented by a single specimen.

The presence of marine shells in this level indicates that there was some contact with the coastal area or with its inhabitants during this period of occupation. The shells bore no traces of human workmanship, and Haury has suggested that they may have been used as containers for liquids. An abundance of bones was found in the lower beds, but none were articulated. Among the animals represented were extinct species of wolf, jaguar, ground sloth, tapir, and horse. Some of these animals may have died of natural causes, but some must have been killed by man. Many of the long bones found in the volcanic layer were split, presumably to obtain marrow, and some were charred. It is not believed that the artifacts or the bones were washed in, but rather that both men and animals were attracted to the cave by the water and shelter it provided. According to Edwin H. Colbert, who studied the fossil vertebrates, the type of extinct animals found in the lower beds suggests that when man first occupied Ventana Cave climatic conditions in southern Arizona differed from those of the present day. He feels that at that time there was more moisture and that there was a grassland environment with persistent streams (Colbert, 1950).

The red sand, which was deposited on the volcanic bed after a long period of erosion, contained leaf-shaped projectile points and a stemmed type that Haury refers to the Amargosa I phase. This is terminology taken from a revised sequence proposed by Malcolm Rogers. Apparently the present Amargosa I correlates with the first part of what Rogers formerly called the Pinto-Gypsum phase which preceded the Amargosa I phase in the old sequence. Rogers has not published any report on his revision, and the situation is completely confused.

In the deepest part of the moist portion of the midden, which lay above, were found a few specimens like those from the red sand level; but the most common type of projectile point had a somewhat expanding stem and a concave base, and was often serrated. There are resemblances between these points, those found in Chiricahua sites, and Pinto Basin types. Associated with them, but occurring in smaller numbers, were specimens with pointed stems that bear some resemblance to the Gypsum Cave type although they are by no means identical. One point was of the Lake Mohave type. Haury assigns these types to the phase designated Amargosa II by Rogers. Milling stones and manos were present in large numbers. They were like those found in Chiricahua Cochise sites.

Grinding stones were less common in the upper part of the moist midden zone. Projectile points were of the San Pedro type. Haury calls this period Amargosa III. Faunal remains were all of modern type. Cultural material, including pottery that may be attributed to the desert branch of the Hohokam Culture, which falls within the Christian Era, was found in the dry portion of the midden.

Kirk Bryan (1950) provided the geological interpretation of the cave deposits. He concurred with Colbert's opinion, based on faunal evidence, that there was more moisture when the cave was first occupied. The nature of the lower cemented beds indicated deposition at a time when the spring had a greater flow than it has had in recent times. This suggested a correlation with a pluvial period. In Bryan's opinion the period involved correlated with the last major climax of the Wisconsin. Since the early Ventana artifacts lay almost at the top of the beds representing the humid period, and since there was evidence that the flow of water decreased toward the end of the period of deposition, Bryan felt that the artifacts were deposited after the pluvial climax had been attained.

The marked disconformity between these lower beds and those above them must represent a long period of erosion, presumably the Altithermal. This dry period may have still been in progress when the red sand was deposited, and it is possible that the artifacts found in this level are of Altithermal age. If Bryan's correlation is correct, and it appears to be, all the artifacts from the midden, including Chiricahua and Amargosa II types, are post-Altithermal in age and are less than 4,000 years old.

The San Jose Complex

In the vicinity of Grants, New Mexico, Kirk Bryan and Joseph H. Toulouse, Jr. (1943) investigated twelve blow-out sites that yielded evidence of a non-ceramic complex to which the name San Jose was given. The projectile points were serrated and had a long tang with an indented base. The edges of the tang were ground. They closely resemble the Pinto-like forms from Ventana Cave. On the basis of geologic studies, Bryan and Franklin T. McCann (1943) suggested that the occupation began during a period of marked erosion. This was probably the Altithermal.*

The Concho Complex

Similar points and points that resemble the Gypsum Cave type are part of the Concho Complex defined by Fred Wendorf and Tully H. Thomas (1951) on the basis of surface collecting from over thirty pre-pottery sites near Concho, Arizona. Associated with them were barbless stemmed points, expanded-base drills, choppers, side and end scrapers, and retouched flakes. No exact date has been assigned to this complex, but it has been suggested that it is of post-Altithermal age.

Age of Stemmed Indented-base Points

It is now possible to return to the problem of the age of Pinto points. Robert Lister (1953), who has published a chart showing seventeen western localities that yielded stemmed points with indented bases, has suggested that such points may serve as a horizon marker somewhere in the period between Folsom and recent times. In the opinion of the writer, although some of the Pinto points found in California may be of pre-Altithermal age, the evidence is not conclusive. None of those found elsewhere appear to pre-date the Long Drought. However, they do seem to be earlier than the pottery-making cultures.

SOUTHERN OREGON

Intensive investigations have been carried on in south central Oregon by L. S. Cressman and his associates. Various sites contained

*In June 1957 in the Texas Journal of Science, Vol. IX, No. 2, pp. 154-156 George Agogino and Sherwin Feinhandler reported the discovery of amaranth (pigweed) seeds in a hearth near Grants, New Mexico associated with grinding implements and characteristic San Jose artifacts. According to Agogino (Personal communication) these seeds were dated at 6,800 ± 400 years ago at the University of Michigan Laboratory.

specimens that lay below pumice deposits which resulted from volcanic action, and it is necessary to have some knowledge of the volcanic history of the area before considering the sites themselves. Cressman has very kindly contributed a statement of explanation of the volcanism in the Cascades which is quoted in the following paragraph.

"The Cascade Mountain range is largely volcanic in origin. While many of the peaks represent remains of long extinct volcanos, some remained active until quite recent times. Two of the cones or sources of pumice have proved to be related to archaeological sites lying east of the mountains and the pumice from them can be readily distinguished and identified as to source. The two sources referred to are Mount Mazama in the crater of which Crater Lake now lies located on the summit of the Cascades well toward the south of the state and a series of cones closely grouped lying north and east of Crater Lake approximately 75 miles and some 50 miles east of the crest of the range. The latter source generally goes by the name of Newberry Crater. The pumice from the final eruption of Mount Mazama has been found in a number of archaeological sites and in a series of caves it has been interbedded between occupational levels. Pumice from the Newberry Crater was first recognized in an archaeological context in the Fort Rock Cave where it, too, was interbedded between occupational levels. It is now recognized that the eruption of Mount Mazama which deposited the pumice in the caves was the final large-scale activity of that volcano. At one point on the boundary of the Mount Mazama pumice, ash from the Newberry eruption was found by Williams overlying that from Mount Mazama, and clearly indicated that this eruption was later than that of Mount Mazama which had deposited the underlying pumice. However, it is now recognized that there were a series of eruptions of the Newberry cones, just as there had been a long series of Mount Mazama explosions, but it was not known which eruption of the Newberry cones deposited the pumice overlying that from Mount Mazama which could be attributed to the final action of the latter volcano. The fortunate discovery of a log or branches of a tree up to one foot in diameter under a cover of three or four feet of pumice from the last explosion within the Newberry Craters during road building operations about 1950 made it possible to get a Carbon 14 date for this final volcanic activity of the Newberry Crater. The date for this eruption is 2054 ± 230 years ago. (Libby, Willard F., Radiocarbon Dating, Second Edition, 1955, University of Chicago Press, P. 120, Sample C-657) and shows clearly that the Newberry Crater continued active after the final eruption of the Mount Mazama volcano. The problem, therefore, in using the pumice from the Newberry Crater as a dating device for archaeological remains is to determine which state of volcanic activity is represented by the pumice fall." (L. S. Cressman).

Four radiocarbon assays made at the University of Chicago on charcoal from a tree killed and covered by pumice from Mt. Mazama averaged 6,453 ± 250 years ago (Libby, 1955). Comparable material submitted to the University of Michigan gave a date of 6,000 ± 700 years ago (Crane, 1956). It was recognized that in the case of these samples there was a possibility of post-depositional contamination through contact with ground water. A dry sample of rodent droppings was taken from immediately below the pumice in Paisley Cave No. 2 (erroneously reported as Paisley No. 3) and submitted to the Geochronological Laboratory at Yale University in an effort to determine if there was any difference in dates from wet and dry samples. This sample produced a date of 7,610 ± 120 years ago (Preston, Person, Deevey, 1955). The difference between this date and those obtained from the samples which had been exposed to water is statistically significant.

Wikiup Damsite No. 1

As early as 1934 artifacts had been found underlying pumice attributed to the explosion that created Crater Lake (Cressman, 1937; Cressman, Williams, Krieger, 1940). At Wikiup Damsite No. 1, on the Deschutes River, John F. Isackson, while digging test pits for U. S. Bureau of Reclamation soil studies, uncovered two knives or scrapers below the pumice. One was of obsidian, the other of fine-grained basalt. They were thin ovoid forms shaped by the removal of large shallow flakes. The edges were retouched only in part. They exhibited less skillful workmanship than specimens of recent age found in the area.

Catlow Cave No. 1

In succeeding years Cressman and his associates excavated a number of cave sites (Cressman, Williams, Krieger, 1940; Cressman et al., 1942). One was a large rock shelter in Harney County called Catlow Cave No. 1. Human bones were found in ancient gravel deposited by a long extinct lake, but there was no conclusive evidence to show whether they had reached this position through deposition or by burial. Smoothed bone splinters were found in the gravels. A fragmentary horse bone was found, but there has been some controversy regarding its provenience (Krieger, 1944b; Cressman, 1944). Although Catlow Cave failed to provide conclusive proof of the presence of Early Man in this area, work in other cave sites showed that there had been some occupation prior to the first pumice deposition and suggested that some of the early inhabitants might have been contemporaries of now extinct animals.

Paisley Five Mile Point Cave No. 1

Paisley Cave No. 1 lies on the east rim of Summer Lake near the village of Paisley. Below a pumice horizon, attributed to the Mt. Mazama eruption, were found fire lenses and occupational debris. Stone artifacts consisted of a fragmentary projectile point, scrapers, one of which was crescent-shaped, and some retouched flakes. Associated with them were a fragment of a shredded sagebrush bark mat, a piece of cordage, made of the same material, that may have been part of a sandal, and a two-ply twisted basketry warp.

Paisley Five Mile Point Cave No. 2

Paisley Cave No. 2 was adjacent to No. 1. Because of the mixing of ash, pumice, artifacts, and debris that resulted from the activities of the inhabitants, the rear of the cave showed no stratification. Toward the front, however, the stratification was clear. It was from this portion of the cave that the sample that provided the Yale radiocarbon date was obtained. It lay immediately below the pumice.

Paisley Five Mile Point Cave No. 3

Paisley Cave No. 3 lies some seventy-five yards north of No. 1 along the face of the cliff. It contained an unbroken stratum of pumice similar to that found in the first cave. Below the pumice five sterile levels, consisting of dust, broken rock, roof debris, and bat guano, overlay two strata that contained a few pieces of obsidian, definitely flaked by man but lacking in diagnostic value, ash lenses, and animal bones. Some of the bones were of existing species, but bones of horse and camel, animals believed to be of pre-Altithermal age, were also found. The presence of a sterile horizon, two and a half feet thick, between the occupation level and pumice layer indicates that a long period of time intervened between the occupation and the Mt. Mazama eruption.

Odell Lake

At the south end of Odell Lake a campsite was found that was overlain by pumice, attributed to Mt. Mazama, which extended into underlying glacial till (Cressman, 1948). In addition to chipped implements, there were flakes, hammerstones, and the remains of fires. There are variations in the projectile point types, but they tend to follow a generalized leaf-shaped pattern. One, which is shouldered on only one side, has been compared to a Sandia point.

Fort Rock Cave

A cave that lies in the Fort Rock Valley, from which it takes its name, contained pumice attributed to the Newberry eruption, believed to have occurred later than the Mt. Mazama. Above the pumice lay wooden artifacts, large and small projectile points, scrapers, drills, and a mano. Below the pumice were found forty-four stemless points and nine stemmed points, seven of which were corner-notched and two side-notched. The former ranged in length from one and a half to three and a half inches, and the latter had an average length of about one and a half inches. There were also eighty-five side and end scrapers, two drills, and four manos. Some bone awls and an atlatl spur made of bone were found. The most common artifacts were well-made sandals of shredded sagebrush bark. There were between seventy-five and a hundred of these specimens, all more or less charred.

Associated with sandals that reportedly lay some distance under the pumice were several fragments of fine twined basketry decorated with false embroidery (Cressman, 1951). The sandals were submitted for radiocarbon dating and produced a date of 9,053 ± 350 years ago (Libby, 1955). This date applies to the specimens, not to the pumice that lay above, which must be younger. It indicates that techniques for the making of sandals and basketry were highly developed in the Basin at an early date.

Willamette Valley

There is no absolute proof of the association of man and mammoth in this area, but it is quite probable that man was present when these animals still existed. In the Willamette Valley pieces of stone, thought to show evidence of human workmanship, were found in a spring that contained mammoth bones (Cressman and Laughlin, 1941). At another locality in the same valley a point which resembles a Scottsbluff but has a slightly contracting stem, and a Sandia-like specimen, were found lying near mammoth bones that had been partially uncovered by water (Cressman, 1947).

Lower Klamath Lake

Leaf-shaped points, large side-notched points, diamond-shaped knives with beveled edges, and pointed implements of fossilized bone that resemble the Clovis specimens, were found in the Lower Klamath Lake bed near the Oregon-California boundary at a locality called the Narrows. Few specimens have been found *in situ*, but Cressman believes most of the objects found have weathered out of blue-gray silts that have yielded bones of extinct fauna. In one case an obsidian knife and a crude scraper were found in an uneroded blue-gray deposit containing fragments of a long bone and tusk of an elephant.

Upper Klamath Lake

Excavations in the Upper Klamath Lake area, sixty miles north of Lower Klamath Lake, were carried out from 1947 to 1951 (Cressman, 1956). In Medicine Rock Cave, a well-made corner-notched point of basalt was found below the Mt. Mazama Pumice. Another important site was a large midden that was named after the adjacent Kawumkan Springs (Cressman, 1956). A long bone implement with a beveled edge, of the type found at Clovis, at Lind Coulee, and in the Narrows locality, was found in the left abdominal area of a skeleton buried in the midden. A large side-notched projectile point with a concave base was found in the skull. It had apparently entered through the right eye. Three small pestle-like objects, a wolf mandible, two fleshers, and a combination mano and pestle were found nearby, but these do not necessarily represent burial offerings, for they may be part of the midden debris.

Excavation was by forty-centimeter levels. Artifacts were obtained from five levels. The midden extended below the water table to an unknown depth. Cressman suggests a minimum date of 7,000 years ago for the skeleton. It was buried into the top of Level IV. The artifacts from this level must be still older than the skeleton, and so must the midden material that lay below.

More than half of the projectile points found in Level IV were long, narrow, leaf-shaped forms with a constricted stem which produced a triangular termination or tang. There were also some unnotched straight-based forms and a few notched and stemmed specimens. Associated with them were chipped cutting, scraping, and chopping tools, and grinding stones. Slab milling stones and manos were more common than mortars and pestles. There was a higher percentage of the latter in the upper levels. Level III, which must represent the period during which the skeleton was buried, contained many of the long, narrow, leaf-like points, slightly more than fifty percent of the total;

but there was a smaller percentage of the square-based type and a larger percentage of notched forms.

Level II, which Cressman attributes to the period beginning about 3,500 years ago and lasting until about 2,500 years ago, showed certain changes. Leaf-shaped forms persisted and still made up more than half of the total number of projectile points, but almost fifty percent of the weapon tips were stemmed or notched. In Level I only slightly more than thirty percent were of the long, narrow, unnotched type which was most common below. Small points were found as low as Level IV, but there were more of them in the two highest levels. They were most common in the uppermost level. Other sites excavated in the area were pre-contact village sites. According to Cressman, the work in the Upper Klamath Lake area shows a continuous occupation from the early post-Pleistocene to historic times, and the adaption of the culture from the characteristic Great Basin pattern to one based on the selective exploitation of the ecological resources of the rivers and marshes.

COLUMBIA RIVER AREA

The Five Mile Rapids Site

The University of Oregon, in cooperation with the National Park Service, and supported by a grant from the National Science Foundation, has carried out, under the direction of L. S. Cressman, excavations about five miles east of the Dalles on the Oregon side of the Columbia River at Five-Mile Rapids, from 1952 until 1957. Cressman has most generously provided the following statement for use in this publication.

"One site at the head of the Rapids has shown continuous occupation from probably before 10,000 years ago until white contact. The site shows change in technological processes from percussion methods of flaking to the varieties of the magnificent stone work characteristic of the Columbia area. In the earliest stage of occupation elk antlers were used for making various kinds of tools and well made burins are associated with this industry. Sedimentation by the river occurs in the bottom two meters of the site in which artifacts occur. Toward the end of this period fish bones begin to appear, together with the bones of large birds. Following the period of sedimentation occurs a level of heavy occupation with great numbers of bones of salmon and large birds, an extinct vulture, condor, bald eagle, and other large varieties. Artifacts show increasing diversification with pressure flaking well developed; lamellar flakes occur through this level, together with bolas, used for taking the birds. Elk bone tools continue. This level is followed by one in which there are fewer artifacts and progressively fewer fish and bird bones. Aerial deposition of fill is now in evidence and a much lighter use of the site. About 6000 years ago, as shown by Radio-carbon dating, an increase in population, or more intense use of the site occurred, together with the beginning of the development of diversified forms of tools and weapons which continued down to historical times." (L. S. Cressman).

The Lind Coulee Site

The salvage program of the River Basin Survey, designed to gain knowledge of archaeological sites threatened by inundation by reservoir waters of various dams, has resulted in valuable discoveries. One of the important sites investigated under this program is the Lind Coulee Site in the Central Plains section of the Columbia Basin in Washington. Excavations, carried on during 1950, 1951, and 1952, were under the direction of Richard D. Daugherty (1956a).

Lind Coulee is a scabland channel carved by melt waters of late Pleistocene glaciers. Bones and artifacts were found eroding out of the channel walls. Test trenches revealed the presence of material in position under some eleven to thirteen feet of overburden. All but the lowest foot of this was stripped off by bulldozers, exposing for excavation a wedge-shaped area 100 feet wide at the front and tapering to approximately thirty-five feet at a distance of fifty feet. The cultural material lay in water-laid sand. Daugherty does not believe the artifacts and bones were washed in. He thinks this was a seasonally occupied campsite, located on the shore of a sluggish stream or lake, which was periodically inundated.

As in other early sites, the recovery of a small amount of material required tremendous effort. Although almost 600 cubic yards of earth were removed, only 186 artifacts were found. Pressure and percussion flaking techniques had been employed in producing the chipped stone artifacts. There were seven complete or nearly complete projectile points and fourteen fragmentary specimens. Twelve could be identified as being stemmed. The stem of one was parallel-sided, but the others had tapering stems that constituted about one-third of the length of the point. Some of the specimens were almost three inches long. In some cases there was evidence of basal grinding. The basal portion of a stemless point with a concave base was found. The shape was much like that of fluted points, but this specimen was unfluted. The flake scars were parallel and were directed obliquely across the face of the blade. There was no basal grinding.

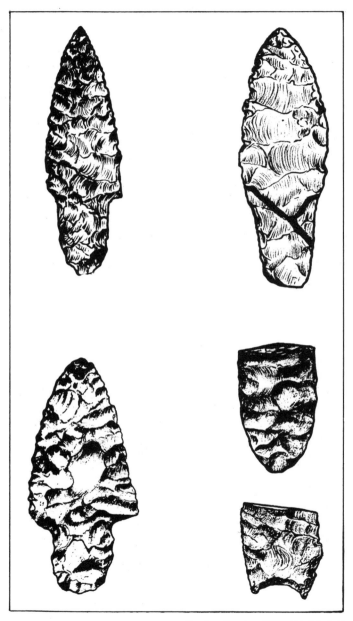

FIG. 57—Projectile points from the Lind Coulee Site, Washington. (From Figs. 19 and 20 pp. 246 and 247, Daugherty, 1956.)

Associated chipped stone artifacts included various crescentic implements, a wide variety of scrapers, many of which were keeled or domed, flake knives and knives with a double bevel, a graver, and massive choppers shaped by percussion. Some implements exhibited ground surfaces that had developed through use, but none of them appeared to have been used in the preparation of food. There were two flat pieces of basalt with fine striations that were stained with red pigment, four handstones that bore traces of red or yellow pigments, and fourteen pieces of hematite and two of limonite.

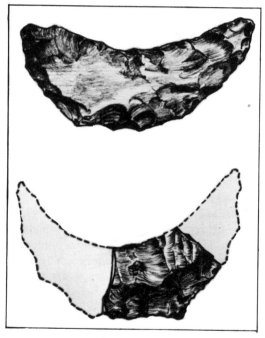

Courtesy American Philosophical Society

FIG. 58—Crescentic implements from the Lind Coulee Site, Washington. (From Fig. 21, p. 248, Daugherty, 1956.)

The few bone artifacts recovered were of unusual interest. They were bone shafts very similar to those found at Clovis and in the Lower Klamath Lake Site, and a fragmentary notched or serrated bone point. Large quantities of unworked bones were found. They were highly mineralized, which, in view of the low calcium carbonate content of the deposits, would suggest some antiquity. Bison bones were most common. They were too fragmentary to permit species identification. The presence of bones of animals and birds such as beaver, muskrat, duck, and goose, suggests that climatic conditions at the time of occupation differed from those of the present.

The nature of the deposits, as well as the faunal assemblage, suggests cool moist conditions. Below the bed in which the cultural material was found was a stratum thought to have been formed during the Mankato period. Above the artifact-bearing bed was a layer of silt and sand believed to have been deposited by wind during the Altithermal period. It contains lenses and pockets of volcanic ash attributed to a northern Cascade source and equated with a period of volcanic activity which is thought to have occurred some 5,000 or 6,000 years ago. The average of two Carbon 14 dates obtained from burned bison bones was 8,700 ± 400 years ago.

NEVADA AND UTAH CAVES

Etna Cave

In Etna Cave near Caliente, Nevada, S. M. Wheeler (1942) found four layers containing cultural debris. These were separated from each other by hard-packed layers that he called floors. The material found above Floors 1 and 2 was said to be of Basketmaker and Pueblo age. Between Floors 2 and 3 were two projectile points that resembled those found in Gypsum Cave, a mano, a worked crystal, an unfinished stone knife, two sandals, and four effigies made by splitting a small twig for most of its length and wrapping the component parts around one another to create an animal form. In the same stratum was dung believed to be that of an extinct species of horse. A lanceolate point with a concave base, a piece of etched slate, a bone bead, two hammerstones, a chopper, and two sandals, were found below the lowest floor. In view of the scantiness of the evidence and the nature of the report, it seems unwise to place too much emphasis on this possible association.

Leonard Rockshelter

Leonard Rockshelter lies seventeen miles south of Lovelock, Nevada, near the northeast end of the Humboldt Lake Basin. Humboldt Lake, which recently became extinct, is one of the remnants of the pluvial Lake Lahonton series. On the floor of the cave lay ancient gravels from Lake Lahonton. The shelter, which lies 4,175 feet above sea level, could have been occupied only after the Stansbury stage when the lake stood higher. Above the gravels was a layer of bat guano two to three feet thick, topped by a thick accumulation of wind-deposited dust and rockfall.

In 1936 Thomas Derby found some artifacts, including a complete atlatl dart and thirty *Olivella* shell beads, in the bat guano (Heizer, 1938). The shells could have come only from the California coast. During the following year additional artifacts were found in this level by a field party from the University of California (Heizer, 1951b). Samples of the bat guano yielded radiocarbon dates averaging 8,660 ± 300 years ago. Fragmentary atlatl foreshafts of wood, found in 1937, were dated at 7,038 ± 350 years ago. Later, a date of 11,199 ± 570 years ago was obtained from bat guano lying immediately upon the Lake Lahonton gravels (Libby, 1955).

More intensive excavations were begun in 1950 under the direction of Robert F. Heizer (1951b). The guano bed that lay on the gravels produced obsidian flakes, a flint knife, *Olivella* shells that had been used as beads, and nets made of cordage. Other evidence for the presence of man in this area at an early time came from an old beach line 3,950 feet above sea level, which is attributed to the Anathermal period. The complex found here was characterized by heavy flake scrapers and hemispherical scraper planes made of basalt.

The higher levels in Leonard Rockshelter also showed evidence of human occupancy. Above the bat guano lay a stratum of wind-blown dust and rockfall with an average depth of about two and a half feet. In it were found carbonized basketry fragments and pieces of cordage, and the skeleton of a newborn infant. Some of the carbonized material produced a radiocarbon date of 2,736 ± 500 years ago. This was completely at variance with the estimate of Ernst Antevs who had undertaken geologic studies of the cave. He was convinced that the layer in which this material was found should be attributed to the Altithermal period and, accordingly, the date should fall between 7,000 and 4,000 years ago. Because of this, a redetermination was made and it was found that material from the same sample produced dates averaging 5,737 ± 250 years ago. Numerous artifacts, mostly of basketry and wood, that resemble specimens from Lovelock and Humboldt caves, were found in a still higher stratum that consisted of wind-blown dust, materials from pack rat nests, and roof falls.

Heizer has proposed the name Humboldt Culture for the material from the deep guano level, Leonard Culture for that from the intermediate level, and Lovelock Culture for the complex represented in the uppermost stratum as well as in Lovelock and Humboldt caves. The heavy flake tools and a basalt core found on the old beach level he assigns to the Granite Point Culture.

Fishbone Cave

During 1952, 1953, and 1954, excavation under the direction of P. C. Orr were carried on in seven small caves in the Lake Winnemucca area of Nevada. These were carved by wave action of Pleistocene Lake Lahonton. Lake Winnemucca, which is now dry, was one of the several remnants of the Lake Lahonton system. One of the caves, called Fishbone Cave, contained artifacts, including some made of normally perishable materials, bones of extinct horse and camel, and human skeletal remains. As yet only brief preliminary reports have appeared (Orr, 1952, 1956), and it is difficult to evaluate the nature of the evidence.

According to Orr, Fishbone Cave contained six levels. The lowest, No. 6, consisted of beach sand laid down during a period when the lake was at a higher level. The fifth level was made up of tufa which fell from the cave roof. Resting on this was Level 4, which consisted of sand, dust, rockfall, guano, bones, and organic debris. Samples of vegetal matter from this level were sent to the Lamont Laboratory, and two radiocarbon dates were secured, 11,555 ± 500 years ago and 10,900 ± 300 years ago.

According to Robert F. Heizer (Personal communication) the caves had been badly torn up by pothunters before they were excavated and the stratigraphic picture was by no means clear. He doubts the validity of the evidence of the association of man and extinct animals and he questions the accuracy of the radiocarbon dates. In Heizer's opinion the cultural material recovered equates with the relatively recent Lovelock complex.

Among the products of human workmanship attributed to Level 4 were fragments of string, netting, and matting, and portions of baskets. There was one awl made from a foot bone, said to be that of a fossil horse, and two stone tools, a side scraper or knife, and a keeled scraper. According to Orr, both of the latter appeared to have been rechipped after having been patinated, indicating that the first flaking was done at a still earlier period. The remains of a human burial consisting of a clavicle, a fibula, and a carbonized left foot were found together with the well-preserved skin of a young pelican. Throughout the deposit were bones of fossil horse and camel, usually split and sometimes burned.

Level 3, which lay above Level 4, contained less sand and more dust. The percentage of dust was greater in the upper portion. This zone produced more artifacts than the lower stratum. Many were of perishable materials such as wood, skin, and plant fibers. Chipped stone artifacts have not yet been described, but one dart point is identified as a Pinto and one as an Amargosa point. It is not clear what the basis for differentiation is. Haury includes Pinto points in his Amargosa II category. This stratum also produced a partial mummy of a child. Level 2 contained only one or two artifacts, and Level 1 was sterile.

Orr attributes Level 4 and the lower portion of Level 3 to the Anathermal period. The presence of juniper and marmot would indicate a colder and wetter climate than prevails today. He assigns the upper portion of Level 3, which appears to have been laid down under very dry conditions, to the Altithermal; and Levels 1 and 2, which show the effect of greater moisture, to the Medithermal.

Bones of extinct horse and camel were found in Level 3. Unlike Charles B. Hunt (1953), who believes that these forms did not survive into the dry period of the Neothermal, Orr is of the opinion that horse and camel were indigenous to the level that he attributes to the Long Drought. The writer feels that the possibility that the fossil bones in Fishbone Cave could have reached a higher level through the activities of the inhabitants of the cave or through disturbance by pothunters cannot be overlooked.

Danger Cave

Danger Cave is a large deep cavern on the western edge of the Bonneville Salt Flats near Wendover, Utah. Excavations were carried on from 1949 until 1951 under the direction of Jesse D. Jennings. As yet only a progress summary has appeared (Jennings, 1953), but this publication serves to indicate that this is an extraordinarily important site. The cave contained fourteen feet of stratified deposits which produced some 2,500 chipped stone artifacts, over 1,000 grinding stones, a great many examples of netting, mats, and basketry; objects made of wood, hide, bone, and shell; and bones of various food animals, including mountain sheep, deer, and antelope. No extinct mammals were represented.

The lowest level in the cave consisted of a thin layer of partially consolidated beach sand deposited when the waters of an ancient lake, part of the Bonneville series that was ancestral to Great Salt Lake, reached a point well above the level of the present lake. The cave, with an altitude of 4,312 feet, lies some 110 feet above the present lake level, and the Stansbury beach line is 220 feet higher than the cave floor. The Provo strandline lies above the Stansbury and the Bonneville shoreline is still higher. The cave became dry only after the water had dropped below the floor level for the last time.

The lower sand itself was sterile, but seven crude artifacts and the remains of four fires were found on its surface, indicating that the cave was occupied soon after the beach sand was laid down. Immediately above this bed lay a thicker layer of unconsolidated sand that was apparently deposited by wind. It contained a few nondescript stone artifacts. Jennings calls both sands Cultural Zone I.

Mountain sheep dung and wood samples from this zone were submitted to the University of Chicago Laboratory for radiocarbon dating. The former was dated at 11,453 ± 600 years ago and the latter at 11,151 ± 570 years ago (Libby, 1955). Later, comparable samples were submitted to the Radiocarbon Laboratory of the University of Michigan. The sheep dung gave a date of 11,000 ± 700 years ago, and the wood provided a date of 10,400 ± 700 years ago (Crane, 1956).

A thin layer of bat guano separated Zone I from an ashy dusty midden deposit, eleven feet thick, that lay above. There were four artifact-bearing zones in the midden that were numbered sequentially from the bottom to the top beginning with Zone II. Between them were layers of rockfall believed to represent periods when the cave was not occupied.

When assayed at the University of Chicago, samples from Zone II produced one Carbon 14 date of 9,789 ± 630 years ago and one of 8,960 ± 340 years ago (Libby, 1955). Most projectile points from this zone were corner- or side-notched forms with a notch at the base that Jennings regards as reminiscent of those found in the Oregon caves. Associated with them were unstemmed points that Jennings feels resemble specimens from the Pinto Basin and the Lake Mohave sites. In the writer's opinion most of the illustrated specimens that Jennings has compared with the California types are sufficiently generalized that they have little diagnostic value. They show no very great similarity to the distinctive forms found in the California Desert; however, since only a few photographs have been published, it would be unfair to try to evaluate the closeness of these resemblances at this time. Slab milling stones and two examples of twined basketry were also found in this horizon.

Zone III, for which no Carbon 14 date is available, contained a higher percentage of stemmed and notched points, but there were also some lanceolate forms. These became dominant in Zone IV, which produced a radiocarbon date of 3,819 ± 160 years ago (Libby, 1955). Here notched forms predominated in the earlier levels, while farther east the lanceolate forms are the earliest (Krieger, 1947). Jennings feels that the cultural material from Zone II indicates some connection with both the western Basin and California. He compares material from Zones II and IV with the Pinto-Amargosa complex represented in California and in Ventana Cave. He also notes that there are similarities between the artifacts from Zones III through V and those found at the McKean Site in Wyoming excavated by William Mulloy (1954). The upper level at the McKean Site has a radiocarbon date of 3,287 ± 600 years ago (Libby, 1955). There is also a lower level which must be considerably older.

Problems Pertaining To The Cave Dates

The early dates for Leonard Rockshelter, for Fishbone Cave, and the two sets from Danger Cave, are essentially consistent within the plus or minus factor of radiocarbon dates, but they present certain problems. The caves became dry only after the lake waters had dropped below floor level, and there is no indication that the caves were ever inundated after occupation had begun. Glacial and pluvial periods have been thought to coincide, and the expansion and shrinkage of lakes in dry regions have been equated with the expansion and shrinkage of the glaciers. It has been believed that the reduction of lake levels below the high strandlines formed during pluvials was a gradual process characterized by minor recessions and readvances and that, after the last pluvial, a considerable period of time elapsed before the water level dropped permanently below such heights as are represented by Leonard Rockshelter (4175 feet altitude) and Danger Cave (4312 feet altitude). The exact height of Fishbone Cave is not known. There is a discrepancy of 105 feet between the estimated elevation given on page 3 and that given on page 10 of Orr's (1956b) report. These are respectively, 4,120 and 4,225 feet altitude.

Recent studies indicate that the geologic history of pluvial Lakes Lahonton and Bonneville is far more complicated than had been thought and that there were some very sudden climatic changes. According to W. S. Broeker and P. C. Orr (1956), radiocarbon measurements have been obtained at the Lamont Laboratory from fossil tufa and from dry cave deposits at Pyramid Lake in the Lake Lahonton area which indicate that the maximum lake level was reached 11,700 years ago, and this was followed by a period of receding lake levels that exposed the caves by 11,200 years ago. It is stated that the data derived from the dry cave deposits indicates rapid desiccation subsequent to this maximum.

Studies undertaken by A. J. Eardley (1956) have suggested that the problems pertaining to the dating of the various beach lines in the Bonneville Basin are extremely complicated. Radiocarbon dates indicate that the Stansbury Beach has various levels and that the climatic minimum, during which the fluctuations occurred that produced these phenomena, lasted from approximately 20,000 to 11,000 years ago. An open file report by J. H. Feth and Meyer Rubin, released by the U. S. Geological Survey on February 21, 1957, which provides radiocarbon dates for wave-formed tufas from the Bonneville Basin obtained at the Washington Laboratory, suggests that the history of rising and falling lake stages is exceedingly complex and that it remains largely undeciphered. Tufas from the Provo level, thought to have post-dated the higher Bonneville shoreline, ranged in age from 11,650 ± 450 to 14,300 ± 300 years ago, while a Bonneville sample was dated at 11,300 ± 300 years ago. Tufas from the Stansbury shoreline which lies at a lower elevation than the Bonneville or Provo, range in age from 14,000 ± 400 to 18,000 ± 1,000 years ago.

In view of the stratigraphic evidence it is difficult to believe that these dates can be correct. If they are, all previous interpretations of the terminal history of Lakes Lahonton and Bonneville must be wrong. For archaeologists the geological situation is one of complete confusion. There is little that they can do but bide their time and await clarification from the geologists.

Utah Caves

There are other caves in Utah that, in the opinion of those who excavated them, were occupied not too long after the lake waters had receded sufficiently to make them habitable. In Black Rock Cave No. 1, which lies above the Stansbury beach line on the south shore of Great Salt Lake, Julian Steward (1937) found charcoal mixed with lake gravels on the floor of the cave. In the two lowest feet of refuse were found a few artifacts including small side-notched points. Larger points were found in higher levels. An infant was buried in the lake gravels. All animal bones found were referred to existing species.

There are two lower caves that emerged from the water at a later date. Elmer Smith (1941, 1952) found artifacts in the horizon just above lacustrine gravel in Deadman Cave, which lies two miles from Black Rock Cave at an elevation of some sixty-three feet above Great Salt Lake. They included large shouldered points or knives with notched or concave bases, and smaller specimens with deep notches and rounded tips.

Promontory Cave II, which was excavated by Julian Steward (1937), is on the north side of the lake, sixty-six feet above the water level. A bed of charcoal which contained several broken bones lay directly on the lake gravels. In the lowest level, six inches above the gravels, was a leaf-shaped point. At a higher level were found stemmed points with bifurcated bases that somewhat resemble the Pinto type.

THE TULE SPRINGS SITE

While conducting palaeontological investigations for the American Museum of Natural History in the Vegas Wash of southern Nevada during 1933, Fenley Hunter found an ash and charcoal bed, uncovered by erosion, which contained split and burned bones of extinct Pleistocene animals, notably camel, bison, and horse. With the bones was found an obsidian flake, produced by man and bearing scars that appeared to have resulted from use. The matrix containing the bones, charcoal, and the flake, was sent to the American Museum of Natural History. Several distinguished scientists were present when the flake was removed (Simpson, 1933).

The locality was visited in 1933 and again in 1952 by Mark R. Harrington (1934 and 1954). He found seven or eight other ash beds in the same general area. One, which lay half a mile up the wash, contained similar bones and a mammoth tooth. Some of the bones were burned at the ends and some apparently split while still green in an effort to obtain marrow. The large extinct camel, Camelops, was the most common form represented. With the exception of one camel's foot, all of the bones were disarticulated. A chopper flaked on both sides, a plano-convex scraper, a roughly circular biface implement, all made of stone, and two awl-like implements and a fragmentary bone tool, were found a few feet away. Harrington believes that they were washed from the bed that contained the bones.

Charcoal thought to be of human origin, taken from the locality investigated by Hunter and Harrington, was submitted to the Chicago

Radiocarbon Laboratory in 1954. According to the determinations of Libby (1955) the charcoal is more than 23,800 years old. How much more is not known. The complex geological history of the area has not been worked out in any detail, but there is some geological evidence that suggests age. This is now an extremely arid, waterless area, but above the various ash beds are deposits of silts, some as much as twenty-one feet thick, which contain fresh-water shells and which must indicate the presence of an ancient lake.

During 1955 Harrington and Ruth D. Simpson conducted further investigations (Harrington, 1955b; Simpson, 1955). Excavations were undertaken in the beds previously discovered and in similar deposits located during this field season. A fire pit, where it is believed a camel was cooked, was found. There were various split and burned bones, and one showed evidence of scraping. One stone tool and one possible artifact were recovered. The first was a disc-shaped biface, the latter an elongated pebble, chipped along one edge, which may have served as a side scraper. In a side canyon of the wash, Simpson found the disarticulated bones of a mammoth. A small bed of charcoal, possibly of human origin, lay on the same level not far from the skull.

SANTA ROSA ISLAND

For some years the Santa Barbara Museum of Natural History has sponsored an archaeological and palaeontological project under the direction of Phil C. Orr on Santa Rosa Island, a large island forty-five miles off the southern California coast (Orr, 1956). The remains of very small mammoths that were only about six feet high have been found in sediments, exposed along the sea cliff, which are attributed to the Pleistocene. These animals were probably not too difficult to kill, and it seems possible they did fall prey to man.

Concentrations of bones, some of which were burned, were found with charcoal-flecked clay that had been burned to a dark brick red. The animals were usually disarticulated, and ribs and vertebrae were often missing. This suggests that the animals were butchered. In some cases skulls were lacking, or the crania were smashed as though in an effort to obtain the brains. The finding of large abalone shells some miles inland, in beds containing mammoth bones, also suggests the presence of man, for it is difficult to see how they could have reached these locations without human agency. One chipped stone was found in a burned area that contained mammoth bones. Four samples of burned bone from Survey Point provided radiocarbon dates averaging 29,650 ± 2,500 years ago. A date secured from a piece of decayed cypress wood that lay below two mammoth skeletons in Tecolote Canyon was 15,820 ± 280 years ago.

Due to the reduction of sea level, Santa Rosa and the other channel islands probably formed a single land mass during late Pleistocene times; but the water between them and the coast is so deep that it is not thought that, at this time, the sea level would have been lowered sufficiently to provide a land bridge to the mainland. However, if the sea were lowered by more than 300 feet, which seems possible, the open water channel would have been only about two miles wide, and no very elaborate watercraft would have been required to reach the island.

Cemeteries containing almost 300 burials were found in dune sands. Many of the bodies had been buried in a sitting position. The skulls were painted bright red. Red abalone was commonly used as a burial offering. A radiocarbon date of 7,070 ± 250 years ago was secured from one of these shells. Artifacts found in the cemetery included well-made bone tools, and shell beads and ornaments. Other red abalone shells from a midden that lay near the top of the sea cliff under twelve feet of alluvium gave Carbon 14 dates that averaged 6,820 ± 160 years ago. Robert F. Heizer (Personal communication) believes that these dates are too early in view of the nature of the associated cultural material, which is characteristic of much later time horizons.

MEXICO

In Mexico is found archaeological material reminiscent of both the Paleo-eastern and the Paleo-western traditions. The tools found with mammoth remains, described on pages 91 to 98, are outstanding examples of the former.

Valley of Mexico

Extremely interesting finds have been made at Tequixquiac, a locality some forty miles northwest of Mexico City, where there are deeply buried deposits rich in Pleistocene fossils. These are found in two formations to which the name Becerra has been given. The one at the bottom is called the Lower or Older Becerra, and the higher, which lies disconformably upon it, is designated the Upper or Younger Becerra. Helmut de Terra, who undertook intensive geological studies in the Valley of Mexico from 1945 to 1947, attributed the Younger Becerra to the last major pluvial, and correlated the first part with the Mankato and the later with the Anathermal (De Terra, Romero, and Stewart, 1949). Wood taken from Younger Becerra deposits at another locality near Mexico City was dated by the radiocarbon method at more than 16,000 years; and peat from the same area gave a date of 11,003 ± 500 years ago (Libby, 1955).

The first discovery at Tequixquiac was made in 1870 when the famous Mexican naturalist, Mariano Barcena, found, at a depth of forty feet, the sacrum of an extinct llama carved to represent the face of an animal, probably a coyote. The specimen was described and photographs were taken, but the object itself was lost for many years. By great good luck, it was rediscovered in 1955 by Luis Aveleyra in a private collection in Guadalajara. He plans to publish a well-illustrated report with a detailed description of this important artifact.

Other artifacts were found by de Terra in the Upper Becerra at Tequixquiac (De Terra, Romero, and Stewart, 1949). One was a flaked tool of chalcedony that could have served as a scraper or graver. There was also a long pointed object of fossilized bone, probably bison, which shows clear evidence of utilization. At the base of the Upper Becerra, Manuel Maldonado and Luis Aveleyra (1949) found a thick triangular tool, worked on both faces, which resembles one of the small hand axes of the European Palaeolithic. A triangular piece of bone, which may possibly have been shaped by man, was found nearby at a higher level. These specimens from Tequixquiac may well be the oldest found in Mexico.

De Terra postulated the existence of three pre-ceramic complexes in Mexico. The artifacts he found at Tequixquiac, and a few specimens from San Francisco Mazapan and El Risco, he assigned to an industry which he called the San Juan. The specimens found at Tequixquiac, mentioned above, are certainly the products of human workmanship; but some of the others, which have been water rolled, could be of natural origin. Artifacts found on high beach levels near the Tepexpan Man Site, discussed on page 238, de Terra attributed to an industry to which he gave the name Tepexpan. Fifty-odd pressure flaked artifacts made of quartz and chalcedony, which included small notched and stemmed points, were recovered. These were surface finds, and, although their presence on high beach levels does suggest the possibility of occupation at a time when the lake level was higher, there is no proof of age.

The name Chalco Culture Complex was given by de Terra to a third group of artifacts largely made of basalt and produced by percussion flaking. A few were found in beds underlying deposits which

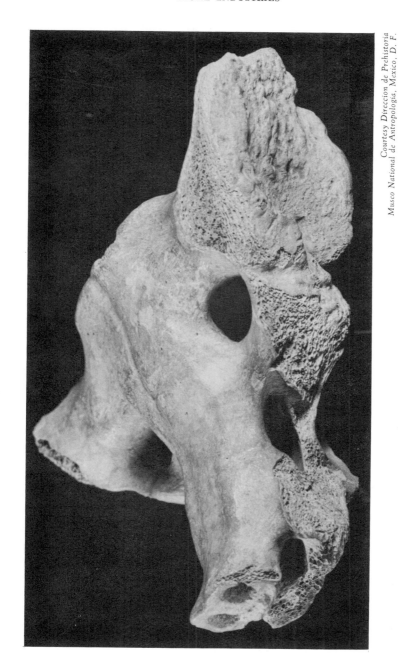

Courtesy Direccion de Prehistoria
Musco National de Antropologia, Mexico, D. F.

FIG. 59—Sacrum of an extinct llama, carved to represent an animal, from Tequixquiac, Mexico. Note the holes drilled to depict the nasal openings.

contained pottery*, but most of them were found on the surface of beach gravels and on hill slopes. Some occurred in caliche soils formed under arid conditions and may be of Altithermal age, while others must be of Medithermal age. Very little is known of the lithic material of the early ceramic cultures in Mexico, and some of the surface finds may belong to that period. These artifacts resemble in many ways those of the Cochise Culture of the southwestern United States. They include a variety of scraper forms, many of which are plano-convex, some choppers, gravers, hammerstones, and a few points. The presence of grinding stones suggests some dependence on plant foods.

Tamaulipas

Richard S. MacNeish (1950; 1955; Personal communication based on a manuscript to be published by the American Philosophical Society) has conducted important investigations in the southern part of the State of Tamaulipas in northeastern Mexico. He has excavated one series of cave sites in the Sierra de Tamaulipas and another in the Sierra Occidental, which lies to the southwest. In both areas he has found deep stratified deposits which have enabled him to develop cultural sequences. Radiocarbon dates, obtained from samples submitted to the University of Michigan, have provided the basis for a chronological framework. Some of the dates are quite early.

In the Sierra de Tamaulipas area, MacNeish recognizes nine complexes. In order of age, beginning with the oldest, they are designated Diablo, Lerma, Nogales, La Perra, Almagre, Laguna, Eslabones, La Salta, and Los Angeles. Material from the Lerma horizon yielded a radiocarbon date of 9,270 ± 500 years ago, a La Perra sample was dated at 4,450 ± 280 years ago, and a Los Angeles sample is 658 ± 150 years old.

In general, the dates are in accord with the geological evidence. The Diablo material was found in gravels of the earliest terrace laid down in Canyon Diablo. The artifacts of the Lerma complex were found in tan calcareous sand and silt that overlay the gravels. Glen Evans and Helmut de Terra undertook brief preliminary studies of the geology of the area and reached certain tentative conclusions. They felt, however, that additional work would be necessary before definite conclusions could be reached. Both agreed that the gravels associated with the Diablo material were laid down during a pluvial period and might be of late Pleistocene age. The Carbon 14 date for the overlying

---

*Charcoal from a pre-ceramic level at Tlatilco that contained Chalco artifacts produced radiocarbon dates with an average of 6,390 ± 300 years ago. (Libby, 1955.)

deposit now suggests that the pluvial during which the gravels were deposited could be a correlative of the Mankato, or, as MacNeish has suggested, they may be still older, and the cutting of the terrace may correlate with the Two Creeks Forest interval of some 11,000 to 12,000 years ago.

Evans and de Terra were not in agreement regarding the climatic conditions that prevailed when the calcareous sand and silt which contained the artifacts of the Lerma Complex were laid down. Evans attributed this deposit to a dry period and de Terra to a moist one. The radiocarbon date, studies of soil samples undertaken in Canada by R. de Will and F. Lionel Peckover, and faunal evidence, are in accord with de Terra's interpretation. The Lerma deposits may equate with the time of the post-Mankato, pre-Altithermal, Cochrane stage. Nogales artifacts were found in deposits indicative of aridity and appear to be of Altithermal age. The radiocarbon date for the La Perra phase indicates that it began at the end of the Altithermal. All of the more recent complexes are of Medithermal age.

The components of the Diablo Complex are crude side and end scrapers, choppers, and bifacial ovoid knives. Lerma Complex artifacts include the doubly pointed laurel-leaf specimens known as Lerma points. As has been noted on page 99, distribution studies of similar projectile points indicate a range from northern Canada to the southern portion of South America. A Lerma point was associated with mammoth at Santa Isabel Iztapan in the Valley of Mexico, and similar points have been found at El Jobo, Venezuela, and in a site in central Argentina. The latter was dated at 7,970 ± 100 years ago by the radiocarbon method.

Artifacts associated with Lerma points in the Tamaulipas sites include snub-nosed scrapers, stemmed end scrapers, side scrapers, gravers, bifacial ovoid knives, square-based knives, some semi-lunar knives, gravers, choppers, and hammerstones. There were some larger triangular points which MacNeish feels were not part of the complex and may indicate trade contacts. Choppers and some of the ovoid knives were flaked entirely by percussion. Most of the other tools appear to have been roughed out by percussion, but they show evidence of a pressure retouch. Many bones, including numerous examples of Mazama deer and beaver, were found in the Lerma levels. The subsistence pattern appears to have been based largely on hunting, although there was probably some collecting of plant foods.

Some Lerma types persisted into Nogales times. A Lerma point, some gravers, square-based knives, and choppers were represented in the earliest component. Distinctive Nogales forms include round-based and triangular projectile points, gouges, small chipped discs, and mortars. Late Nogales components contained large chipped discs, battered nodules, skin smoothers, and manos, which are more typical of later horizons. Shell beads and an antler flaker were found with Nogales artifacts in one site. Hunting appears to have played a larger role in the life of the early Nogales people than in that of the later people who depended to a greater extent on the gathering of wild plant foods.

Many Nogales traits were represented in the succeeding La Perra Complex. Triangular projectile points, large disc choppers, battered nodules, and skin smoothers predominated in this horizon. Examples of cordage, netting, matting, and basketry were recovered in some sites. A few cobs of domesticated corn and squash seeds (Cucurbita pepo) indicate some dependence on agriculture, but hunting and the gathering of wild plants appear to have continued to be most important in the economy.

On the basis of data derived from three caves with stratified deposits in the Ocampo district in the Sierra Oriental, MacNeish recognizes eight complexes in that area.* They are named, in order of age from early to late, Infiernillo, Ocampo, Flacco, Guerra, Mesa de Guaje, Palmillas, San Lorenzo, and San Antonio. Samples from levels of the Infiernillo phases, assayed at the University of Michigan, produced dates of 8,540 ± 450 years ago and 8,200 ± 450 years ago. MacNeish's tentative dates for the time range of this phase are from 9,000 to 7,500 years ago. Artifacts included leaf-shaped and diamond-shaped projectile points, very large and crudely flaked choppers and scrapers, and some nets, mats, and baskets. The Infiernillo people were essentially gatherers of wild plants who also did some hunting. They may have planted some squash.

Estimated dates for the succeeding Ocampo Complex are from 6,000 to 4,300 years ago. Carbon samples have provided dates of 4,580 ± 350, 5,230 ± 350, and 5,650 ± 350 years ago. These are in accord with Carbon 14 dates obtained from other sites with a similar cultural complex. Artifacts recovered included large triangular and leaf-shaped dart points as well as a variety of scrapers, choppers, and gouges, and perishable materials. The Ocampo people were primarily

---

*A brief summary of the archaeological sequence and a most interesting discussion of the cucurbit materials recovered in these sites will be found in Whitaker, Cutler, and MacNeish (1957).

wild plant collectors and hunters, but they may have planted some of the beans and squash recovered in levels attributed to this phase.

Coahuila

In northern Mexico, in the State of Coahuila, there is a site known as Frightful Cave. This was excavated by Walter W. Taylor. Wood from the lowest level produced a Carbon 14 date of 8,870 ± 350 years ago (Crane, 1956). The final report on this site has not appeared, and the nature of the cultural material associated with the wood is not known.

Campeche

In Campeche, in southern Mexico, Jorge Engerrand (1912) found a series of artifacts which he called the industry of La Concepcion. All were heavily patinated. Some percussion flaked specimens were shaped like palaeolithic hand axes. Scrapers made from retouched flakes showed signs of intense utilization. No manos or metates were found. These were surface finds and there is no proof of age; but the absence of grinding stones, which would seem to indicate a lack of dependence on plant foods, may be significant in an area where agriculture developed early.

CANADA

Discoveries of artifacts characteristic of the Paleo-eastern tradition in Alberta, Saskatchewan, the Northwest Territories, and eastern Canada have already been discussed. Canadian sites with Paleo-northern affiliations will be considered in a later section. There are some sites in Ontario, of probable antiquity, that will be considered here.

George Lake Sites

Emerson F. Greenman and George M. Stanley have reported on two sites that lie on the north shore of Lake Huron near Killarney, Ontario (Greenman, 1941; Greenman and Stanley, 1943). These sites, named after George Lake which lies nearby, were associated with beaches that lay well above the recent level of the Great Lakes. One was 320 feet above the present water level of Lake Huron, the other was 297 feet above it. Some of the artifacts were abraded. If they were battered and ground by wave action, as some geologists believe, they must have been present when a further rise in water level made it possible for waves to beat against the sites (Greenman, 1954). It is believed that, for these beaches to have been formed, the waters of Lake Huron must either have been impounded by ice or the land surface must have been tilted in such a way as to prevent drainage. The time of occupation of the higher site may fall within a period when ice sheets were still relatively close. The problem is to date this period. It is said to correlate with the Algonkian Lake stages which are probably more than 8,000 years old.

An artifact that resembles a Scottsbluff point was found on the lower terrace. Two single-shouldered points and other artifacts were found at the higher site. The latter have little broad diagnostic value, although they are typologically distinct from others found in the same area. All are made of quartzite. They include biface semi-lunar, ovoid, and quadrangular cutting or scraping tools, choppers, perforators, and retouched flakes.

Sheguiandah Site, Manitoulin Island

On Manitoulin Island, some twenty miles from the George Lake Sites, Thomas E. Lee found evidence of prehistoric Indian activity over an area of approximately twenty-six acres (Lee, 1954, 1955). The island contains quartzite outcroppings which were quarried by the Indians. They left vast quantities of blocks, chips, and worked fragments.

One section appears to represent a habitation area. Due to various factors, there has been a good bit of disturbance of the soil, and the stratigraphy is by no means clear. On the basis of his excavations, however, Lee believes he can recognize five components that represent different periods of occupation. The most recent is the Point Peninsula, an early stage of which has been dated elsewhere by the radiocarbon method at more than 4,000 years ago. The second is characterized by large biface tools which resemble specimens found at George Lake. Below were found large notched points with pronounced grinding along the basal edges. They resemble certain Archaic forms. Still lower were found large, thin, bifacial tools with a secondary retouch. The evidence for Lee's fifth component consists of a few flakes and chipped stones incorporated in what some geologists regard as glacial till.

Near the highest point of the site were four small swamps which contained clays overlain by peat. Artifacts were found in the clays. A sample taken from the base of the peat bed in one of the swamps provided a Carbon 14 date of 9,130 ± 250 years ago (Lee, 1956). It is not clear to which component the specimens found in the clays, which must be older than the peat, would be assigned, but Lee states that they are much more recent than some found in another part of the site.

British Columbia

Two sites in British Columbia, on which only a paragraph has been published (Garfield and Duff, 1951), may be of some importance. One lies on the north shore of Natalkuz Lake and the other on Euchu Lake. The numerous artifacts recovered were chipped chiefly by percussion and were made of yellow rhyolite. This manufacturing technique and this material were not normally used in the production of tools and implements of the more recent cultures in the area.

THE PALEO-NORTHERN TRADITION

A number of sites found in the Arctic have yielded polyhedral cores (cores with many plane faces), the small prismatic flakes derived from them, which are called microblades, and tools manufactured from these blades. The microblades have sometimes been called lamellar flakes, but this is a most unfortunate term which can only produce confusion, and it should be dropped. The technique employed in preparing the cores from which the blades were struck was the same as that employed in the preparation of cores found in Siberia and Mongolia. In some of these sites were found burins. These were tools used to produce grooves on bone and hard organic materials such as ivory and antler, probably to facilitate splitting. They were made from flakes on which a sharp cutting edge was produced by the removal of small needle-like slivers at one end. These slivers are called burin spalls.

The Campus Site

The first evidence of a core and blade industry in Alaska was found in 1933 on the University of Alaska campus near Fairbanks. Excavations were conducted here and at two apparently related sites between 1934 and 1936 by Froelich Rainey (1940). The Campus Site contained end scrapers, small polyhedral cores, and blades struck from these cores, which, as N. C. Nelson (1937b) pointed out, closely resembled those he had found in the Gobi in Mongolia. Rainey noted that there were very strong similarities between these specimens and some found in the Lake Baikal area of Siberia. A re-examination of the material from the Campus Site revealed the presence of three objects that might possibly represent two burins and a burin spall (Irving, 1955). The specimens are rather amorphous, and it seems by no means certain that the removal of the side flakes was not fortuitous.

The Dixthada Site

Deposits at the Campus Site provided no clues as to possible age; but at the site of Dixthada, in the upper Tanana Valley, Rainey found a few similar cores and microblades in the lower levels of a midden built up by recent Athapaskan Indians. This at first suggested a very moderate age for the complex. Other Athapaskan sites in the area, however, did not yield similar material, and later, after such artifacts had been found under circumstances indicating antiquity, Rainey (1953) came to the conclusion that the recent Athapaskans at Dixthada had cut into a much older site when excavating their house pits.

The Denbigh Flint Complex

Between 1936 and 1948 there were a few other discoveries of polyhedral cores and blades in Alaska, but they were found under such circumstances that there was no way of determining their age. It was not until 1948 that J. L. Giddings, Jr. found such artifacts in position in a site that lent itself to geological studies and yielded material suitable for radiocarbon dating (Giddings, 1951, 1954).

This site, which is called Iyatayet, lies on a high beach or terrace on the west side of Cape Denbigh in Norton Sound. The upper levels contained Eskimo material of no very great age; but just below were two to eighteen inches of sterile, laminated, sandy clay, beneath which lay deposits that contained a remarkable series of artifacts to which Giddings gave the name Denbigh Flint Complex. Approximately 1,500 artifacts were recovered. Some of these were reminiscent of Old World forms of Upper Palaeolithic and Mesolithic age, while others were similar to Paleo-Indian types from the New World.

Among the Old World forms were burins resembling types found in Europe in Upper Palaeolithic sites of the Aurignacian period and in Mesolithic sites in Europe and Siberia. Most of the tiny spalls removed in the production of burins were, themselves, used as tools, for photographic enlargements have revealed that the tips had been so formed as to resemble chisels. Large numbers of microblades were found. There were many end and side blades—little diagonally flaked implements that were probably set into the grooved sides of antler or bone implements. Some of the tiny diagonally flaked tools were pointed at both ends, others were crescentic or triangular in outline. The delicacy of the flaking is extraordinary. In one case a specimen about an inch and a quarter long bears more than twenty ribbon-like scars on each face. Two polyhedral cores were recovered. There was also a variety of scrapers and some triangular forms that may have been used on harpoon heads.

FIG. 60—Artifacts of the Denbigh Flint Complex from the Iyatayet Site, Alaska.

Specimens reminiscent of Paleo-Indian types included a fluted point of approximately the same size as a Folsom but essentially triangular in outline. More evidence is needed before triangular forms may be regarded as characteristic of fluted points in the north; but it is worth noting that a fluted point found near the Utukok River north of Bering Strait by R. M. Thompson (1948), and two found near the Kugururok River by Milton C. Lachenbruch (Solecki, 1951b), were of the same general shape. So was a specimen found near Edmonton, Alberta, by James MacGregor. In the Iyatayet collection were three flakes with tiny projections at the end that closely resembled the gravers found at the Lindenmeier Folsom Site, a point reminiscent of the Scottsbluff type, one which resembled a Plainview point, and the upper portion and several bases of large points, probably lanceolate in outline, which bore parallel flake scars directed obliquely across the face of the blade.

Although these specimens are very much like those made farther south, they do not necessarily prove contemporaneity of the Denbigh people and the early Paleo-Indians. In the United States these types are attributed to different complexes. These artifacts could, as Henry B. Collins (1953) has suggested, be relics of an earlier period. It is also possible that this may represent a peripheral area where, at a later period, there was a mingling of traits that were elsewhere, at an earlier time, chronologically distinct. If the writer is correct in believing that the tradition of fluting developed in the Southwest or in the Plains, the fluted specimens found in the extreme north may represent the spread of a trait through diffusion or a later northward movement of people who employed this technique. In this case they would be more recent than those found farther south.

D. M. Hopkins undertook geological studies at the Iyatayet Site in an effort to relate the archaeological sequence to a geologic and climatic chronology (Hopkins and Giddings, 1953). Below the layer that contained the artifacts were deposits that Hopkins attributed to a period when cold and frost action were intense, presumably a late Wisconsin substage. He believed the soil immediately below the artifact-bearing layer was formed and the cultural layer deposited during a warmer period. In the Denbigh flint layer were complex folds that Hopkins felt must have been formed during a cold period that occurred long after the occupation had ended.

On the basis of this evidence Hopkins suggested that there were two possible correlations. (1) The culture layer could be of pre-

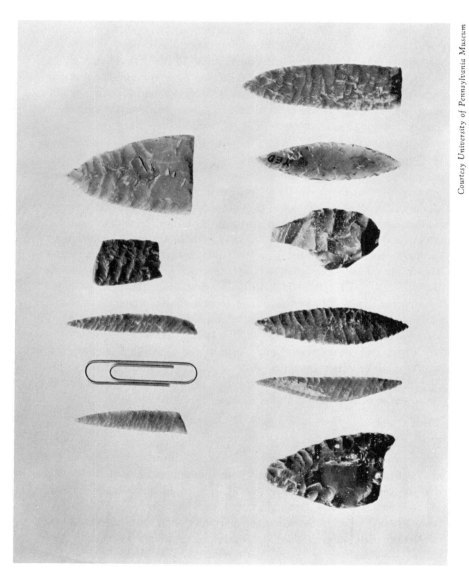

Courtesy University of Pennsylvania Museum

Fig. 61—Artifacts of the Denbigh Flint Complex from the Iyatayet Site, Alaska.

Mankato age and the folding could have occurred during this substage. (2) The culture layer could date from a warm interval represented by muck in the Seward Peninsula dated at about 8,000 or 9,000 years ago, and the folding could have occurred during a minor cold interval of post-Mankato age. From the beginning Hopkins favored the second alternative. In 1954, in a personal communication to Giddings, he stated that the first correlation could be ruled out completely, that the Denbigh Complex was more than 5,000 years old and less than 9,000 years old, and that he believed a date of 8,500 years ago would be of the right order of magnitude (Giddings, 1955).

In 1952 Giddings found two hearth areas containing small flecks of charcoal which could be used for radiocarbon dating. Since living grass roots penetrated the old layer, even at its deepest point, it seemed reasonable to assume that there was contamination; but Giddings felt that a radiocarbon assay would provide a "stop date" and the complex could be no more recent than the date obtained from the samples, although it could be older (Giddings, 1955). The samples collected by Giddings were tested at the University of Chicago Laboratory. Dates from Sample I averaged 3,509 ± 230 years ago. The first run on Sample II, collected in a section some fifty feet away from the first, provided a date of 4,253 ± 290 years ago. A second run on material from the same sample, that had been washed with acid, gave a date of 5,063 ± 340 years ago (Giddings, 1955; Libby, 1955).

Cores and blades resembling those of the Denbigh Complex have been found in other localities in Alaska, the Yukon Territory, the Aleutians, and the Northwest Territories. Burins have been found as far to the east as Greenland (Meldgaard, 1952).

Trail Creek

In 1950 Helge Larsen (1951 and Personal communication) excavated two caves on Trail Creek on Seward Peninsula. No final report has been published, but apparently four different periods of occupation were represented. In the lowest level were found microblades similar to those found at Cape Denbigh, but there were none of the distinctive cores usually associated with them, nor were there any burins. These caves also yielded good sized projectile points with exceptionally fine oblique parallel flaking. Some are reminiscent of the Angostura type discussed on page 139. A date of about 6,000 years ago was obtained at the University of Chicago radiocarbon laboratory from willow twigs found in the bottom of one of the caves, but there was no direct connection with the artifacts, so this does not serve to date the complex.

Courtesy National Museum of Denmark

FIG. 62—Artifacts from Trail Creek, Seward Peninsula, Alaska.

Aleutians

Artifacts that differed from those of the prehistoric Aleuts, as regards both form and material, were found in the course of re-examining a collection made in 1938 (Laughlin, 1951). They came from a blow-out site on the south end of Ananiuliak Island. This site lacked the midden material that characterized most sites in the Aleutians, and it was located in the center of the island instead of at the edge as are most Aleut villages. Included in the collection were a polyhedral core, microblades, end scrapers, and a bifacially flaked knife.

In 1952 W. S. Laughlin and members of another expedition revisited the site (Laughlin and Marsh, 1954). They came to the conclusion that the site represented a manufactory for the production of microblades. Test pits and trenches revealed that these flakes occurred only on the surface. Among the 1,652 pieces recovered were retouched and unretouched microblades, polyhedral cores, larger cores of a different pattern, two scrapers, and a knife. There was no means of dating this site. Excavations in two nearby Aleut village sites, where tools made from microblades were found in the lower levels, suggested to the investigators that this blade-producing technique was used by some of the prehistoric Aleuts but has not been used for some 1,500 or 1,600 years.

Northern Alaska

Ralph Solecki (1951b) found two surface sites on the Kukpowruk River in northwestern Alaska that produced cores and microblades. During the 1950 season, on the Kugurok River, which lies to the north of the Arctic Circle, Milton C. Lachenbruch found a surface site on a hilltop that produced two fluted points and a polyhedral core (Solecki, 1951b). The material of which they were made is thought to be of local origin. They must be of post-glacial age since they were found in a locality that would have been ice-covered prior to the glacial recession in the mountain valleys.

At the mouth of Anaktuvuk Pass in the Brooks Range, Robert J. Hackman found a site that contained material closely resembling that from the Iyatayet Site and the tip of a projectile point that appeared to have been fluted (Solecki and Hackman, 1951). The artifacts represented include burins, polyhedral cores, the microblades derived from them, end and side blades, and end scrapers. Many of these specimens bore fine obliquely directed flake scars.

On a knoll overlooking the Anaktuvuk River, about twenty miles from its source, William Irving (1951) found material of the Denbigh Complex. Among the sixty-five artifacts found on the surface were microblades, side blades, burins, and burin spalls. Two fragmentary side blades and a polyhedral core were found near a hearth in a small test pit.

Central Alaska

During 1944 Frederick Johnson conducted an archaeological survey of the region traversed by the Alaskan Highway. On the southwest shore of the Little Arm of Kluane Lake he found some microblades (Johnson, 1946). Johnson also found evidence of a core and blade industry in several sites in the Shakwak Valley of Yukon Territory (Rainey, 1953).

Ivar Skarland and J. L. Giddings, Jr. (1948) reported the discovery of a site at Birch Lake, sixty miles southeast of Fairbanks, that contained microblades and a prepared core. The artifacts were in mucks thought to be of post-glacial age. Earth-moving machinery had, however, removed the overburden and there was no way of determining the exact age of these deposits.

CANADA

The Pointed Mountain Site

For a number of years Richard S. MacNeish has been conducting archaeological investigation in the Northwest Territories of Canada. In 1952 he excavated a site in the southwest corner of the Territories, some twenty miles north of Fort Liard (MacNeish, 1954). It lay on the top and along the sides of a moraine against the eastern slope of Pointed Mountain, for which it was named. The zone of occupation was in a loess deposit. Some geologists have attributed a similar wind-laid deposit in the Peace River Town region to the Altithermal period. If the loess deposit at the Pointed Mountain Site is of Altithermal age, the artifacts must be less than 7,000 years old, perhaps around 5,000 years old, since they were found in the upper third of the deposit. Other students, however, believe that the forest invaded the mountain area during the Altithermal and that the loess deposits are more than 7,000 years old. MacNeish has suggested that the time of occupation probably falls sometime between 8,000 and 5,000 years ago.

Among the specimens recovered were some that MacNeish identified as burins although they are rather amorphous and lack the distinctive features of the Eurasiatic types and those of the Denbigh Complex. He also found polyhedral cores and retouched and unretouched microblades, fairly large and heavy projectile points, some with contracting stems and some with side notches, and a variety of side and end scrapers. There were also some large ovoid biface implements, some percussion flaked choppers, and battered hammerstones. Side and end blades were lacking. MacNeish has suggested that the people who lived inland in the Northwest Territories, Central Alaska, and the Yukon Territory, had undergone some specialization toward forest living, while the specialization of those who lived on the coast was directed toward adaption to coastal conditions, but the two might have had a common ancestral culture.

The Engigstciak Site

During the summers since 1954, MacNeish has been excavating a very important multi-component site about sixteen miles from the Arctic Ocean on the Firth River in the Mackenzie drainage. In a preliminary progress report MacNeish (1956b) has described nine different archaeological cultures. The artifacts occurred in pits and refuse areas and in some series of thin lenses of refuse separated by sterile deposits. In no one area were all nine complexes found one on top of the other and the tentative sequence for the five lower levels was worked out by correlating a number of short stratigraphic columns with some overlap. The relative chronological position of the three most recent complexes was assumed on the basis of chronological order in excavations in Alaska and one of the complexes was placed in chronological position on the basis of seriation. Further excavation may lead to some revision of the conclusions regarding the various components for there must have been some mixing of materials due to the pits dug by the occupants of the site.

To the earliest complex, which is represented by only a small sample, MacNeish has assigned the name British Mountain. The artifacts, which consisted largely of crude choppers and scrapers, lay under gray clay. Two lanceolate points were found. They were erroneously referred to the next complex in the progress report (MacNeish, Personal communication). One which was made from a prismatic flake and retouched only along the edges, resembles specimens found by A. P. Okladnikov (1950) in Neolithic sites in Siberia. The other, which was bifacially flaked, had a flute extending its whole length on one surface.

Lanceolate points were also found in the next complex in the sequence, called the Flint Creek. One has been classified as a Plainview, and there were twelve fragmentary points, some of which have good oblique flaking, that MacNeish has assigned to the Angostura category. On the basis of the illustrations available, it appears probable that this attribution is correct. Two fragmentary points were apparently tear-shaped. Among the other artifacts recovered there were crude prismatic blades, a microblade, a fragment of a polyhedral core, and five crude artifacts that may have served as burins. The latter resemble the specimens found at the Pointed Mountain Site. The associated artifacts, consisting of scrapers, choppers, knives, and awls have little diagnostic value.

More than 600 artifacts recovered were assigned to the third preceramic complex, to which the name New Mountain has been given. There were small side and end blades, many with delicate oblique flaking, a wide variety of burin types, many burin spalls, small microblades and large, crude, prismatic blades thought to have been struck from polyhedral cores. Some projectile points, believed by MacNeish to be arrowpoints, were small lanceolate forms with straight or slightly convex bases. There were also some large points with lanceolate or triangular shapes. The trait list is not identical with that for the Denbigh Complex, but the similarities are sufficient to indicate some relationship. In the next assemblage in the sequence were small tools of types which suggest derivation from the New Mountain Complex. It and the succeeding horizons all produced pottery and are beyond the scope of this book. Further work at this site may throw new light on various aspects of Arctic archaeology and may contribute to the solution of problems concerning the development of the Woodland Pattern in the eastern United States.

Alberta

In the collection made near Cereal in southern Alberta by Russell A. Johnston, who has saved many flakes as well as completed artifacts, the writer has seen one delicate prismatic flake with three faces on one surface, and parallel sides, very much like the best examples in the Cape Denbigh collection, and a few specimens that resemble burins. Accidental breakage may give the impression of a burin stroke, so the latter are not necessarily significant. It is difficult to see, however, how the microblade could have come from anything but a specially pre-pared polyhedral core. These few specimens do not provide proof of a southward extension of the Paleo-northern Tradition, but they do suggest that, as work continues in western Canada, it would be desirable to examine the flakes that are found with some care.

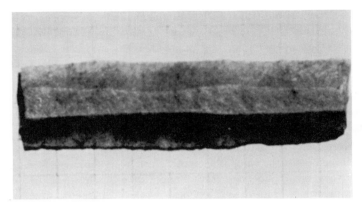

FIG. 63—Microblade found near Cereal, Alberta, Canada. Russell A. Johnston collection. Length nine-tenths of an inch.

COLUMBIA RIVER

The Five Mile Rapids Site which lies near The Dalles on the Oregon side of the Columbia River is discussed on page 186. Burins were found in the earliest levels. Radiocarbon dates for samples collected there have been obtained at the Yale Geochronometric Laboratory and will be included in Cressman's forthcoming publication on the site. They have not yet been released and cannot be quoted here, but they do serve to indicate that burins were being used in this area at a very early date.

NON-PROJECTILE POINT ASSEMBLAGES

Some sites that appear to be of considerable antiquity and that do not contain projectile points have already been discussed. To this group should be added Freisenhahn Cave, which lies near the inner margin of the Texas Coastal Plain (Sellards, 1952; Krieger, 1953). This cave contains the bones of a very large number of Pleistocene animals. A great many Pleistocene genera are represented. So large a representation certainly does not suggest a fauna on the verge of extinction, and these deposits may date well back in the Wisconsin. Crudely flaked stones which could be the products of human workmanship have been found there. One object, possibly a crude scraper, lay under the skeleton of a large tiger.

There are other purportedly pre-projectile point assemblages. Some contain artifacts that resemble Palaeolithic tools, others are so crude that it is a matter of opinion whether they were produced by man. These discoveries have been regarded as extremely old, probably of pre-Wisconsin age, by some students of the subject. Those who accept these claims constitute a distinct minority. The writer is not one of this group, but feels that, with our present limited knowledge, it would be unwarranted to say that evidence of the presence of man in America in early Wisconsin times or prior to the Wisconsin will not be found. This possibility should certainly continue to be investigated, but before it can be regarded as anything more than a possibility acceptable evidence will have to be found.

The Black's Fork Finds

In the course of four seasons of surface collecting in the Black's Fork Basin of southwestern Wyoming, the first in 1935 and the last in 1939, E. B. Renaud found some seventy localities which yielded thousands of artifacts that are typologically similar to Old World Palaeolithic tools of great antiquity (Renaud, 1938, 1940). The Palaeolithic forms are dated in terms of hundreds of thousands of years by some archaeologists, and even the most conservative estimates place them far back in the Pleistocene.

Included in the Black's Fork collection are fist axes, choppers, scrapers, and flakes that do bear a resemblance to Early and Middle Palaeolithic tools. However, most archaeologists have been reluctant to place much dependence on these typological resemblances, for a variety of reasons. All of the artifacts described by Renaud lay on the surface of the ground, and there is absolutely no geological or palaeontological proof of antiquity. Furthermore, work in other parts of Wyoming and in Montana indicates that when similar implements were found in excavated sites they were part of comparatively recent complexes (Mulloy, 1953). In Saskatchewan, Allan J. Hudson (Personal communication) has found many such specimens in an area covered by ice during the Wisconsin advances. They were found on or near the surface, but there is no evidence that they were subjected to ice or water action. Similar specimens found in other parts of western

Canada where the writer has worked also appear to be of no very great age.

It is true that many of Renaud's artifacts were found on high terraces and showed definite signs of abrasion. If it could be proven that this was the result of water action it might provide some evidence of age, for a considerable length of time has elapsed since water last reached these terraces. However, if the smoothing was due to wind erosion it provides no evidence of real antiquity although the fact that some artifacts are worn, while others in the same location are not, suggests that there are definite age differences between the worn and unworn specimens. E. H. Stephens, who studied the geology of the sites, stated, "In all the specimens examined the wear was by wind abrasion, thus eliminating the possibility of dating them by the time of the abrasion as might have been done if the wearing was by water action" (In Renaud, 1940, p. 17).

As is often the case where surface sites are concerned, there is reason to believe that various lithic horizons are represented. On the basis of typology and patination Renaud feels that he can recognize three cultures, but his attribution of age by typology has not been substantiated by other chronological data. To what he has called the "Typical Culture" he attributes artifacts that show typological similarities to those of Early and Middle Palaeolithic cultures of the Old World. Some specimens he places in a category referable to what he calls the "Peripheral Culture." This is not at all clearly defined. A third group of artifacts he assigns to the "Sand Dune Culture." It is pre-ceramic but presumably of no great antiquity. Arrowpoints, milling stones, and fireplaces are found on sites attributed to this culture.

The Los Encinos Complex

Artifacts reminiscent of ancient Old World types were found by Kirk Bryan (1938, 1939) in a chert quarry on the southwest side of a peak called Cerro Pedernal, which lies in north central New Mexico. They included large axe-like objects, flaked on both faces, that resembled artifacts made during the Lower Palaeolithic period in Europe. Some could represent partially fabricated implements, but others show signs of use. Other specimens were chipped flakes which resemble those of an ancient European industry known as the Levallois.

The fact that these specimens differed from the implements of relatively recent prehistoric cultures which were known in this area suggested that they might be of some antiquity. Before even the most tentative conclusions could be reached regarding the age of the artifacts it was necessary that similar objects be found in position in deposits which might lend themselves to geological dating. In the valley of a small stream that flows nearby, the Rio de los Encinos, Bryan found three alluvial fills. The Early Alluvium yielded a fragment of a tusk, possibly of mastodon or mammoth, but it contained no evidence of human occupation. In the Intermediate Alluvium were found some implements that resembled those from the quarry, and many large flint chips. The Late Alluvium contained numerous small flint chips and a few charcoal hearths which Bryan thought were left by later Pueblo people.

Bryan believed that the Palaeolithic-like implements found in the quarry and the specimens found in the Intermediate Alluvium formed a cultural unit to which he gave the name Los Encinos Complex. The artifacts found in the intermediate fill would appear to have only a very moderate antiquity. A similar three-fold sequence of alluvial deposits has been recognized in many places in the Southwest, and the Intermediate Alluvium is believed to have formed immediately prior to the beginning of the Christian Era (Hack, 1941; Hunt, 1953).

Little Colorado Drainage

Katharine Bartlett (1943) has reported the discovery of some seventy sites in the Little Colorado Valley of Arizona that contained rough percussion flaked biface implements, flakes reminiscent of Lower Palaeolithic forms of Europe, and keel-shaped scrapers. There is a complete absence of arrow-points and blades. The three well-flaked dart points recovered are not thought to be part of the complex. There is no association with the pottery-making cultures which, in this area, date from approximately 500 A. D. All the implements were found on the surface, so there is no way of fixing their age at present, but it seems probable that they pre-date the Basketmaker-Pueblo Culture.

Discussion

In the case of the finds discussed above there is no proof of antiquity and there is some evidence that suggests relative recency; but there is no question whatsoever that we are dealing with stones flaked by man. The possibility that some could be blanks or rejects rather than actual tools may warrant consideration, but they are indubitably the products of human effort. In the case of some of the other assemblages that lack projectile points and for which great antiquity is claimed by some, the situation is different. In general it may be said that while some of the specimens in the collections discussed below might be regarded as stones possibly utilized by man if they were linked with some clear-cut evidence of human occupation, by themselves they fail to carry conviction.

One often overlooked fact deserves consideration. Well-made hand axes and flake implements were being produced in the Old World during the third interglacial and even earlier. There is no question as to whether they are tools or not.* If, as we believe, the stone-working traditions of the New World followed those of the Old, the crude American specimens, believed by some to have been made by man, would, if they were the only implements produced, belong to a far, far earlier period than the third interglacial.

Southern California

The chief champion of Interglacial Man in the New World is George F. Carter, who is convinced that Lower Palaeolithic-like cultures are widely distributed in America. He has suggested that man could have entered America as early as the beginning of the third (Illinoian) glaciation and have penetrated far into America before the Wisconsin began (Carter, 1951 and 1952). Ruth D. Simpson (1956) is also firmly convinced that there are pre-projectile point cultures that go far back into Pleistocene times.

Carter first worked in the La Jolla area. Here he found burned areas, flakes, and a mano, in deposits which he believed dated far back in the Wisconsin. One sample collected by Carter produced a radiocarbon date of 21,500 years ago, but two others were dated at 500 and 600 years ago (Carter, 1955). In the opinion of James B. Griffin (Personal communication) the localities that provided the recent dates are sites, while the level dated in excess of 20,000 years does not contain evidence of occupation.

Carter's most intensive work has been in the San Diego area where there is a series of terraces, some of which must be of Pleistocene age (Carter, 1952). He believes the valley fills represent interglacial periods. Those found at about twenty-five and sixty-five feet he attributes to the third interglacial, the intervening period between the Illinoian and Wisconsin glaciations. In a number of localities Carter

---

*E. F. Greenman (1957) has discussed this matter in a recent article.

has found stones which he considers to be artifacts, in deposits which, on the basis of studies of eustasy, climatology, pedology, and geology, he believes to be of third interglacial age. Most archaeologists, including the writer, are not convinced that they were made by man. Among those who feel sure that these are not products of human workmanship and that sites are not present in the formation are James B. Griffin, Robert F. Heizer, Frederick Johnson, Clement Meighan, T. D. Mc-Cown, and Kenneth Oakley.

The site which Carter regards as of the greatest significance is commonly referred to as the Texas Street Site (Carter 1954a). It lies on the south side of the San Diego River, at the foot of the Texas Street grade, where there is a prominent bench composed of a lower unit of coarse gravels, an intermediate unit of coarse sands, and an upper one of fine silty sands. By 1954 Carter had collected 140 objects, largely battered quartzite cobbles, at various places along the exposed face, including the basal gravels. He believes these are artifacts. Areas of burned earth and rocks, ranging from six to one hundred feet in diameter, he has identified as hearth areas. He attributes the stones and the burned areas to the third interglacial.

Most archaeologists believe that these phenomena were produced by natural agencies, but there are some who share Carter's opinion. John Witthoft (1955) is convinced, on typological grounds, that the specimens gathered by Carter at the Texas Street Site are clearly the purposeful products of human hands. He believes that two distinct lithic industries are represented. Ruth Simpson (1954) believes that a few of the specimens are true artifacts while many are cores and quarry rejects altered but not fashioned by man.

The finding of definitely prepared hearths would indicate the presence of man. The writer has not seen the site and is not able to judge the nature of the burned accumulations classified by Carter as hearths. Burned areas as large as one hundred feet in diameter, and several feet thick, would, however, suggest the possibility of fires caused by natural agencies.

The desert area of southern California provides evidence that most, if not all, of the major basins that are now dry were once filled with water. Terraces indicate that at various times the lakes stood at different levels. On some of the old beaches, that must correlate with a time of greater precipitation and cooler climate, and which are attributed to the Pleistocene, Lydia and Thomas Clements have found flaked rocks which they believe represent three primitive lithic industries characterized by extremely simple uniface tools and lacking projectile points and grinding stones (Clements and Clements, 1953; Clements, 1954). They believe them to be more ancient that the artifacts from Lake Mohave and the Pinto Basin. An assemblage found on Manly Terrace in Death Valley they regard as the oldest; material found at Pisgah, along the Colorado River near Earp, and near Carson's Well in the Turtle Mountains, they think is intermediate in time between this and a "Yellow-jasper Culture" best represented in Panamint Valley. The writer would hesitate to classify the specimens exhibited by the Clementses at the Great Basin Conference held in Los Angeles in 1955 as artifacts, but she has not seen the total collection. With such crude material it is impossible to evaluate specimens on the basis of illustrations.

Michigan

Carmen Baggerly (1954, 1956) has collected more than 5,000 fractured stones from sand bars and a moraine along the Imlay Channel, an outlet of Glacial Lake Maumee. They bear evidence of the action of wind, water, and ice. Baggerly very kindly sent a collection to the Denver Museum of Natural History. Most of the stones do not seem to show any evidence of human workmanship, and there are none that the writer is prepared to say are unquestionably artifacts, but there are a few debatable specimens that do resemble choppers. Alex Krieger, George Engerrand, and Glen L. Evans, who examined specimens sent to the University of Texas by Baggerly, found it difficult to state that any of the specimens were artifacts, but they noted that the fracture facets found on a few specimens were difficult to explain on the basis of accident or rocks knocking against each other (Krieger, Editor, 1953b). The University of Michigan has had collections for some years from these deposits. Archaeologists there are sceptical as to their association with man.

Summary

In the opinion of the writer, and in the opinion of the great majority of archaeologists, no evidence has yet been presented that proves the existence of man on this continent in pre-Wisconsin times. This, however, does not mean that it is impossible that such evidence should be found at some future date. We do not know when man first reached the New World.

Chapter V

HUMAN SKELETAL REMAINS

The finding of skeletal remains claimed to represent geologically ancient inhabitants of North America has been reported for many years. Each find has had its individual champions, but few of their claims have won any widespread acceptance. The influence of the late Ales Hrdlicka, who for many years was the best known and the most vocal of the anthropologists who denied the antiquity of man in the New World, had a salutary effect in the sense that it forestalled the too ready acceptance of many unwarranted claims. However, his firm belief that skeletons more than a few thousand years old must differ markedly from those of more recent times, and must be considerably more primitive, is regarded as unjustified by present-day anthropologists. There is ample evidence that modern types of men were present in the Old World during the late Pleistocene, and North American skeletons need not show particularly archaic features in order to be attributed to that period. Only through geological evidence or radiocarbon dating will it be possible to establish the antiquity of skeletal remains found in the Western Hemisphere.

Unfortunately, such evidence has not been readily available because so many of the finds so far reported have been made by people untrained in scientific methods and have been removed from their original locations before having been witnessed by geologists and anthropologists. It cannot be impressed too strongly upon the minds of all those interested in archaeology that when bones are found they should not be touched under any consideration until they have been viewed in position by someone whose training qualifies him to make all necessary observations.

Among the discoveries of presumed antiquity which were widely discussed at one time were a famous hoax, the Calaveras Skull, allegedly found 130 feet below the surface in deposits of Tertiary age (Hrdlicka, 1907; Heizer, 1950a); "Homo novusmundus," a skeleton found fourteen miles from the Folsom type locality but under circumstances that did not make it possible to date the bones (Figgins, 1935b; Roberts, 1937a); and skeletons from Texas with very long, narrow heads (Hooton, 1933; Roberts, 1945; Woodbury, 1935). Some of the latter were found in deeply buried silts, but there is no certainty regarding the age of the deposits. Human skeletal remains reportedly found in deep deposits containing bones of extinct animals in a cave on Bishop's Cap Peak in southwestern New Mexico (Byran, 1929) may be important, but no adequate report has been published. None of these will be considered here. Only a few finds that have won some measure of acceptance will be discussed in any detail. There are controversies regarding even most of these.

The Natchez Pelvis

It now appears probable that one of the earliest discoveries of a human bone, originally believed to be quite old, may indeed be ancient (Richards, 1951). Sometime prior to 1846 a fragmentary human pelvis was found near Natchez, Mississippi, by a physician, Dr. M. W. Dickeson. It reportedly lay in a bed of loess-covered blue clay which contained remains of sloth, mastodon, horse, and big-horned bison. As early as 1895 it was known that fluorine tests indicated that the human bone and one of the sloth bones were of substantially the same age. Little attention was paid to these findings until 1951 when the matter was reinvestigated by T. D. Stewart.

In 1954 George Quimby attempted to relocate the site where the pelvis was unearthed, with the hope that other evidence of early man might be found in the vicinity (Quimby, 1956). Unfortunately, it appears that erosion destroyed the locus of the find at a much earlier date. However, in this general area, fossil bones and teeth are still occasionally found in the blue clay, believed to have contained the pelvis, and further discoveries of human bones or artifacts may yet be made.

The Vero and Melbourne, Florida, Finds

In deposits near Vero, Florida, E. H. Sellards, in 1916, found human skeletal remains and artifacts in association with an extinct fauna including mammoth and mastodon (Sellards, 1917, 1937, 1940a, 1947, 1952). Three strata were recognized. The lowest, the Anastasia, is a marine formation which produced no vertebrate remains or artifacts. The middle bed, to which the name Melbourne has been applied, was a non-marine sand stratum in which were found bones of extinct animals and a few of the human bones and artifacts. This stratum was separated from the one above by a marked erosional disconformity. The uppermost bed, which consisted of sand and muck, is known as the Van Valkenburg. It contained pottery and other artifacts.

In Sellards' opinion the undisturbed cross-bedding of the deposits above the human bones precluded the possibility of intentional burial, and the facts that the bones, though broken, were largely complete and that some were too fragile to have been moved by flood waters without greater breakage made it seem improbable that they had reached their position through secondary deposition (Sellards, 1947). Sellards believes the human bones and those of the extinct animals are of Pleistocene, i. e., of pre-Altithermal, age.

James W. Gidley and Frederick B. Loomis (1926) accepted the contemporaneity of the men and the extinct animals here and near Melbourne, Florida, where they worked in comparable desposits, but they suggested that the animals had not become extinct until after the end of the Pleistocene. On the basis of more recent investigations in the Indian River area and studies of sea level changes, Irving Rouse (1952) has come to the conclusion that the Melbourne formation in which the bones were found was laid down during the Anathermal and the first half of the Altithermal.

In any case, Rouse (1951) does not believe that the human bones were deposited at the same time as the extinct fauna. He notes that, while a partially complete skeleton is represented, the bones did not lie in anatomical order but were broken and scattered in such a way as to suggest that they had been dug out of the ground. Since Sellards' cross-sections show a hole in the top of the Melbourne stratum at this point, Rouse suggests that Indians lived at the site while the Melbourne stratum was at the surface, dug a pit into it, encountered a primary burial while so doing, and scattered the bones around the edges of their excavation. This would account for the fact that Sellards found most of the human bones on rather than in the Melbourne stratum and that the bones were disturbed but not water-worn.

Rouse believes that the burial was made and then subsequently dug up during a period of erosion after deposition of the Melbourne formation had ended but before the overlying Van Valkenburg stratum had begun to accumulate. Since the stone and bone artifacts found with the human bones are typical Archaic forms and the custom of digging "wells" is also known from the nearby Archaic site of South Indian Field, he concludes that the burial dates from the Archaic period.

Sellards found a hundred or more pieces of broken pottery in the Van Valkenburg bed. In 1952 Ripley P. Bullen (Personal communication) found three potsherds resting directly on the surface of the

Melbourne formation. They were not of the fiber-tempered type, which occurs during the latter part of the Archaic period in the area, but of later, sand-tempered and chalky (untempered) varieties. This suggests that the surface of the bone bed may have been exposed even more recently than Rouse had thought. Bullen believes that the bone bed is a reworked deposit, that the animal bones and artifacts are not necessarily of the same age, and, like Rouse, he feels that the human bones reached their location through burial and subsequent disturbance by human agency, but from the contact zone, not the present surface.

The results of chemical analyses have been inconclusive (Sellards, 1952). In 1916 a human tibia, a wolf bone, and a sloth bone from Vero, and a human tibia from an Indian mound of relatively recent age were analyzed. Specific gravity, amount of moisture, volatile matter, phosphoric acid, and calcium oxide showed a reasonable consistency for human and ancient animal bones from Vero and indicated that they differed markedly from the more recent human bone. The human bone from Vero contained a considerably higher percentage of iron and aluminum oxides than did any of the other bones. There was a greater percentage of insoluble matter and silica in the wolf bone than in any of the others. Fluorine content was not determined at this time. Fluorine analyses made at the University of Florida in 1951 indicated that small differences were apparent when the human bones and animal bones from the upper level were compared with those from the Melbourne formation, but the variations were too slight to provide valid evidence of age differences. Despite recurring rumors that a Carbon 14 date was obtained from a sample from Vero, Sellards and the writer have been unsuccessful in their efforts to find a record of such a date.

Discoveries of a similar nature were made at a later date in comparable deposits near Melbourne, Florida, some thirty miles from Vero. Frederick B. Loomis, in 1923, found artifacts in the same horizon with bones of extinct animals including mammoth and mastodon. In 1925 James W. Gidley and Loomis (1926) found a locality on the Melbourne golf course where a crushed human skull lay in the upper portion of the Melbourne bed below an apparently undisturbed stratified deposit. In the same level, although not in direct association, were the remains of extinct horse, turtle, and tapir.

Gidley (1929, 1930, 1931) undertook further work at intervals between 1926 and 1930. Unfortunately, both Gidley and Loomis died without leaving detailed reports on their research, and the evidence is very difficult to evaluate. As far as can be judged, according to

Rouse (1951), who has made a detailed study of all available evidence, the hole in which the bones of "Melbourne Man" were found was dug from the surface down, and evidence of a burial pit would probably have been recognized. Furthermore, in modern times this locality has been a swamp where it would be unlikely that a grave would be placed, and the incompleteness of the skeleton does not suggest intentional burial. Rouse, however, suggests that the finds date from the dry interval represented by the disconformity between the Melbourne and Van Valkenburg beds. He believes that the human bones are intrusive in the deposit and thinks that they might have reached their location through the digging of wells, as at Vero, or that they could have been trampled into the Melbourne horizon.

Rouse also suggested that the artifacts, which include a stemmed point and a bone pin of types usually attributed to the Archaic, were intrusive from the contact zone. However, while his report was in press he added a footnote quoting from a personal communication of William Edwards who stated that in the Melbourne formation near South Indian Field he had found Suwanee points together with stemmed points of the type already reported. Suwanee points resemble Clovis and Plainview points as regards shape and are thought to be fairly early although their exact position in Florida cultural chronology is not known (Goggin, 1950). It may well be that here, as in certain other areas, there was some overlap of Paleo-Indian and Archaic traditions.

Analysis of fluorine content and other constituents by Robert F. Heizer and S. F. Cook (1952) suggested that the human bones could be as old as those of the extinct animals. There are, however, no bones from the upper bed with which to compare them. Rouse (Personal communication) has suggested that, were this to be done, it is possible that here, as at Vero, no significant differences would be apparent. Material from the Melbourne locality has not been dated by the radiocarbon method. Persistent rumors that such a date exists possibly stem from the report that a date was obtained for skeletal remains found near Melbourne, Australia.

The Vero and Melbourne skulls were first submitted to Ales Hrdlicka, an implacable foe of all claims for the antiquity of man in North America. In his examination he failed to find the markedly primitive features which he insisted must be present before a skull could be granted any claim to age (Hrdlicka, 1918, 1937a). The Vero skull was clearly narrow relative to its length, but, on the basis of a reconstruction done by one of Hrdlicka's technicians, the Melbourne skull appeared to be relatively broad. More recently T. D. Stewart (1946) has re-examined the skulls and done another reconstruction of the badly crushed Melbourne skull. It is now apparent that it was also dolichocranic. These skulls are comparable to those found in Archaic sites in the area, but are quite unlike those found in later sites which were occupied by predominantly broad-headed people. They do not have any distinguishing features that provide proof of great age, but neither do they have any characteristics that would prevent their placement in the Paleo-Indian category. The case for considerable antiquity for Melbourne Man is somewhat better than that for Vero Man, but, unless further evidence is obtained, neither can be placed in the first rank of contenders for the "Early Man" title.

The Stanford Skull

A discovery made more than thirty years ago may be of some importance. It had been largely neglected until recently when Robert F. Heizer (1950) gathered together data pertaining to it. In 1922 Bruce Seymour, a Stanford University Student, found a human skull twenty feet below the surface in the bank of San Francisquito Creek near Stanford, California. It was cemented in a gravel stratum on which an alluvial cone had been formed. Bailey Willis visited the locality and came to the conclusion that a considerable period of time must have been required for the formation of the alluvial cone which overlay the gravel, and for the cutting of the present creek bed. He suggested that the skull might have been deposited more than 4,000 years ago. Willis was a capable geologist, he had worked closely with Hrdlicka, and was likely to be extremely cautious in supporting claims for the antiquity of human remains.

The skull, which was studied by T. D. McCown (1950), was that of a male between thirty-five and forty-five years old. The absolute dimensions were moderately long and narrow, and it was barely mesocephalic. McCown found nothing that would distinguish it from skulls of other aboriginal inhabitants of the area, but neither did he find any evidence that would make it appear impossible for it to be of relatively great age. The physical and chemical condition of the specimen made it appear unlikely that it could be very recent.

Los Angeles Man

Various finds have been made in the Los Angeles area that may be of some antiquity, but in most cases the inadequacy of the reports available makes it impossible to evaluate them. Among the localities which might profitably be reinvestigated is the Rancho La Brea asphalt deposit where, in 1914, a human skeleton, some animal bones, and some artifacts were found in one of the tar pits. The fauna, which contained some extinct forms, was attributed to the Neothermal period, but it could be of Anathermal age. Another potentially important locality is Angeles Mesa where, ten years later, six skeletons were found at depths of from nineteen to twenty-three feet below the surface. The bones must have been interred when the land level was lower than it is at present (Heizer, 1950a).

The skeleton from this area that, in the light of present knowledge, seems to have the best claim to antiquity, has been called "Los Angeles Man." In 1936 workmen on a W. P. A. project, while digging a storm drain along the Los Angeles River near the city of Los Angeles, found human bones at a depth of twelve to thirteen feet below the surface. A partial human cranium and seven fragments of other bones were recovered. They were mineralized and heavily coated with sandstone and conglomerate. Ivan A. Lopatin (1939), of the University of Southern California, conducted excavations in the same area in an effort to find further bones, but only a few very small decayed fragments came to light.

Less than two months after the original discovery, project workers found large animal bones in the same stratum. Lopatin undertook further excavations and unearthed two teeth which were identified as those of an Imperial Mammoth. Later two more teeth and some bone fragments were found. Thomas Clements, who studied the geology, came to the conclusion that the stratum that contained the bones was of Pleistocene age. The fluorine dating method was applied to the human bones and those of the mammoth. The results suggested that the two were of approximately the same age (Heizer and Cook, 1952). Absolute proof is lacking, but there is a high degree of probability of antiquity. The cranium was so badly damaged that it yielded little information beyond the fact that it was a representative of Homo sapiens, probably female, and either dolichocephalic or mesocephalic.

The Tranquillity Site

Another site in California has yielded mineralized human skeletons and bones of extinct horse and camel which, on the basis of chemical analysis, appear to be of approximately the same age (Heizer and Cook, 1952). The statement made in the third edition of this book, that the tests indicated lack of contemporaneity, was incorrect. The situation is complicated, however, by the fact that associated artifacts have been attributed by Heizer (1952) to the Middle Culture Horizon which is thought to be, at most, a few thousand years old.

This site, which lies near Tranquillity in Fresno County, was investigated in the course of a number of visits between 1939 and 1944 by Gordon W. Hewes (1946). A surface collection of artifacts was made, four burials exposed by erosion were removed, and the remains of camelops were found imbedded in a hardpan matrix. Horse teeth and fragmentary bison bones were also found. No excavation into undisturbed deposits was attempted by Hewes. In 1944 a field party under the direction of Linton Satterthwaite, Jr. undertook controlled excavations, and a fifth burial was exposed. No report on these excavations has been published, so the stratigraphic situation cannot be evaluated. Hewes has stated, however, that the deposits did not provide proof of the contemporaneity of the men and the extinct animals. The skeletons have not been described.

Minnesota Man

The first skeleton in North America that could be adequately studied, and which occurred in geologically dated deposits attributed to the Pleistocene, was found three miles north of Pelican Rapids, Minnesota, on July 16, 1931 (Jenks, 1936). Highway workers, while digging a roadbed, uncovered an almost complete skeleton associated with two artifacts at a depth of ten feet in glacial silts. Unfortunately, the skeleton was not witnessed *in situ* and was removed before being examined by a trained observer. However, the workmen who uncovered it gave it intelligent care and it was brought to the attention of the late A. E. Jenks of the University of Minnesota. In subsequent redigging of the site under Jenks' direction, bone fragments were found *in situ* which could be fitted with parts previously removed.

The skeleton was that of a girl approximately fifteen years old, who is believed by some to have drowned in a glacial lake, Lake Pelican, at a time when the last major glacier of the Wisconsin had retreated only a short distance. The name "Minnesota Man," which was first given to the skeleton, has been retained in the literature, although there can be no doubt that it is that of a female. The importance of the find and the need for presenting certain disputed points in connection with the site warrant considering the problem in some detail.

The artifacts associated with the skeleton are such as to give no clue as to the age. One was a dagger or knife eight or nine inches long, made of elk antler, and perforated at one end. The other was a conch shell with two perforations, which lay among the ribs and vertebrae in the abdominal area of the skeleton. It is assumed that these objects may have been suspended from a thong and tied around the neck or on a girdle. This would account for their being found directly associated with the skeleton, even if the girl met her death by drowning. The conch shell suggests interesting possibilities, for it is a Gulf Coast species which would seem to indicate some contact with regions farther south.

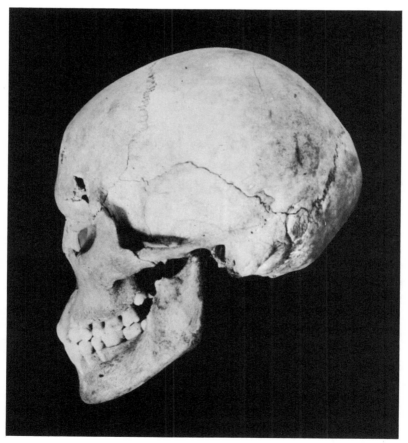

Courtesy University of Minnesota Press

FIG. 64—Skull of Minnesota Man.

The skeleton, which was carefully described by Jenks, exhibited, in his opinion, certain primitive morphological characters. Among those which he considered the most important was the lack of reduction of the jaw and teeth. The teeth are, in fact, extraordinarily large, even larger than those of certain Paleolithic men. The cusp pattern of the molars is of a primitive type. The upper incisors are shovel-shaped, a trait ordinarily associated with Mongoloids. There is a marked protrusion of the portions of the upper and lower jaws which contain the front teeth and a pronounced backward extension of the skull which is narrow relative to its length. Jenks stated, "The measured and observed morphological characters of the skeleton proclaim it to be a primitive type of *Homo sapiens* of an early type of evolving Mongoloid suggesting American aborigines, especially the Eskimo, more than the present Asian Mongoloids."

Hrdlicka (1937b) attacked Jenks' conclusions on a number of points. On the basis of the measurements and observations published by Jenks, he believed the skeleton to be that of a modern Sioux Indian and felt that it represented a comparatively recent burial. He attempted to refute the theory of accidental burial on the grounds that the skeleton was found lying on its side, a position that he did not feel suggested drowning, and on the basis of the completeness of the skeleton, for he believed that, had the body decomposed in the lake, the bones would have been scattered by wave action.

Jenks answered these observations in a later review (Jenks, 1938). He maintained that the Minnesota skull differed sufficiently from modern Indian skulls, on morphological grounds, to warrant giving it a Pleistocene dating. He pointed out that Hrdlicka, in comparing the skull with a series of modern Sioux crania, had presented only skulls containing one or two primitive characters. While all the primitive traits of the Minnesota cranium could be found in a large series of Sioux skulls, he felt that no single Indian skull showed anything approaching the same number of primitive characters. Furthermore, the fact that it fell within the range of variation of the Sioux series was not significant, for the series provided a wide range in which many skulls, known to be totally unrelated, could be fitted.

Jenks further pointed out that he had long been familiar with Sioux burials and there was every reason to suppose that he would recognize an intentional burial of this nature. Doctors and police officials confirmed his belief that neither the position nor the condition of the skeleton precluded the possibility of death by drowning. Particularly in cold water, the rate of decomposition of a body may be slow enough to allow it to be covered by water deposits which will prevent the bones from being separated from each other after the flesh and cartilage have decayed.

Earnest A. Hooton (1946) accepted a late glacial dating for this find. He questioned the Eskimoid character of the skull, but he believed that the Minnesota skeleton showed generalized Mongoloid characteristics. He regarded the unusually large size of the teeth as the most distinctive feature of the skull. As Hooton pointed out, it is regrettable that this individual was an adolescent female, for the skull of an adult male would have shown racial characteristics more clearly and would have provided a better subject for studies by physical anthropologists.

An attempt was made to obtain a radiocarbon date from a section of the elk antler dagger found with the skeleton, but its carbon content was largely inorganic carbonate and it was not possible to determine the age. Such a degree of mineralization would, however, suggest antiquity (Wilford, 1955). Once more it is necessary to consider the geological evidence. It is accepted that the deposits in which the skeleton was found are varved clays laid down in glacial Lake Pelican shortly after the last major advance of the continental ice sheets. At the time of the discovery, a date of some 25,000 years ago was accepted for the Mankato, and the clays were dated at approximately 18,000 to 20,000 years ago. With the new dates assigned to the Mankato on the basis of radiocarbon dating, most geologists would regard these deposits as being less than 11,000 years old; but their place in the Pleistocene sequence is not in question. The basic controversy regarding the age of this skeleton has centered around the problem of whether it was of the same age as the deposits or whether it was intrusive.

The greater part of the discussion involves the question of the disturbance or internal deformation of the varve layers. Ernst Antevs (1937a) believes that the deposits in which the skeleton was found were disturbed and that the skeleton is probably intrusive and of a later period. He has suggested two theories: (1) that intrusion was caused by a landslide; (2) that intrusion was through burial in an ancient gully now filled. He states that evidence of the presence of such a gully was found in a survey before the road was built.

Kirk Bryan and Paul MacClintock (1938), on the other hand, while admitting that the deposits were somewhat disturbed, felt that such a disturbance did not necessarily provide evidence of landsliding or intentional burial and could be accounted for on the basis of settling which would follow the melting of the ice, or by ice override. They also suggested the possibility that in a relatively shallow lake, such as Lake Pelican, wave action might result in some disturbance of lake sediments.

The same authors also showed that the theory of accidental burial through landsliding offered further difficulties since it necessitated the assumption of a number of remote contingencies. It was necessary to assume either that the girl fell or was placed in a crack ten feet or more deep, and that the crack closed over again without crushing or disturbing the bones; or that the body was in position below a hill and that a portion of the cliff moved out laterally across it without disturbing the associated artifacts, crushing or disturbing the bones, or including beach sand or cliff debris. Assuming, however, that such were the case, the dating of the skeleton need not be much later since the special climatic and topographic conditions necessary to induce landsliding would be associated with a period almost as remote as the time of the varve formation.

Bryan and MacClintock also questioned the theory of intentional burial in a gully. They felt that had there been an ancient gully, evidence of its presence would have remained despite the disturbance of the deposits by the road crew. On the basis of interviews with the men who made the original find, as well as the published observations of Jenks, Thiel, Kay, Leighton, and others, they felt that such evidence was lacking. They concluded that the hypotheses brought forward to explain the deep burial of the skeleton required belief in a combination of circumstances beyond reasonable probability. The writer agrees. She believes that "Minnesota Man" represents an individual who drowned in the waters of Lake Pelican not long after the Mankato maximum.

Similar Skulls from Wyoming

Since the discovery of "Minnesota Man" was reported, four skeletons have been found near Torrington, Wyoming, which, according to W. W. Howells (1938), who studied and reported upon them, closely resemble the skeleton found at Lake Pelican. It is most unfortunate that these bones were found by untrained workmen in the course of blasting activities. Not only was all geological evidence lost through the explosion, but artifacts, reportedly found with the bones, were taken by the workmen and have not been available for study by archaeologists who might have been able to identify them. The little information which is available indicates that intentional burials were represented and that they lay within a cave or crevice. There is, of course, no way of determining the age of these skeletons, but there is at least a possibility that they may be of reasonable antiquity, and the resemblance to "Minnesota Man" makes them of interest. The close similarities between the Browns Valley points found in Minnesota and the points found at the Jimmy Allen Site in Wyoming (see pages 144 to 146) do suggest that there may have been some connection between the early inhabitants of these areas.

The remains of four individuals were recovered, but one of the skeletons was that of a young child and the bones were extremely fragmentary. The adult skeleton included one male of early middle age, a young female, and a middle-aged female. These individuals were somewhat more long-headed than the Minnesota girl and their jaws were slightly more protruding but, in general, they appear to be representatives of the same racial group and all seem to be of a slightly more primitive type than recent Indians.

Browns Valley Man

The circumstances concerning the discovery in Browns Valley, Minnesota, of a human skeleton and artifacts thought to be of some antiquity have been discussed on page 143. The skeleton is that of an adult male believed to have been between twenty-five and forty years of age. The skull is dolichocranic (long and narrow), and the nose is leptorrhine (narrow). It possesses certain unusual characteristics, notably an asymmetrical combination of a long skull with a short face, prominent brow ridges, and a wide mandible and skull base.

Sauk Valley Man

Another possibly ancient skeleton was found in Minnesota, but it was not seen in position by a trained observer, and the geological evidence is not conclusive (Bryan, Retzek, and McCann, 1938; Jenks and Wilford, 1938). It was found in a gravel pit by workmen engaged in caving off an overhang on the gravel face. The bones were claimed by Daniel W. Frazier, the owner of the land, and later turned over to the Reverend Henry Retzek for study. Later in the year the site was examined by Kirk Bryan and Franklin T. McCann.

As far as can be determined, there was no evidence of burial, and the position of the skeleton in the grave was due to natural processes of entombment. Within the skull case was found limonitic sand. Under present climatic conditions calcium carbonate is being deposited, and had the skull been laid down under these conditions it would be expected that the sand within the skull would contain a lime cement, which was not present. Bryan and McCann thought it probable that the skeleton was deposited during or before the period of limonite deposition, or previous to a more humid climate that antedated the present semi-arid type of climate. They believed that the depth of the occurrence and the presence of the limonitic gravel might indicate considerable antiquity, although this did not provide conclusive proof. Jenks and Wilford reported that the skeleton was that of a middle-aged male and that it showed some Mongoloid traits.

Tepexpan Man

An interesting find of human skeletal remains was made in the Valley of Mexico near the village of Tepexpan (De Terra, Romero and Stewart, 1949). In 1949 Helmut de Terra began a series of geological and archaeological studies in the Valley of Mexico. Some of his discoveries are discussed on pages 200 to 202. It came to his attention that fossil elephant remains had been uncovered in ancient lake flats near Tepexpan and he found a few artifacts in deposits which previous work initiated by Kirk Bryan and A. R. V. Arellano had indicated were of Pleistocene age. De Terra, Arellano, and their associates undertook excavations in this area and discovered a human skeleton lying in a silty clay deposit with some sixteen inches of the same lake sediments above.

The skeleton lay face down, with the legs drawn up to the stomach. Many of the foot bones, the major portion of the pelvis, the shoulder blades and collarbones, and most of the vertebrae and ribs were missing. The long bones were all represented, but most of them were incomplete. The skull, which, from the anthropological point of view, is of the greatest importance, was essentially complete although the facial portion was in a somewhat fragmentary condition and was detached from the skull. This has since been restored. De Terra came to the conclusion that this individual had met an accidental death, and that the body had rested face downward in the mud. The shoulders, back, and hips were exposed and, through the scavenging activities of animals and birds, some of the skeletal parts disappeared.

The silts in which the skeleton lay belonged to the Younger Becerra formation and corresponded with similar deposits nearby which yielded mammoth remains and a worked obsidian flake. Above the

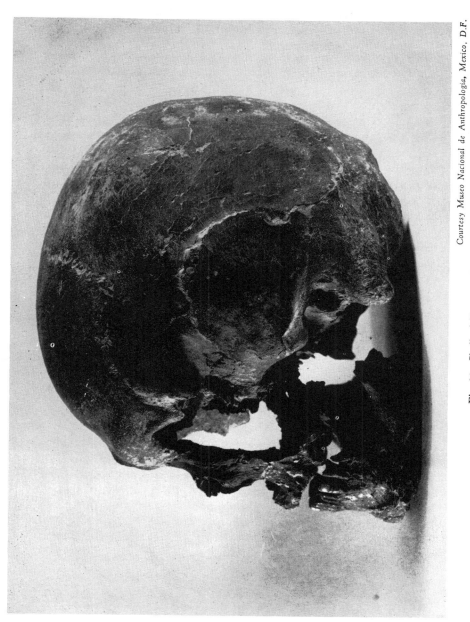

Courtesy Museo Nacional de Antropología, Mexico, D.F.

Fig. 21—Skull of Tepexpan Man.

silts was a layer of caliche. The silts are marsh deposits which must have been formed during a moist period, while the caliche deposits indicate a dry climatic phase. De Terra attributed the caliche to the Altithermal period. He felt, however, that in a subtropical region, such as the Tepexpan area, the Altithermal period would have been earlier than farther north, and he estimated the date at which the caliche began to form at about 9,000 or 10,000 years ago. Since the skeleton lay beneath sixteen inches of marshy lake sediments, he postulated that this individual lived during a moist period; but for a marsh or swamp to have formed there, it would have been necessary for the lake waters already to have receded from the higher point which is shown by ancient beach levels. De Terra came to the conclusion that the age of the deposit containing the bones must lie between the date of the Pluvial maximum and that of the beginning of the dry period, and closer to the latter. He dated this deposit and Tepexpan Man at about 11,000 to 12,000 years ago. Peat from another locality, believed to be attributable to the same general topographic level as the one that contained the human skeleton, produced a radiocarbon date of 11,003 ± 500 years ago. The age of a wood sample collected a short distance away from the first was given as more than 16,000 years (Libby, 1955). De Terra (1951) has suggested that this wide time range is the result of the composite nature of the fan deposit from which the samples were taken.

For a skeleton to be assigned the same age as the deposit in which it is found, it is considered essential that it be a primary inclusion. This point of view is clearly seen in the controversy regarding the age of "Minnesota Man." The methods of excavation employed in removing the Tepexpan skeleton have been severely criticized (Black, 1949; Krieger, 1950). It has been suggested that, due to the manner of exhumation, an intrusive grave pit might have been present although it was not recognized. It has been noted that the caliche level was absent immediately above the skeleton. The position of the body, the absence of mortuary offerings, and the general physical appearance of the individual, can be duplicated in burials of the Archaic period.

On the other hand, de Terra has stated that root canals of swamp plants extended from the top of the clay level and penetrated the skull. If there was no evidence of disturbance, this would indicate continuous sedimentation, and the age of the roots must be less than that of the skeleton. Samples of stems and roots of aquatic plants gathered at this locality, although not in the excavation that produced the body, provided radiocarbon dates that averaged 4,118 ± 300 years ago (Libby, 1955). Javier Romero has pointed out that the degree of fossilization of the bones cannot be duplicated in those from Archaic burials in the locality (De Terra, Romero, and Stewart, 1949). A. R. V. Arellano, who assumed much of the responsibility for the exhumation, has more recently provided additional data (Arellano, 1951a). He made borings that showed that the caliche layer, which was absent above the skeleton, was similarly absent in other nearby areas. He tested material from the various levels with hydrochloric acid. All of the more recent deposits reacted vigorously, but the deposits surrounding the bones did not fizz when exposed to the acid. In the digging of a burial pit it would be expected that some material from overlying limey deposits would be incorporated in the fill.

The criticism of the manner in which the skeleton was excavated is justified, and it will never be possible to obtain absolute proof of the antiquity of Tepexpan Man. Nevertheless, the discoveries at Santa Isabel Istapan have provided incontrovertible proof that men and mammoths lived in this area at the same time. After talking with those who were present at the time of excavation, and visiting the site, the writer believes that it is highly probable that Tepexpan Man is of late Pleistocene age and was correctly dated by de Terra.

Studies by physical anthropologists indicate that the Tepexpan skeleton is that of a man between fifty-five and sixty-five years of age who was about five feet seven inches tall. The skull exhibits no markedly primitive features, but this has little bearing on the antiquity of the bones, since it is generally conceded that a skeleton some 11,000 years old would be of modern form. The fact that Tepexpan Man was moderately round-headed has led to some discussion, since it has been generally believed that the earliest migrants were long headed. As T. D. Stewart has pointed out, however, there is a range of variation in any group, and even an essentially long-headed population contains some individuals who are moderately round-headed (De Terra, Romero, Stewart, 1949).

The Midland Discovery

The name "Midland Man" has been commonly applied to the partial human skeleton that has been most generally accepted as representing a very early inhabitant of North America (Wendorf, Krieger, Albritton, Stewart, 1955). "Midland Man," however, like "Minnesota Man," was actually a female. The skeletal remains, which consist of parts of a skull, two fragmentary ribs, and three metacarpals, represent the first adequately documented human bones attributed to the pre-Altithermal period.

The first discovery was made in 1953 when Keith Glasscock found fragments of human bone and two artifacts lying in the bottom of a sand blow-out on a ranch near Midland, Texas. The site was named in honor of the landowner, Clarence Scharbauer. Glasscock, a capable amateur archaeologist, picked up only the fragments that were being jeopardized by high winds, and left those that were still in position in place for observation by specialists. He brought the discovery to the attention of Fred Wendorf who visited the site with Alex Krieger and a number of other well-known archaeologists. From the beginning of the investigations the site was extremely well-documented.

In the course of the first visit, three more skull fragments, a rib section, a metacarpal, and many tiny fragments of bone too small for identification were recovered. A third artifact was found on the surface some seventy feet away. This specimen, like one of those found by Glasscock, resembled a classic Folsom point as regards shape, size, and flaking, but it was unfluted. On page 41 is a brief discussion of these and similar specimens found at this site and now called Midland points. An examination of other localities in the area revealed the presence of less deeply eroded blow-outs. It became apparent that only through excavation would it be possible to gain the necessary data that would enable the investigators to determine the geologic age of the human remains. During most of the period of excavation, from February 1 to 28, 1954, Wendorf was in charge of the work, but Krieger revisited the site, and the final report on the archaeology and the general synthesis is the work of both authors. Claude C. Albritton undertook the geological studies, and T. D. Stewart described the human skeletal remains. Further investigations were undertaken during November and December by E. H. Sellards, who reported on his work in an appendix in the reference cited above. Additional work by Wendorf and Krieger was conducted in October and November, 1955. The results of this last excavation have not yet been published, but the major results have, most generously, been made available for summary here.

There were five major subdivisions in the sand deposits, which had an aggregate thickness of fifty-five to sixty feet. The sands that made up the deposits were separated from each other by disconformities. They lay in the following order:

Unit 5	Tan Sand	}	
Unit 4	Light brown Sand		Monahans Formation
Unit 3	Red Sand	)	
Unit 2	Gray Sand	}	Judkins Formation
Unit 1	White Sand	)	

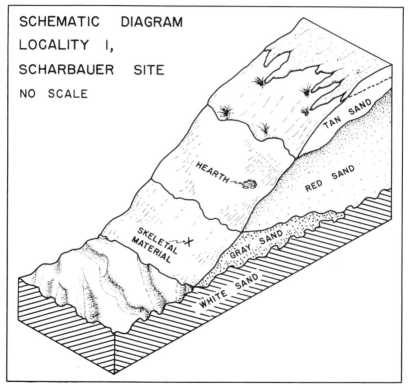

SCHEMATIC DIAGRAM

LOCALITY I,

SCHARBAUER SITE

NO SCALE

TAN SAND

HEARTH

RED SAND

SKELETAL MATERIAL X

GRAY SAND

WHITE SAND

Courtesy University of Texas Press

Fig. 66—(Fig. 9 p. 37 in Wendorf, Krieger, Albritton and Stewart, 1955.)

The human skeletal remains lay on and just beneath the eroded surface of the gray sand. From adjacent hummocks of gray sand it could be determined that this deposit had once stood at least two feet higher at that spot. This bed yielded some chipped artifacts, a smoothed piece of sandstone, burned rocks, horse teeth, and fragmentary bones of horse, extinct antelope (Capromeryx?), and bison. The antelope bones were burned. The presence of gray sand in the internal auditory aperture and other sinuses of the skull provided confirmation that the bones were in primary association with this stratum rather than with one of the overlying beds. Chemical analyses were run on the human bones, bones of extinct animals from the lower zones, and bones from above. The human bones were shown to contain approximately the same amounts of fluorine, nitrogen, and organic carbon as those from the lower horizons, but there were significant differences when they were compared with bones from a humic zone that occurred at the top of the red sand and those found on the modern surface.

Seven fluted Folsom points and twenty unfluted specimens that closely resembled them, a Milnesand point, a Meserve point, a ground limestone disc, and a probable mano were found on the surface of the red sand. It was originally believed that the Folsom material occurred only at the contact zone of the red and light brown sand and, accordingly, the human remains, which were found below, were regarded as being of pre-Folsom age. In the course of later investigations, however, a basal fragment of a Midland point was found in the gray sand that contained the skull fragments. This suggests that some such points were of the same age as the human bones but that they were still being made after the period during which the red sand was deposited. Unfortunately, there is no way of determining how long a time was involved in the deposition of this unit.

At the locality that yielded the human bones, a hearth, apparently essentially in place, was found on the surface of the red sand. It consisted of a concentration of burned lumps of caliche. The remains of another were found resting on the gray sand, but the stones were scattered, and it is thought that they had reached this position through a process of deflation as sand was cut from under the stones by wind action. Various other hearths were found in nearby localities. It is possible, but by no means certain, that some could be of Folsom age.

In the white sand that underlay the gray were found a small broken flint and the fragmentary leg bone of a horse which bore a series of sharp grooves. These cuts are believed to have been made while the bone was still fresh. Among the other fossil bones that came from this level were those of mammoth, camel, bison, and an extinct form of antelope, *Capromeryx*. Sellards believes that this horizon correlates with the lowest artifact-bearing stratum in the Clovis area which yielded Clovis points and mammoth remains.

Claude C. Albritton attempted to reconstruct the geologic history of the site. Each sand is separated from the one above by a disconformity caused by wind erosion. A standing body of water appears to have been present when the white sand was laid down. This would indicate a climate more moist than that of the present. Apparently the lake disappeared for a time and there was a drier period during which the lake bed was scoured by wind. There was somewhat greater moisture during the following period when the gray sand accumulated, but it is thought that only an ephemeral lake or playa was represented. Next came a period of erosion followed by one during which the red sand was deposited by wind action. This deposit indicates a long period of aridity that permitted the formation of dunes. Toward the close of the period somewhat more humid conditions must have prevailed, for there was enough moisture to permit a soil zone to develop. These relatively moist times were followed by another period of aridity marked by wind erosion and dune formation. Since it is of post-Folsom age, it seems probable that it is the latter period that correlates with the Altithermal. If this is the case, the long arid period attested to by the earlier red sand is of particular interest, for it suggests that there was a major drought preceding the one that began some 7,000 years ago. This pre-Folsom drought seems to correlate with the disappearance of the horse, elephant, camel, and many other late Pleistocene animals from the Southern High Plains. Of these late Pleistocene animals, only the giant bison remains have been found in Folsom sites in this area. It would appear that the geologic history of this and adjoining areas is far more complex than has been realized.

The evidence derived from radiocarbon samples is far from satisfactory. Great difficulties were encountered in obtaining organic carbon from the hard fossils. A mixed bone and tusk sample from the gray sand, submitted to the University of Michigan Laboratory, was dated at between 4,000 and 5,000 years on the basis of a forty-eight hour run; but after being placed in the counter for two more weeks it produced a date of 7,100 ± 1,000 years ago. Another Carbon 14 date was obtained from the fat and carbon absorbed by the caliche rocks used in cooking and found buried in the gray sand. A considerable amount of carbon was extracted from these caliche stones, and this carbon yielded a date of 20,400 ± 900 years. Wendorf regards this as too old. Bones from the top of the white sand yielded dates averaging 8,670 ± 600 years ago. Fresh-water snail shells from this formation, submitted to the Lamont Laboratory, provided a date of

12,500 ± 1,200 years ago. Palaeontological and archaeological evidence suggests that the latter is probably closer to the right order of magnitude, but when there are such discrepancies it is difficult to place much reliance on the radiocarbon dates. New uranium isotope dates and the results of chemical analyses undertaken by Kenneth Oakley to determine the extent of uranium absorption, which will be published by Wendorf and Krieger in their forthcoming report on the 1955 excavations, should help to clarify the situation.*

T. D. Stewart, who reassembled the fragmentary calvarium, insofar as was possible, and described the human remains, has stated that the degree of mineralization is consistent with considerable burial age. He believes the bones are those of a female about thirty years old. The condition of the teeth suggests a diet with a strong abrasive content, perhaps one that included seeds or some form of vegetable matter ground on stone. The skull is quite long relative to its breadth. It is, in fact, more dolichocranic than any of the other American skulls with a good claim to antiquity. It closely resembles certain long-headed skulls found in Texas in deposits which are of uncertain age but could be quite old.

The Turin Skeletons

A discovery which has had a great deal of publicity in newspapers and magazines was made by Asa Johnston in August, 1955, in Turin, Iowa. Johnston, a gravel pit operator, was using his bulldozer to remove loess that overlay gravel deposits, when he saw a part of a human skull roll down the slope. Part of the skeleton, that of an adult, remained in the bank, but it was, unfortunately, removed by the County Coroner who thought it might be the body of a local inhabitant who had disappeared some years before. The discovery was reported to the State University. Reynold J. Ruppe, an archaeologist from that institution, and Weldon D. Frankforter, a palaeontologist from the Sanford Museum, examined the bones and visited the site.

A few weeks later Johnston noted the top of a second skull exposed in a large block of loess that had fallen from the bank. Frankforter investigated immediately and called in a number of scientists

---

*Kreiger (Editor, 1957b) states that John N. Rosholt, who has developed a new dating method utilizing the daughter products of uranium, has made a test of fossil bones from the Midland locality. Measurement of three different uranium isotopes found in minute quantities in the fossils produced dates of 19,000, 17,000 and 15,000 years ago.

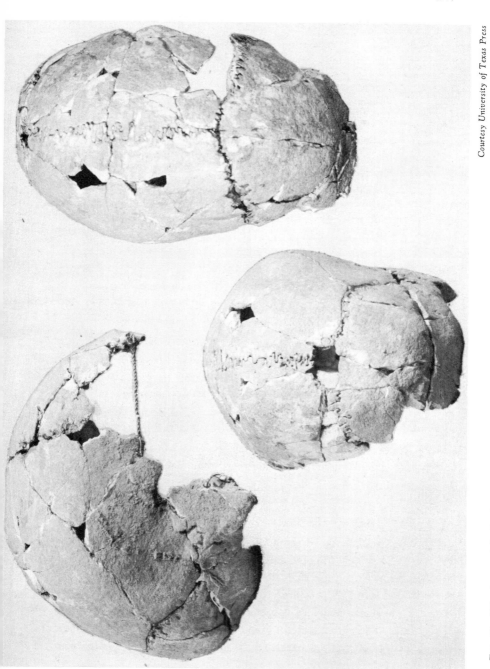

FIG. 67—Side, top, and back views of the Midland Calvarium. (Fig. 27, p. 78 in Wendorf, Krieger, Albritton and Stewart, 1955.)

from institutions in Nebraska. The skeleton was exposed and found to be lying in a flexed position on the left side. A little over a week later Johnston reported finding a third skull still *in situ.* Telegrams were sent to a number of specialists, and a group of archaeologists, palaeontologists, and geologists gathered at the site. The circumstances under which the other bones had been found had been less than ideal, but, although some of the bones had fallen from the cliff face, much of this skeleton was still in position and it was excavated under optimum conditions with only highly skilled and experienced individuals doing the digging under the direction of Ruppe and Frankforter. The excavation, which was begun at the top of the cliff and continued fifteen feet below the surface to the point where the skeleton lay, revealed that this individual, an adolescent, had been buried in a flexed position on the left side in a pit. Red ochre had been placed in the grave. In the course of the excavations the skeleton of an infant, buried in the same position, was found near the third. No attempt was made to clear the bones completely in the field. Still encased in the surrounding matrix, they were jacketed in burlap and plaster and sent to the University of Iowa for final cleaning and study.

The fact that these skeletons were found in loess deposits at a considerable depth below the surface suggested the possibility of some antiquity, for the presence of loess is thought to indicate a fairly cool climate, and the material for such beds was often derived from outwash glacial plains. The problem, however, was to determine the position of the loess bed in the geologic sequence. The underlying gravels yielded evidence of a Pleistocene fauna including mammoth, horse, and camel. The only animal bones found in the loess were those of bison, which lay at a lower level than the burials. They were so fragmentary that it was not possible to determine whether they belonged to an extinct species.

When the skeleton of the adolescent was cleared of matrix in the laboratory, a projectile point was found in association. It was a large notched point of a type that closely resembled some of those of the Archaic period. This, however, does not serve to provide a definite date for the skeletons, since it is not known how far back the Archaic horizon may date in this area. Plans have been made to submit some of the bones for radiocarbon analysis (Ruppe, Personal communication).

Chapter VI

THE PEOPLING OF NORTH AMERICA

It is now generally accepted that man did not originate in the New World and that he first came to America by way of Bering Strait, but it should be mentioned that other theories have been advanced, although none is widely held. Among the best known, although the least accepted in scientific circles, are those that take for granted the former existence of now submerged land masses, such as the legendary continents of Mu and Atlantis, which would have provided a link between the hemispheres. Another theory is that at one time North and South America were attached to Europe and Africa but later broke away and moved to their present positions. Most scientists simply classify these as fairy tales, or, at most, admit that land distribution has differed from that of the present but at such remote times in the past that it would not serve to explain the presence of man in the Western Hemisphere.

The possibility of trans-oceanic voyages has also been suggested. Trans-Pacific voyages have been most widely advocated on the basis of certain cultural traits that are common to both Oceania and South America. While it is entirely possible that there was some contact in more recent times, it seems inconceivable to most scientists that people could have reached the New World by this route at any very early date or in sufficient numbers to account for the populating of the New World. The possibility of trans-Atlantic migrations is generally thought to be even more remote.

Still another theory sometimes suggested is that the early migrants crossed from Asia by way of the Aleutian and Komandorski Islands. As there is no geological evidence that ice sheets formed here, even in the glacial period, boats would have had to be used. It is possible that this route was followed by some groups, but it is not generally accepted that the earliest men, or many of the later migrants, arrived by this route. It would have required great skill in navigation, since there are treacherous currents, rocky shore lines, and much fog and wind. Also, some of the islands are so far apart as to be invisible from each other even in the clearest weather.

If, as archaeologists believe, Bering Strait was the only possible route available to people who did not have the watercraft and the navigational skill that would have enabled them to traverse oceans or to go through very difficult waterways, the first people must have come to America from Siberia by way of the Strait. At this point Asia and America are separated by only fifty-six miles of sea broken by three islands. The widest expanse of unbroken sea is only twenty-five miles, and land is in sight on even moderately cloudy days. The gap between the two continents is not thought to have been wider since a time before the last glaciation, and there were times when it did not exist at all.

Although the crossing could have been accomplished by means of very primitive watercraft and with little knowledge of navigation, or by walking across on the winter ice, it is difficult to see what the incentive would have been for such a movement, at least for hunters of grazing animals. It seems more probable that such people would have crossed the Strait at a time when it was possible for the animals on which they depended for food to cross. They would have been able to do so when the two continents were joined by a land bridge. At the height of a glaciation much water was abstracted from the sea to feed the ice sheets, and there was some rise of the ocean floor. A general lowering of sea level resulted, and shallow portions of the ocean became land surfaces.

The floor of Bering Strait would be above water if sea level were reduced by only 120 feet. Due to low precipitation in much of Alaska, glaciers formed largely in the mountains. If the land bridge and adjacent areas were unglaciated they could probably have provided food for grass-eating animals and for men. Palaeontological evidence indicates that in the plains and valleys of Alaska man would have found animal and plant foods to supply his needs (Smith, 1937).

There is also the problem of how men reached the areas farther south in which evidence of their presence at an early date has been found. During glacial stages there were ice sheets covering large parts of North America. These would have presented a barrier to the movements of men and animals. During interstadials, however, the ice retreated and ice-free corridors were opened. During one or more of the interstadials that preceded the Mankato, as well as in post-glacial times, the Mackenzie Valley was probably free of ice. Those who reached it by moving along the low northern coast line of Alaska could have followed the valley and gained access to the northern Plains. People who moved up the Missouri could have reached the Snake River Plain and the Great Basin. At a later date, movement along the Yukon and down the Liard and Peace River valleys to the Plains, or along the Frazer River to the Great Basin, may have been practicable.

It should be noted, however, that while it is very simple to plot migration routes while sitting in an office and looking at a map, the problem assumes new dimensions when one is in the field in this northern country. It takes only a fraction of a second to draw a line half an inch long on a map. However, if that line represents a non-existent path through a hundred miles of muskeg, the situation become extraordinarily complicated if one attempts to follow it in person.

As Froelich Rainey has pointed out, "Northwestern America and northeastern Asia, under present climatic conditions, together form one of the most formidable barriers to human communication one can find anywhere in the world" (Rainey, 1953, p. 46). Undoubtedly, there were times when it was possible for people to move through this country, but there must have been times when such movement was not practical. In this connection the theory of Ewing and Donn discussed on page 11 is of particular interest. If they are correct in believing that during stages of widespread continental glaciation the Arctic Ocean was not frozen these might have been the times most favorable for movement by man.

Glib statements pertaining to migrations into the New World often convey an impression of masses of people moving swiftly across the Strait and marching briskly down the continent in search of a pleasanter climate or in pursuit of animals that were rushing south. This is probably far different from the true picture. People dependent on hunting and food gathering cannot move together in large numbers. Furthermore, to the primitive the unknown and the unseen are strange and terrifying, and primitive man does not willingly depart from known familiar things to face the unknown. Only some strong compulsive force, such as the need for food, will cause him to make a drastic change. Also, a warmer climate, even were it known to exist in some distant region, would not necessarily provide an irresistible attraction. In general, people are more likely to make an effort to adapt to conditions in the country that they know.

It seems probable that, as J. L. Giddings (1952) has suggested, the peopling of the New World was the result, not of migrations, in the sense of predetermined movements, but rather of a spread of population that resulted from the gradual extension of the hunting and gathering ranges of various groups. Population growth would lead to an increase of the range exploited. Variations in climate would, at times, have changed the ecological situation and led to movements into new areas by game animals and the men dependent upon them. Droughts in arid areas could have forced people with some dependence on food gathering into new territory. Radiocarbon dates from Patagonia indicate that men had reached the tip of South America some 8,000 years ago (Bird, 1951); and, if we eliminate the idea of swift purposeful movement to the south, many thousands of years must have elapsed since the ancestors of these people first reached the Western Hemisphere. The diversity of culture and language among the American Indians also serves to indicate the passage of a very long period of time.

Believing, as we do, that the early American population was derived from northeastern Asia, it is, of course, highly desirable to know something of the archaeological remains found on the Siberian side of Bering Strait. Unfortunately, the writer is unable to read Russian, and it has been impossible to do a proper analysis of the literature pertaining to Siberian sites. All that has been available are the summaries in English published by Lawrence Krader (1952) and Chester S. Chard (1956), and illustrations and partial translations of some of the books of A. P. Okladnikov, which appear to be excellent reports. Scanty as this information is, it serves to indicate that no very early sites have been found; most are attributed to the Neolithic. This is scarcely surprising, however, for Siberia is much like Alaska and northwestern Canada. Those who have worked in the north realize how extraordinarily difficult it is, in such country, to find the scanty traces left long ago by small groups of hunters and gatherers with few possessions and no permanent habitations. The fact that early sites have not been discovered does not mean that they do not exist.

What of the culture of the early people who moved into North America? We shall never be able to gain information about many of their traits, but it is possible to make certain inferences. As John R. Mather (1954) has pointed out, people without warm clothing could not survive a winter under present climatic conditions. Even if, as has been suggested, the Arctic Ocean was ice-free during times of widespread continental glaciation, it is reasonable to assume that people entering the New World during the Wisconsin had suitable clothing. Probably, particularly during the winter, they also needed some sort of shelter and a means of heating it.

There is also the question of what items were to be found in the tool kits of the first comers. We have seen that in the United States there were two traditions of stone working, one in the east that placed a greater emphasis on flakes and bifacially flaked implements, and one in the west where cores and chopping tools were important. In the

Old World, too, there were distinct traditions. In southeastern Asia chopping tools made from cores, and pebbles were typical implements, while in other parts of the Old World bifaces and flakes were widely utilized (Movius, 1949). It seems more than coincidental that two similar traditions should be found in the New World. It is not unreasonable to consider the possibility that both traditions had reached the area from which the first Americans came, and that some of these people were followers of one tradition and some of the other. They could have come at different times and followed different routes as they moved farther south.

The people who first occupied the area east of the Rocky Mountains probably had projectile points, but we can only speculate as to the types. It would be tempting to envisage some connection with the Upper Palaeolithic Solutrean culture, for, as various archaeologists have noted, there are extremely striking resemblances between Solutrean points found in western Europe and the single-shouldered Sandias and the laurel-leaf points found in North America. However, no Solutrean sites have been found east of the Dneister River and, according to Hallam L. Movius (Personal communication), nothing even remotely resembling the Solutrean has turned up in Siberia or anywhere in Asia.

In the opinion of the writer, however, Sandia points were among the earliest forms, and they may represent the prototype from which various types of later points developed. This is pure conjecture, but the fluted single-shouldered points found at the Lucy Site suggest that the technique of fluting may have been developed by the makers of Sandia points. Clovis Fluted points could have developed from this type. It is also possible that the fluted Sandias reflect a Clovis influence. The Folsom type probably represents a later refinement of the Clovis pattern that was made in a limited area where there were large herds of bison.

There are problems pertaining to Plainviews and the various types of lanceolate points with parallel flaking used by other ancient bison hunters. They closely resemble certain Siberian specimens, particularly those found in the Lake Baikal area. Do these forms reflect influences from Asia, or did they originate in the New World, perhaps being derived from the Clovis type? We do not know. However, no great antiquity is attributed to the Siberian sites that contain such types. None of them is indubitably pre-ceramic, and they are classified as Neolithic. In general, they are not thought to be more than 4,000 years old. It is entirely possible that earlier sites containing these types will ultimately be found there, but, on the basis of present evidence, the possibility that some influences spread from Alaska to Asia cannot be overlooked.

The first people who lived on the western side of the Rocky Mountains probably possessed choppers and scrapers. We cannot be sure whether they had stone projectile points, although they probably depended on animal foods to some extent. It is impossible to develop even a hypothetical sequence of projectile points except in certain limited areas where, in general, notched and stemmed forms seem to have preceded lanceolate forms. In the eastern United States the sequence is apparently reversed. There is a question as to the manner in which grinding stones became a part of the Paleo-western tradition. They do not appear to be early in northeastern Asia. Perhaps they were first developed in the Great Basin or in the Southwest. (Hurt, 1953). However, until further evidence is available, and until sites with such artifacts are accurately dated, both in Asia and in America, the question cannot be answered.

Old World connections are somewhat clearer in the case of the core and blade industry of the Arctic, although there are definite problems in regard to distribution. The closest resemblances are to be found when comparisons are made with material from the Lake Baikal area and Outer Mongolia, which are geographically remote; but this tradition surely must have come from an Asiatic source, for the similarities are too close to be coincidental. Quite probably the people of the Paleo-northern tradition were later comers who arrived after the other early groups had moved farther south.

To continue in the realm of conjecture, we may consider the physical types of the first Americans. Due to the extreme rarity of physical remains thought to possess some degree of antiquity, there is little to be learned from early skeletal remains. Physical anthropologists have been forced to pursue various lines of evidence in attempting to construct theories pertaining to the earliest inhabitants and the development of later American Indian types. As is often the case when data are very scanty, there are almost as many theories as there are anthropologists concerned with the subject. On two points, however, there is some general agreement. Anthropologists feel that the absence of any higher anthropoids and of sub-human forms precludes the possibility that man originated in the New World. They agree that most American Indians are basically Mongoloid in appearance, although certain features that are not characteristically Mongoloid are present and are more commonly found in some regions than in others.

There can be no question that there are marked physical differences between various Indian groups, particularly as regards head shape, facial features, and body build. Although these were recognized by the late Ales Hrdlicka (1923, 1937a), he remained a firm believer in the unity of the American Indian race, and he was convinced that Mongoloid physical characters were fundamental in all groups. He believed that variations did not indicate any non-Mongoloid increment but were due to environmental or genetic factors. This opinion was shared by Clark Wissler.

Many anthropologists are convinced that, although American aborigines must be placed in the general Mongoloid division of mankind, they represent a composite race. Some, notably Roland B. Dixon (1923), sought to explain the mixture of various racial elements by postulating a series of separate migrations, each of an essentially pure race, followed by a later period in the New World when races became mixed. Others are of the opinion that a great deal of racial mixing had occurred in Asia before the first people came to America.

The late Earnest A. Hooton (1946) stated that present-day Indians have a generally Mongoloid appearance, particularly as regards hair form, skin color, and structure of cheek bones; but he noted that, as one goes farther south from the Eskimo area, Mongoloid features become attenuated until they reach their lowest point of development in the jungles of South America. Since there is a general belief that the types most closely resembling the first to come into a country will be found in peripheral areas farthest from the original point of entry, he did not think that the earliest people could have been predominantly Mongoloid. In his opinion there had already been much race mixture in Asia, and various racial elements, possibly including a Negroid strain, were present in the early population of the New World and were carried "in solution." Later groups introduced additional Mongoloid elements which served to obscure the presence of other racial strains.

William W. Howells (1940) believes that when man first came to America there existed in eastern Asia an only slightly specialized population in which Mongoloid and possibly certain Caucasian forms were simply incipient. In both Asia and America, as time went by, evolutionary processes continued and specialization increased. In Howells' opinion, later influences may have reached America from Asia after certain Asiatic types had become more highly specialized; but he believes that definite Mongoloid elements were already present in the basic American population and may have become more fully developed here.

Another hypothesis has been presented by Joseph Birdsell (1951), who has sought to redefine the problem and to try new methods of analysis. He has tried to determine which racial elements were present in Asia when the first movements into America occurred, and, instead of concentrating exclusively on American data, he has utilized data that he has obtained in Australasia. Birdsell is in agreement with Carlton Coon, who believes that originally only the eastern branch of the Caucasoid race, which is called the Amurian, was represented in northeastern Asia. Late in the fourth glacial period, in response to stringent environmental factors, the Mongoloid race developed there from the archaic Caucasoid stock and evolved with great rapidity (Coon, Garn, and Birdsell, 1950). There were then two racial groups in the area. Birdsell regards the American Indian as a hybrid, produced by a combination of Amurian and Mongoloid strains, in which Mongoloid features came to predominate and mask the presence of the Caucasoid element. If man reached the New World before the Mongoloid type developed, only the Caucasoid strain would have been represented. At a later date people moving into America would have had a Mongoloid component. Still later migrants might be expected to have had an even more pronounced Mongoloid strain. Among living Indians in North America the Cahuilla tribes of inland southern California, and the Pomo and Yuki of northern coastal California, are thought to show the greatest number of Amurian traits. Perhaps, if enough early skeletons are ever discovered, we shall find that there were physical as well as technological and economic differences between the Paleo-Indians who lived on the eastern side of the Rocky Mountains and those who lived to the west.

Studies of blood groups are still in their infancy, but they may eventually throw some light on problems pertaining to the peopling of the New World. The absence, or extreme rarity, of Blood Group B among pure-blooded American Indians is of particular interest (Boyd, 1950). It seems unlikely that the mutation which produced Blood Group B is a relatively recent one, which took place after America was populated, for this group is found among other primates. Also, it is extremely common in Asia. For it to have reached its present development there in a very short time would have required what appears to be an impossibly rapid rate of mutation. Blood Group B, though originally present in the American Indian population, could have been lost because it was not a favorable factor, and those who possessed it did not survive. There is no evidence, however, that blood groups have a selective value, and the fact that B is increasing in Asia and Europe makes it appear unlikely that it is an unfavorable factor. If this group was rare in the population, it could have been lost by chance either in America or in that part of Asia from which the ancestors of the American Indian came. If such loss occurred, however, assuming that selective factors are not involved, the absence or rarity of Group B may have some bearing on the question of how many different population movements from Asia to America produced the American Indian population. The larger the number of such movements, the greater would be the probability that this blood group would be introduced, and the possibility that it would be lost by chance would be correspondingly reduced. It is interesting to note that Blood Group B is found among the Eskimo, who probably stem largely from a different population source in Asia.

It must sometimes appear to the reader that the Paleo-Indians simply float in time with no connections with the Indians of later periods. Until far more knowledge is available, we cannot trace the connections with any degree of accuracy; but people must have ancestors and, in the normal course of events, they have descendants. The way of life of many groups in the Great Basin and in California, even in historic times, is strongly reminiscent of that of the Paleo-Indians who occupied the area. Many archaeologists are now convinced that a relationship can be shown between the Southwestern cultures of the Christian Era and the "Desert Culture" that goes far back in time (Jennings, Editor, 1956). The Cochise Culture is thought to have been ancestral to the Mogollon and probably the Hohokam. The Basketmaker Culture, too, was probably derived from a manifestation of the Paleo-western (Desert Culture) tradition. Important changes occurred when southern traits, notably pottery and agriculture, were acquired by these groups. There are also questions about the ancestors of the people to the south who first domesticated corn and made pottery. Perhaps they, too, came from this common base at an earlier period.

Corn is thought by many botanists to have been first domesticated in Mexico or South America. Much time must have elapsed before it was grown as far north as New Mexico, and the early dates from Bat Cave serve to indicate that it was domesticated a long time ago. If people in whose economy the gathering of plant foods was important moved into the southern portion of the hemisphere at an early period, it is not so difficult to explain the first domestication of plants and the development of agriculture in the New World. It seems much more logical that it should be people who were already dependent on plant life who should become the first agriculturists, rather than that hunters, chiefly concerned with animal life, should make so radical a change. People who emphasized hunting in their economy, however, were also present in Mexico and South America at an early period.

We also wonder about the Indians who lived in the area that now comprises the United States east of the Rocky Mountains. Doubtless, descendants of the early hunters who made fluted points continued to live there, but in cultures of the Archaic Stage we see dependence on gathering, a use of stemmed and notched points, percussion flaking, and the addition of grinding and polishing techniques. The similarities between the Archaic Cultures of the east and the Desert Cultures of the west are such that it seems certain that there was some connection, but the nature of the relationship is by no means clear. Perhaps, there were influences from the west and the Archaic shows the results of the hybridizing of two traditions that have here been called Paleo-eastern and Paleo-western. Perhaps, some of the traits that the two held in common were as early or earlier in the east. We need many more dates from both areas.

The Archaic doubtless provided the base for the later cultural developments in the east, but there were important differences between this stage and the succeeding Woodland Stage. Did some of the traits which characterize the latter, such as cord-marked pottery and the building of mounds over the dead, have an Asiatic source? They probably did, but we do not know how they were transmitted. There must also have been some influences from the south and some southern traits, including agriculture, became part of the eastern patterns. Again, we do not know exactly how this was accomplished, but the fact that the earlier people had augmented their diet by the gathering of wild foods probably led to a readier acceptance of agriculture. As time went on, there was increased specialization in different areas and the cultures of various groups became increasingly divergent.

There seems to be a definite connection between the Paleo-northern tradition, which was derived from Eurasia, and the later Eskimo pattern of culture (Collins, 1954, 1956). Burins, the small spalls struck from them, microblades, and small side and end blades used on slotted bone points, which are major elements in the Denbigh assemblage, are present in many prehistoric Eskimo sites. Studies in the fields of physical anthropology, linguistics, and ethnology have also suggested that the Eskimo are more closely related to Old World groups than to the American Indian, and that their culture is more Asiatic than American in character.* It is interesting to note that there is a percentage of the Eskimo population that possesses Blood Group B, which is common in Asia but apparently lacking in the American Indian population.

In the whole field of the study of Early Man in North America we have made a bare beginning, and an immense amount of work remains to be done. More evidence must be uncovered, and new techniques must be developed, before we may reach even a partial solution of the multitude of problems which we still face. We must arrive at more accurate dates and learn the time at which certain climatic conditions prevailed; and the period in which certain animals became extinct must be ascertained. Sensitive index fossils are badly needed. We must learn a great deal more of the archaeology and geology of Asia and the northern portion of this continent. The relationship between ancient complexes, those already known, and those still to be discovered, and the relationship between these and more recent cultures must be established through stratigraphic and distributional studies. More authentic finds of human skeletal remains, whose age may be ascertained, must be made so that we may know something of the physical appearance of the early people and their racial affinities.

It will be many years before even a portion of these problems may be solved, but new finds are constantly being made and new techniques being perfected, not only in archaeology, but in other fields. Archaeology is not and never can be entirely independent, but must rely upon other sciences. Probably one of the most important factors in the ultimate solution of many of the problems linked with the study of ancient man will be the recognition of this dependence and an increasing cooperation of geologists, palaeontologists, botanists, physicists, and other scientists, with the archaeologist.

To the casual observer the growing list of unanswered questions regarding the ancient inhabitants of North America may seem appalling; actually it should be regarded as encouraging. With a new subject the tendency is to oversimplify through lack of knowledge. Only with increased knowledge comes the realization of the complexity of

---

*However, as has been noted in a footnote on page 152, the suggestion has been made that the Old Copper and related Indian cultures are representatives of an ancient boreal forest culture which contributed to the development of Eskimo Culture.

the problem, for with each solution which is reached new fields are opened and new perplexities arise. To find an answer, one must first have sufficient knowledge to formulate the question.

Illustrations and Definitions

of

Certain Key Projectile Point

and Knife Types

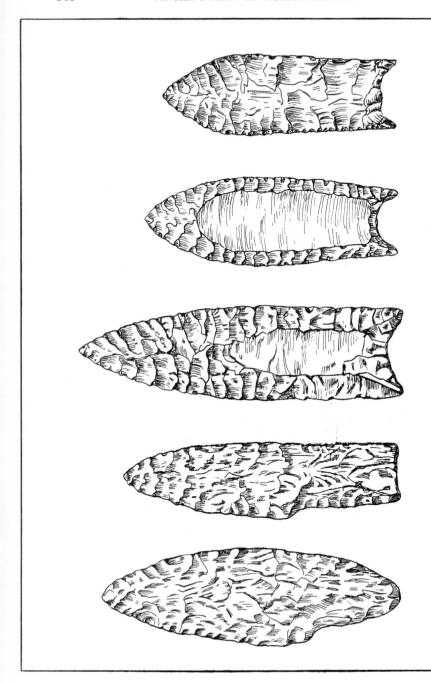

FIG. 68—Sandia points, Types I and II, Clovis point, Folsom point, Midland point.

DEFINITIONS OF CERTAIN KEY PROJECTILE POINT AND KNIFE TYPES

Sandia Points: (Fig. 68, Nos. 1 and 2)

Lanceolate points characterized by an inset on one side which produces a single shoulder. They range in length from two to four inches with an average of about three inches. Some are rather crudely flaked. Two sub-types were recognized in Sandia Cave. Type 1 was rounded in outline (Fig. 68, No. 1). Type 2 had sides that were more nearly parallel and the base was straight or slightly concave (Fig. 68, No. 2). At the Lucy Site specimens were found that resembled Type 2 in general outline, but they had more deeply concave bases and were fluted (Fig. 30, Nos. 4 and 5, page 88). For a further discussion of Sandia points see pages 85 to 91.

Clovis Points: (Fig. 68, No. 3)

Fluted lanceolate points with parallel or slightly convex sides and concave bases. They range in length from one and a half to five inches, but are usually some three inches or more in length and fairly heavy. The flutes sometimes extend almost the full length of the point but usually they extend no more than half way from the base to the tip. Normally, one face will have a longer flute than the other. The fluting was generally produced by the removal of multiple flakes. In most instances the edges of the basal portion show evidence of smoothing by grinding. Certain fluted points found in the eastern United States resemble the Clovis type, but they have a constriction at the base which produces a fish-tailed effect (Fig. 29, No. 3, page 82). These have sometimes been called Ohio points or Cumberland points. Many of these specimens tend to be somewhat narrower relative to their length than other fluted forms. For a further discussion of Clovis points see pages 43 to 59.

Folsom Points: (Fig. 68, No. 4)

A more specialized type, of excellent workmanship, thought to be derived from the Clovis type. There is some overlap in size between Clovis and Folsom points, but the latter are lighter and usually smaller. They range in length from three quarters of an inch to three inches with an average of about two inches. They are lanceolate in outline and have concave bases usually marked by ear-like projections. There is frequently a small central nipple in the basal concavity. The points were fluted through the removal of longitudinal flakes. The flutes usually extend over most of the length of the point. In most cases one major channel flake was removed from each face but sometimes only one face was fluted. Most specimens have a fine marginal retouch. The lower edges usually bear evidence of grinding. For a further discussion of Folsom points see pages 23 to 41.

Midland Points: (Fig. 68, No. 5)

Points which were originally called "Unfluted Folsoms" because they closely resemble classic Folsoms as regards shape, size, and general method of flaking, but are very thin and unfluted. Some resemblances to Plainviews are also apparent, but, in general, these specimens are smaller, thinner, flatter, and narrower. For a further discussion of Midland points see page 41 and pages 241 to 246.

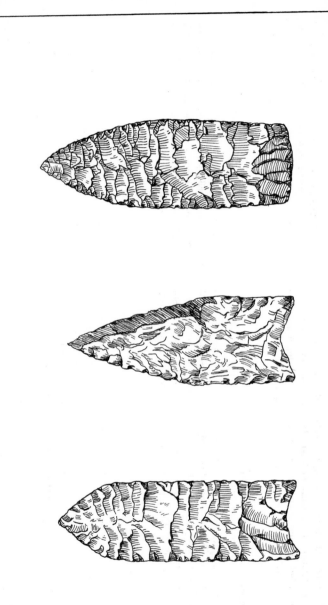

FIG. 69—Plainview point, Meserve point, Milnesand point.

Plainview Points: (Fig. 69, No. 1)

Lanceolate points with parallel or slightly convex sides and concave bases. Essentially the shape is the same as that of the Clovis, but these points are unfluted. They range in length from one and three quarters to three inches. Flaking is sometimes parallel, particularly at the distal end, but is more often irregular. Basal edges are almost always ground and there is usually some thinning of the base accomplished by the removal of small vertical flakes. For a further discussion of Plainview points see pages 107 to 111.

Meserve Points: (Fig. 69, No. 2)

Points with sides essentially parallel for approximately a third of the length and with steeple-shaped upper portions which are unifacially bevelled, usually to the right. The lower portion, which is ground along the edges, is usually three quarters to one and three quarters inches long. There is some variation in the length of the pointed upper portion. Most specimens are between two and three inches long. Some points give the impression of being reworked Plainviews. Similarly shaped points with serrated upper portions found in Missouri have been called Dalton points. For a further discussion of Meserve or Dalton points see page 113.

Milnesand Points: (Fig. 69, No. 3)

Points which resemble Plainviews but that have straight or very slightly convex or concave bases. More and smaller flakes were removed in thinning the base, resulting in a bevelled appearance. Basal grinding goes farther up the sides than on most Plainviews, often extending more than half the length of the point. Flaking is of the transverse parallel type, but some specimens have fairly pronounced median ridges. The general range in length is between one and a half and three inches. Most points are between two and three inches long. For a further discussion of Milnesand points see pages 111 to 112.

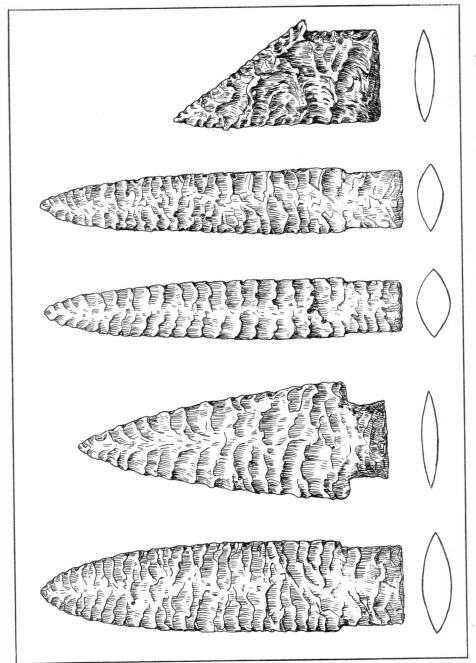

FIG. 70—Artifacts of the Cody Complex. Scottsbluff Type I, Scottsbluff Type II, Eden with collateral flaking, Eden with transverse flaking, Cody Knife.

Artifacts of the Cody Complex

Scottsbluff Points: (Fig. 70, Nos. 1 and 2)

Type I—Points with somewhat triangular or parallel-sided blades, small shoulders and broad stems. The flaking is usually of the transverse parallel type, but it may be more irregular. The cross-section is a thick oval. The stem edges are usually ground. The range in length is from two to five inches. Most specimens are between three and four inches long and about one inch wide. Many of those that are less than three inches long compare with the longer specimens in breadth and may represent points that were reworked after the tips had been broken. (Fig. 70, No.1).

Type II—Points that Resemble Type I but that have wider triangular blades, are thin and lenticular in cross-section, and have more clearly defined shoulders. (Fig 70, No. 2). For a further discussion of Scottsbluff points see pages 118 to 123 and pages 136-137.

Eden Points: (Fig. 70, Nos. 3 and 4)

Points that resemble the Scottsbluff types, but which are narrower relative to their length. The insets that produce the stems are very slight; in some cases the apparent stemming may be only the result of pronounced basal grinding. Most Eden points are characterized by collateral flaking and have pronounced median ridges and a diamond-shaped cross-section. (Fig. 70, No. 3). In rare cases the flaking is of the transverse parallel type and the median ridges are less clearly marked. (Fig. 70, No. 4). Those found in the Plains area of the United States are usually three to four and a half inches long and one half to three quarters of an inch wide. Eden points of similar size occur in the Prairie Provinces of western Canada, but some specimens have been found there that are as little as two inches long and five sixteenths of an inch wide. For a further discussion of Eden points see pages 124 to 135 and pages 136-137.

Cody Knives: (Fig. 70, No. 5)

Knives with transverse blades that are usually shouldered on one side, but are sometimes characterized by a parallel-sided base without an inset. There is virtually no published information on this type and it is difficult even to estimate the size range, but most of the specimens seen by the writer have been two to three inches long. For a further discussion of Cody knives see pages 128 and 129.

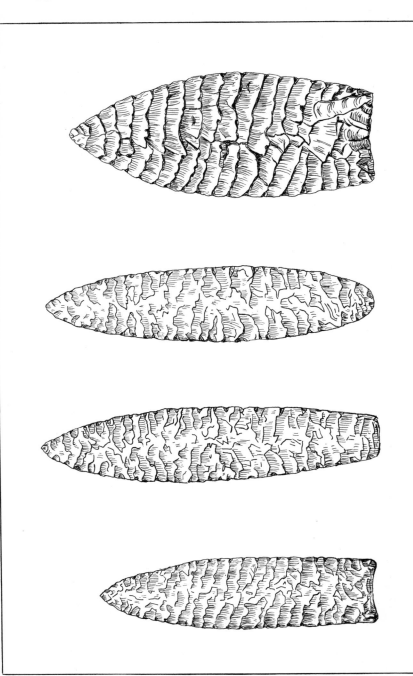

FIG. 71—Angostura point, Agate Basin points, Browns Valley point.

Angostura Points: (Fig. 71, No. 1)

Slender lanceolate points, the symmetrical sides of which incurve to the tip and taper to the narrow base forward from the base about two-fifths to one half of the total distance from base to tip. The base is either shallowly concave or irregularly straight. Normally each face bears parallel ripple flake scars running obliquely from upper left to lower right. The ripple flake scars are usually of approximately equal length and the cross-section is lenticular, but in some instances the presence of flake scars of unequal length has produced one or two longitudinal ridges and some specimens are asymmetrical or trapezoidal in cross-section. In a few cases the flake scars are horizontal. Points range in length from two and a half to three and a quarter inches. The bases were thinned by the removal of small longitudinal flakes. The lower portion of the lateral edges, but not the basal edge, were smoothed by grinding. (Condensed from "Description of the Angostura Point Type" in "Archaeological Remains in the Angostura Reservoir Area, South Dakota, and in the Keyhole and Boysen Reservoir Areas, Wyoming", by Richard Page Wheeler, Manuscript, 1957). For a further discussion of Angostura points see pages 138 to 141.

Agate Basin Points: (Fig. 71, Nos. 2 and 3)

Long slender points with sides slightly convex or almost parallel. The maximum breadth of specimens with curved sides is usually above the mid-point. Bases are straight (Fig. 71, No. 2), or convex. In some instances the bases are almost as pointed as the tips (Fig. 71, No. 3). Flaking is usually of the horizontal parallel variety, and there is a fine marginal retouch and pronounced grinding of the lower lateral edges; the base is rarely ground. There is a considerable variation in size with a range of between two and a half and six inches. For a further discussion of Agate Basin points see page 141.

Browns Valley Points: (Fig. 71, No. 4)

Thin, broad, lanceolate points that are widest at the mid-section. The bases are slightly concave. Flaking is of the oblique parallel variety. The basal edges were ground. There is little information regarding the dimensions of this type for few specimens have been reported. The type specimens from the Browns Valley site were three and a half inches long and one and a half inches wide. For a further discussion of Browns Valley points and a similar type see pages 143 to 146.

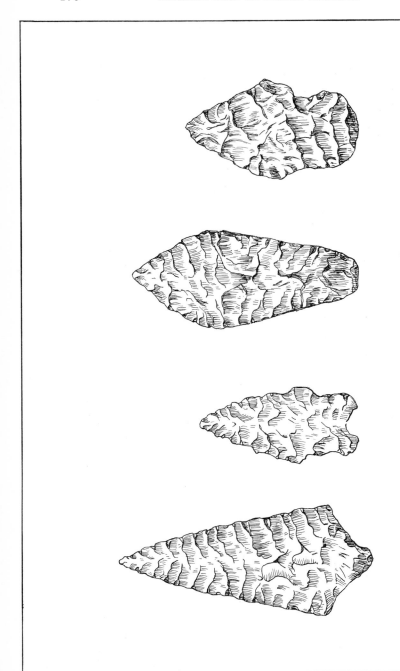

FIG. 72—Gypsum Cave point, Pinto Basin point, Lake Mohave point, Silver Lake point.

Gypsum Cave Points: (Fig. 72, No. 1)

Lozenge or diamond-shaped points with small stems that slope abruptly back from the shoulders to a rounded end forming the butt. They are usually about two to two and a half inches long. These are sometimes called simply Gypsum points. For a further discussion of Gypsum Cave points see pages 157 to 160.

Pinto Basin Points: (Fig. 72, No. 2)

Thick, rather short points, slightly shouldered, with bifurcated bases. Blade edges are often serrated and sometimes there are some side nocks below the shoulders. Many are crudely flaked and some were probably produced by percussion. An effort was made to thin some of the bases. The points range in length from one to two and a half inches; most specimens are about one and a half inches long. These are sometimes called simply Pinto points. For a further discussion of Pinto Basin points see pages 165 to 169 and page 180.

Lake Mohave Points: (Fig. 72, No. 3)

Points characterized by long, slender stems, produced by a very slight shouldering. The blade portion is usually somewhat smaller than the stem portion, and the maximum breadth is generally slightly above the mid-point. The base is rounded. Some specimens appear to have been flaked by percussion, others have a pressure retouch. Points range in length from one and three quarters to three inches. These are sometimes called simply Mohave points. For a further discussion of Lake Mohave points see pages 161 to 164.

Silver Lake Points: (Fig. 72, No. 4)

Points that resemble the Lake Mohave type but which have less basal taper and more clearly defined shoulders. The area of maximum breadth is somewhat lower. For a further discussion of Silver Lake points see pages 161 to 164.

GLOSSARY

Altithermal—A term applied by Ernst Antevs (1948) to the second temperature age of the Neothermal; a period distinctly warmer than the present, dated at about 7,000 to 4,000 years ago. In the western United States, where it is sometimes called the Long Drought, there was a pronounced increase in aridity as well as warmth. The term Climatic Optimum is sometimes applied to the correlative warm period in Europe. This period has also been referred to as the Thermal Maximum.

Anathermal—A term applied by Ernst Antevs (1948) to the first temperature age of the Neothermal; a cool period that became progressively warmer, which is dated at about 9,000 to 7,000 years ago. In the Great Basin and the Southwest there appears to have been more moisture than at present during most of this period. According to Antev's calculations, the Anathermal is of post-Cochrane age. Many other geologists would now place the Cochrane substage in this time span.

Archaic—As used in this publication in connection with discoveries in the eastern United States, the term is applied to the pre-agricultural, pre-ceramic stage which preceded the Early Woodland in the developmental sequence. The eastern Archaic was characterized by a marked dependence on food gathering as well as on hunting. Most projectile points were large notched or stemmed forms. Some of the complexes assigned to this stage contain polished stone tools, but others do not. For a discussion of the way in which the term is used by various writers, see page 4. The early pottery producing cultures of Mexico are sometimes also designated as Archaic.

Articulated—Two or more bones are said to be articulated when they are held in position by the ligaments or when they are found in a deposit lying in the same position they held before the decay of the connective tissues.

Artifact—A product of human workmanship. Commonly used by archaeologists in speaking of prehistoric tools, implements, etc.

Aspect—A unit of the McKern (1939) classification. A group of foci that share a preponderance of traits. See also Phase.

Atlatl—An Aztec word meaning spear-thrower. Atlatls are throwing sticks which have a handle on one end and on the other a spur which fits into a pit or cup drilled into the basal end of a dart shaft. When the dart is thrown the atlatl remains in the hand. The benefit of this device over the use of the spear or javelin alone is that the atlatl gives more leverage and speed in casting by adding length to the user's arm.

Basal Grinding—The smoothing of the butt edges of stone points to prevent cutting of the binding used in hafting.

Basal Thinning—The removal of small longitudinal flakes from the basal edge of stone artifacts.

Blade—The unhafted portion of a stemmed projectile point or knife. This term is also used by many American archaeologists to refer to thin bifacially flaked cutting or scraping tools. In this book it is used in the sense employed by Old World archaeologists to designate thin, narrow prismatic flakes with essentially parallel sides that were struck from specially prepared cores. Small specimens are called microblades. These have sometimes been called lamellar flakes by American archaeologists, but it is now generally conceded that this is an undesirable term.

Blank—A roughly shaped stone artifact, still in the process of manufacture, which has been blocked out to the approximate shape and thickness desired for a completed tool.

Blowout—A section of land which has been denuded of top soil and scoured into a more or less bowl-shaped depression by wind action.

Breccia—A rock consisting of angular fragments of older rocks held together by a matrix of natural cement.

Burin—A tool made from a flake from which sliver-like spalls were struck at one end to form a cutting edge. Burins are thought to have been used to form deep grooves in bone, antler, and ivory, in preparation for splitting.

Calcium Carbonate—A chemical combination of calcium, carbon, and oxygen. The substance of limestone; also a common hardening and cementing agent in other types of deposits.

Caliche—A crust, or succession of crusts, of calcium carbonate that forms within or on top of the soil of arid or semi-arid regions.

Ceramic—Pertaining to pottery and its materials.

Channel Flake—A long spall removed longitudinally from the face of a point to form a grove.

Chronology—The study of the method of arranging past events or the material representing them in a sequence of their happenings in relation to years or in relation to each other.

Collateral Flaking—Produced by the removal of broad conchoidal spalls which begin at either edge and extend to the mid-section where they meet and form a dorsal ridge. The flakes, which lie at right angles to the long axis of the point, are parallel to each other.

Complex—A group of related traits or characteristics that combine to form a complete activity, process, or cultural unit. Lithic complexes are identified by the presence of several key implement or tool types in association. In some cases the elements that constitute what is called a complex in this publication would be the elements that constitute a focus as defined below (phase in the terminology of some archaeologists), but in many instances the scantiness of available data makes it seem unwarranted to use this more specific term.

Component—A site or a level within a site that represents one manifestation of a geographically and chronologically limited cultural unit known as a focus (phase in the terminology of some archaeologists).

Conchoidal—Having elevations or depressions in form like one-half of a bivalve shell; applied principally to a surface produced by fracture in homogenous substances such as glass or finely granular substances such as flint.

Core—A stone from which flakes have been struck; a nucleus. Artifacts made from cores are called core tools.

Correlate—In geological work, to determine the relationships of strata which are not continuous, or not known to be continuous, although possibly of the same age. To establish connecting links between related cultures of different areas or between cultural and geological events are among the many correlation problems of archaeology.

Cross-bedding—Individual layers of a deposit which lie at an angle to the planes of deposition of the principal beds.

Deposit—Any natural accumulation of rock material laid down by wind, water, ice, snow, volcanic action, or by any other agency.

Dendrochronology—A system of establishing an absolute count of years by utilizing the pattern combinations of tree-rings, invented by Dr. A. E. Douglass.

Diatom—A kind of algae with a siliceous skeleton, microscopic in size. Diatoms are helpful in indicating climatic conditions and in aiding to date geologically strata in which they occur.

Diffusion—The transference of elements of culture from one society to another.

Disconformity—A disconformity is said to exist between two beds when the lower has been eroded before the deposition of the upper.

Dolichocephalic or Dolichocranic—Terms applied to heads or skulls narrow relative to their length.

Eolian—Made by wind; a term applied to deposits of blown sand or silt.

Erosion—Gradual wearing away or destruction by weathering or water action.

Fauna—The animal life belonging to any specific geological period, formation, or region.

Flake—A spall removed from a larger stone by percussion or by pressure. Artifacts made from flakes are called flake tools.

Flora—The plant life belonging to any specific geological period, formation, or region.

Fluted—Grooved or channeled.

Focus—A group of components that are characterized by similar traits. The trait lists need not be identical, but they must be sufficiently similar to make it possible to differentiate between earlier and later foci or contemporary foci from other areas. There may be great variation in the time and space dimensions of different foci. It is assumed that a focus will be manifested in more than one component, but it may be defined initially on the basis of a single component. See also Phase.

Graver—A small sharp-pointed implement used for engraving, incising, or marking stone, bone, antler, or ivory.

Great Basin—An area of internal drainage comprising Nevada, eastern California, southeastern Oregon, and western Utah.

Ground Stone Tools—Tools smoothed by usage.

Hematite—A red oxide of iron often used by primitive people as a pigment. When soft called red ochre.

Horizon—In a site, a level or stratum. In a culture, a particular level of development.

In situ—Term applied to an object found in its natural position or place in the rock or earth in which it was first placed or formed.

Intrusive—Term applied to an object found in a stratum in which it was not originally formed or deposited.

Lacustrine—Of or pertaining to, growing in, or deposited in lakes or inland seas.

Lamellar Flake—See Blade.

Laminations—lamina (singular) laminae (plural). Thin, flat, sedimentary beds or strata, usually of clay, fine sand, or shale.

Limonite—A brown oxide of iron often used by primitive people as a pigment. When soft, called yellow ochre.

Lithic—Of or pertaining to stone; or an adjective suffix denoting pertaining to or characteristic of a specific stage in the use of stone, as Palaeolithic or Neolithic.

Loess—A yellowish fine-grained, slightly calcareous, loamy clay believed to be a deposit of wind-blown dust.

Malar—The cheekbone or zygomatic bone.

Mano—A handstone used for grinding. Some writers use this name only for stones used with a backward and forward motion for grinding grains on a metate, others apply it to all handstones including those which are used with milling stones and which may be employed to grind seeds, paints, etc.

Medithermal—The term applied by Ernst Antevs (1948) to the third temperature age of the Neothermal that began some 4,000 years ago and which is still in progress. It is characterized by moderate temperatures. In the western United States the beginning of the period was also marked by an increase in moisture.

Mesolithic—Pertaining to the Middle Stone Age in the Old World; a period between the Palaeolithic and the Neolithic. Microliths were a characteristic form.

Metate—Commonly used to refer to a grinding stone with a more or less trough-shaped depression resulting from the use of a mano with a backward and forward motion. These were usually used to grind corn. See also Milling Stone.

Microblades—See Blades.

Microliths—Very small stone tools formed from small prismatic flakes. They occur in geometric forms, triangles, trapezoids, etc. Few of them could be used without hafting. They were often set in rows in slots cut in wood, bone, or antler implements.

Midden—A refuse deposit.

Milling Stone—A stone slab on which a mano was rubbed with a rotary motion, producing a shallow bowl-shaped depression. Used primarily in the crushing and grinding of wild plant foods.

Mongoloid—One of the major racial divisions of mankind. In general, individuals belonging to this group are characterized by the possession of narrow, obliquely directed eyelid openings, yellow to yellowish brown skin, straight, coarse, black head hair, sparse body hair, broad faces, very low nasal roots and bridges. The head form is normally round and low but it is variable. In the examination of skulls all these traits cannot be observed. The principal criteria are broadly flaring malars, low nasal root and bridge, broad low palate, shovel-shaped incisors, broad low heads. It is a combination of traits rather than any single feature which is of the most diagnostic value.

Moraine—An accumulation of earth, stones, etc., carried and finally deposited by a glacier.

Morphology—The science of structure or form. A morphologically modern type of skeleton is one which is modern in form.

Neolithic—Pertaining to the New Stone Age in the Old World. Generally characterized by the domestication of plants and animals and the use of polished stone implements and pottery.

Neothermal—A term applied by Ernst Antevs (1948) to a period beginning some 9,000 years ago which he divides into three main temperature ages, the Anathermal, Altithermal, and Medithermal.

Oblique Flaking—Similar to transverse flaking, but the flake scars are directed diagonally across the face of the specimen, usually from upper left to lower right.

Ochre—See *Hematite* and *Limonite.*

Palaeolithic—Pertaining to the Old Stone Age of the Old World which extended throughout the Pleistocene. The men of the Old Stone Age were primarily hunters and had no knowledge of agriculture, the domestication of animals, or the use of metals. They used tools and weapons of flaked stone and of bone. Percussion was the earliest stone flaking technique. It was later largely replaced by pressure flaking.

Patina—(Patination). In an archaeological sense, the surface or surface crust produced on an object by weathering.

Percussion Flaking—The technique of shaping a stone through removing flakes by blows struck with another stone or with a heavy bone or piece of wood.

Phase—A term used in different ways by various writers. Some (Phillips and Willey, 1953) use phase as an approximate equivalent of focus as defined above. For others (McKern, 1939) it is a more generalized term, and they group related foci into larger units, called aspects, and aspects with common traits into still larger units, called phases. Still others (Suhm and Krieger, 1955) use the word phase to refer to a slight change in culture which took place during the life span of a given focus. It is in the latter sense that it is used in this publication.

Playa—A shallow basin or dry lake bed, in an arid region, in which water collects after rains and stays until evaporated.

Planoconvex—Flat on one side, convex on the other.

Pluvial—Pertaining to or due to the action of rain; also used to designate periods of wetter climate in arid regions.

Polished Stone Tools—Artifacts that were intentionally smoothed through abrading and polishing.

Pressure Flaking—The technique of shaping a stone by pressing flakes from it by means of a pointed instrument, often made of bone or antler, which is forced against the edge of the stone.

Projectile Point—An arrow point, spear point, or dart point.

Retouch—A secondary removal of small flakes from a stone artifact for the purpose of sharpening or resharpening the edge.

Scraper—An artifact used for rasping or cleaning hides, bone, wood, etc. In archaeological references unless otherwise specified these are usually of stone. They are named by the position of their cutting edge, as end scraper, side scraper; or by their shape, turtle back (flat on bottom and rounded on top), snub-nosed or thumb scraper (thumb-shaped) and keel scraper (keel-shaped).

Serrated—Notched or toothed on the edge like a saw.

Shaman—An individual who is believed to derive power directly from the supernatural which he often uses for purposes of healing. He is sometimes called a medicine man.

Silt—Earthy material whose grains range in size between those of sand and clay.

Site—Any location that provides evidence of human occupation.

Stage—A level in a historical-developmental sequence. A given cultural stage may be reached at different times in different areas.

Stratification—The characteristic of being in layers or strata and the processes by which such material is deposited. A single layer is called a stratum, more than one, strata. When undisturbed the lowest stratum is the oldest since it was laid down first.

Terrace—A benchlike feature, bordering a stream valley, which is a remnant of a former valley floor now dissected by the stream. When terraces occur in series in a steplike formation the highest is the oldest.

Till—Unstratified glacial material deposited directly by the ice and consisting of clay, sand, gravel, and boulders in any proportion; also known as boulder clay.

Tradition—"A major large-scale space-time cultural continuity, defined in reference to persistent configurations in single technologies or total (archaeological) culture, occupying a relatively long interval of time and a quantitatively variable but environmentally significant space." (Phillips and Willey, 1953, p. 628). In general, the term has been used in this publication in a broader sense than can be justified in terms of this definition. With greater knowledge it will become increasingly apparent that significant variations exist in what have been loosely called here the Paleo-eastern, Paleo-western, and Paleo-northern traditions, and it will be recognized that many separate traditions, as defined above, are represented in each of these very generalized categories.

Trait—Any single element of culture.

Transverse Flaking—Horizontal parallel flaking produced by the removal of narrow flakes which begin at either edge and join so smoothly that they often give the impression of forming a single flake scar. The scars lie at right angles to the long axis of the specimen.

Typology—The study of any system of arrangement according to types.

Varves—Paired laminations consisting of a silty or sandy lower component and a clay upper component, formed in lakes fed by glacial water. Each varve is the result of one summer's melting and represents one year. Counting the varves makes it possible to determine the number of years required to deposit any one body of laminated beds.

Bibliography

Albritton, Claude C., and Kirk Bryan.
1939 Quaternary Stratigraphy in the Davis Mountains, Trans-Pecos, Texas. Bulletin Geological Society of America, vol. 50, pp. 1423-1474.

Allison, I. S.
1945 Pumice Beds at Summer Lake, Oregon. Bulletin Geological Society of America, vol. 56, pp. 789-808.
1952 Dating of Pluvial Lakes in the Great Basin. American Journal of Science, vol. 250, pp. 907-909. New Haven, Conn.

Allison, Vernon C.
1926 The Antiquity of the Deposits in Jacob's Cavern. Anthropological Papers American Museum of Natural History, vol XIX, pt. VI. New York.

Amsden, Charles Avery.
1935 The Pinto Basin Artifacts *in* The Pinto Basin Site. Southwest Museum Papers, no. 9, pp. 33-50. Los Angeles.
1937 The Lake Mohave Artifacts *in* The Archaeology of Pleistocene Lake Mohave: A Symposium. Southwest Museum Papers, no. 11, pp. 51-97. Los Angeles.

Antevs, Ernst.
1935a The Occurrence of Flints and Extinct Animals in Pluvial Deposits near Clovis, New Mexico, pt. II, Age of Clovis Lake Beds. Proceedings Philadelphia Academy of Natural Science, vol. LXXXVII, pp. 304-311.
1935b The Spread of Aboriginal Man to North America. The Geographical Review, vol. XXV, no. 2, April, pp. 302-309.
1937a The Age of "Minnesota Man." Carnegie Institute of Washington Yearbook, no. 36, pp. 335-338.
1937b Age of the Lake Mohave Culture *in* The Archaeology of Pleistocene Lake Mohave: A Symposium. Southwest Museum Papers, no. 11, pp. 45-49. Los Angeles.
1937c Climate and Early Man in North America. Early Man, J. B. Lippincott & Co., Philadelphia.
1945 Correlation of Wisconsin Glacial Maxima. American Journal of Science, vol. 293-A, Daly Volume, pp. 1-30.
1948 The Great Basin, with Emphasis on Glacial and post-Glacial Times: Climatic Changes and pre-White Man. University of Utah Bulletin, vol. 33, no. 20, pp. 168-191. Salt Lake City.
1949 Geology of the Clovis Sites. Appendix *in* Wormington, Ancient Man In North America, 3rd Edition.
1952 Climatic History and the Antiquity of Man in California. University of California Archaeological Survey Report, no. 16, pp. 23-29. Berkeley.
1953a Artifacts with Mammoth Remains, Naco, Arizona, II: Age of the Clovis Fluted Points with the Naco Mammoth. American Antiquity, vol. XIX, no. 1, pp. 15-18.
1953b Geochronology of the Deglacial and Neothermal Ages. Journal of Geology, vol. 61, no. 3, pp. 195-230.
1954a Geochronology of the Deglacial and Neothermal Ages: A Reply. Journal of Geology, vol. 62, no. 5, pp. 516-521. Chicago.
1954b Climate of New Mexico During the Last Glacio-Pluvial. Journal of Geology, vol. 62, no. 2, pp. 182-191. Chicago.
1955a Geologic-climatic Dating in the West. American Antiquity, vol. XX, no. 4, pp. 317-335.
1955b Geologic-climatic Method of Dating *in* Geochronology, Terah L. Smiley, Editor. Physical Science Bulletin, no. 2, pp. 151-169. University of Arizona Press, Tucson.

1957   Geological Tests of the Varve and Radiocarbon Chronologies. The Journal of Geology, vol. 65, no. 2, pp. 129-148.

Arellano, A. R. V.
1946   Datos Geologicos sobre la Antiquidad del Hombre en la Cuenca de Mexico. Memorio del Segundo Congresso Mexicano de Ciencias Sociales, vol. 5, pp. 213-219. Mexico, D. F.
1951a   Some New Aspects of the Tepexpan Man Case. Bulletin Texas Archeological and Paleontological Society, vol. 22, pp. 217-224. Lubbock.
1951b   The Becerra Formation (Latest Pleistocene) of Central Mexico. International Geological Congress, "Report of the Eighteenth Session, Great Britain, 1948," pt. XI.

Arnold, James R.
1954   Scintillation Counting of Natural Radiocarbon: I—The Counting Method. Science, vol. 119, no. 3083, pp. 155-157.

Aschmann, Homer.
1952   A Fluted Point from Baja, California. American Antiquity, vol. XVII, no. 3, p. 262.
1954   Report on the Los Angeles Symposium on Early Man. American Antiquity, vol. XIX, no. 4, pp. 417-418.
1955   Comment on Quimby's "Cultural and Natural Areas Before Kroeber." American Antiquity, vol. XX, no. 4, pp. 377-378.

Aveleyra-Arroyo de Anda, Luis.
1950   Prehistoria de Mexico. Ediciones Mexicanas, Mexico, D.F.
1955   El Segundo Mamut Fosil de Santa Isabel Iztapan, Mexico, y Artefactos Asociados. Instituto Nacional de Antropologia e Historia, Mexico, D.F.
1956   The Second Mammoth and Associated Artifacts at Santa Isabel Iztapan, Mexico. American Antiquity, vol. XXII, no. 1, pp. 12-28.

Aveleyra-Arroyo de Anda, Luis, and Manuel Maldonado-Koerdell.
1952   Asociacion de Artefactos con Mamut en el Pleistoceno Superior de la Cuenca de Mexico. Revista Mexicana de Estudios Antropologicos, vol. 13, no. 1, pp. 3-29.
1953   Association of Artifacts with Mammoth in the Valley of Mexico. American Antiquity, vol. XVIII, no. 4, pp. 332-340.

Baggerly, Carmen.
1954   Waterworn and Glaciated Stone Tools from the Thumb District of Michigan. American Antiquity, vol. XX, no. 2, pp. 171-173.
1956   Artifacts from Drift of the Wisconsin Glaciation. New World Antiquity, vol. 3, no. 1, pp. 3-7. Markham House Press, London.

Barbour, E. H., and C. Bertrand Schultz.
1932   The Scottsbluff Bison Quarry and Its Artifacts. Bulletin 34, vol. 1, Nebraska State Museum, Lincoln.

Bartlett, Katharine.
1943   A Primitive Stone Industry of the Little Colorado Valley, Arizona. American Antiquity, vol. VIII, no. 3, pp. 266-268.

Beardsley, Richard K.
1948   Culture Sequences in Central California Archaeology. American Antiquity, vol. XIV, no. 1, pp. 1-28.

Bell, E. H., and M. Van Royen.
1934   An Evaluation of Recent Nebraska Finds Sometimes Attributed to the Pleistocene. Wisconsin Archaeologist, New Series, vol. 13, no. 3, pp. 49-70.

Bird, Junius.
1938   Antiquity and Migrations of the Early Inhabitants of Patagonia. Geological Review, vol. 28, pp. 250-275.
1951   South American Radiocarbon Dates *in* Radiocarbon Dating, Frederick Johnson, Editor, Memoirs of the Society for American Archaeology, American Antiquity, vol. XVII, no. 1, pt. 2.

Birdsell, Joseph B.
1951 The Problems of the Early Peopling of the Americas as Viewed from Asia *in* Papers of the Physical Anthropology of the American Indian. Wenner-Gren Foundation, New York.

Black, Glenn A.
1949 "Tepexpan Man," a Critique of Method. American Antiquity, vol. XIV, no. 4, pp. 344-346.

Bliss, Wesley L.
1939a An Archaeological and Geological Reconnaissance of Alberta, Mackenzie Valley, and Upper Yukon. Yearbook of the American Philosophical Society.
1939b Early Man in Western and Northwestern Canada. Science, vol. 89, pp. 365-366.

Bode, Francis D.
1937 Geology of Lake Mohave Outlet Channel *in* The Archaeology of Pleistocene Lake Mohave: A Symposium. Southwest Museum Papers, no. 11, pp. 109-118. Los Angeles.

Borbolla, Sol Arguedas R. de la, and Luis Aveleyra-Arroyo de Anda.
1953 A Plainview Point from Northern Tamaulipas. American Antiquity, vol. XVIII, no. 4, pp. 392-393.

Botelho, Eugene.
1955 Pinto Basin Points in Utah. American Antiquity, vol. XXI, no. 2, pp. 185-186.

Boyd, William C.
1949 The Blood Groups and Types *in* The Physical Anthropology of the American Indian, pp. 127-137. Wenner-Gren Foundation, New York.
1950 Genetics and the Races of Man. Little-Brown and Co., Boston.

Braidwood, Robert J.
1948 Prehistoric Man. Chicago Natural History Museum Popular Series, Anthropology, no. 37.

Brainerd, George W.
1952 On the Study of Early Man in Southern California. University of California Archaeological Survey Report, no. 16, Berkeley.
1953 A Re-examination of the Dating Evidence for the Lake Mohave Artifact Assemblage. American Antiquity, vol. XVIII, no. 3, pp. 270-271.

Broecker, W. S., and P. C. Orr.
1956 Late Wisconsin History of Lake Lahonton. Geological Society of America Bulletin U. 67, no. 12, pt. 2, pp. 1675-1676 (Abstract).

Browne, Jim.
1938 The Antiquity of the Bow. American Antiquity, vol. III, no. 4, p. 358.
1940 Projectile Points. American Antiquity, vol. V, no. 3, pp. 209-213.

Bryan, Kirk.
1937 Geology of the Folsom Deposits in New Mexico and Colorado. Early Man, J. B. Lippincott & Co., Philadelphia, pp. 139-152.
1938 Prehistoric Quarries and Implements of Pre-Amerindian Aspect in New Mexico. Science, New Series, vol. 87, no. 2259, April 15, pp. 343-346.
1939 Stone Cultures near Cerro Pedernal and Their Geological Antiquity. Bulletin Texas Archeological and Paleontological Society, vol. II, pp. 9-42.
1941 Correlation of the Deposits of Sandia Cave, New Mexico, with the Glacial Chronology: Evidences of Early Occupation in Sandia Cave, and other Sites in the Sandia-Manzano Region. Smithsonian Miscellaneous Collections, vol. 99, no. 23.
1950 Geological Interpretation of the Deposits *in* The Stratigraphy and Archaeology of Ventana Cave, Arizona, pp. 75-125. University of New Mexico Press, Albuquerque.

Bryan, Kirk, and Paul MacClintock.
1938   What is Implied by "Disturbance" at the Site of Minnesota Man. The Journal of Geology, vol. XLVI, no. 3, April-May, pp. 279-292.

Bryan, Kirk, and F. T. McCann.
1943   Sand Dunes and Alluvium near Grants, New Mexico. American Antiquity, vol. VIII, no. 3, pp. 281-290.

Bryan, Kirk, Henry Retzek, and Franklin T. McCann.
1938   Discovery of Sauk Valley Man of Minnesota, with an Account of the Geology. Bulletin Texas Archeological and Paleontological Society, vol. 10, pp. 112-135. Abilene.

Bryan, Kirk, and Louis L. Ray.
1940   Geologic Antiquity of the Lindenmeier Site in Colorado. Smithsonian Miscellaneous Collections, vol. 99, no. 2.

Bryan, Kirk, and Joseph H. Toulouse, Jr.
1943   The San Jose Non-Ceramic Culture and its Relation to Puebloan Culture in New Mexico. American Antiquity, vol. VIII, no. 3, pp. 269-280.

Bryan, W. A.
1929   The Recent Bone Cavern Find at Bishop's Cap, New Mexico. Science, New Series, vol. 70, no. 1802, July 12, pp. 39-41.

Burmaster, E. R.
1932   *In* Reports of Archaeological Field Work in North America during 1931. American Antiquity, vol. 34, p. 491.

Byers, Douglas S.
1954   Bull Brook—A Fluted Point Site in Ipswich, Massachusetts. American Antiquity, vol. XIX, no. 4, pp. 343-351.
1955   Additional Information on the Bull Brook Site, Massachusetts. American Antiquity, vol. XX, no. 3, pp. 274-276.
1956   Ipswich, B. C. Essex Institute Historical Collections, Essex, Massachusetts.

Campbell, Elizabeth W. Crozer.
1949   Two Ancient Archaeological Sites in the Great Basin. Science, 109:340.

Campbell, Elizabeth W. Crozer, and William H.
1935   The Pinto Basin Site. Southwest Museum Papers, no. 9. Los Angeles.
1937   The Lake Mohave Site *in* The Archaeology of Pleistocene Lake Mohave: A Symposium. Southwest Museum Papers, no. 11, pp. 9-43. Los Angeles.
1940   A Folsom Complex in The Great Basin. The Masterkey, vol. XIV, no. 1, pp. 7-11. Southwest Museum, Los Angeles.

Campbell, John Martin, and Florence Hawley Ellis.
1952   The Atrisco Sites: Cochise Manifestations in the Middle Rio Grande Valley. American Antiquity, vol. XVII, no. 3, pp. 211-221.

Campbell, Thomas N.
1948   The Merrell Site: Archaeological Remains Associated with Alluvial Terrace Deposits in Central Texas. Bulletin Texas Archeological and Paleontological Society, vol. 19, pp. 7-35.

Carter, George F.
1951   Man in America: A Criticism of Scientific Thought. The Scientific Monthly, vol. LXXIII, no. 5.
1952   Interglacial Artifacts from the San Diego Area. Southwestern Journal of Anthropology, vol. 8, no. 4, pp. 444-456. Albuquerque.
1954a   An Interglacial Site at San Diego, California. The Masterkey, vol. 28, no. 5, pp. 165-174. Southwest Museum, Los Angeles.
1954b   More Evidence for Interglacial Man in America. New World Antiquity, no. 8, pp. 1-4. London.
1955   Early Man in America. New World Antiquity, vol. 2, no. 1, pp. 8-9. Markham House Press, London.

Chapman, Carl H.
1950 Missouri Archaeology *in* Missouri, Its Resources, People, and Institutions, pp. 190-200. University of Missouri, Columbia.

Chard, Chester S.
1956 The Oldest Sites of Northeast Siberia. American Antiquity, vol. XXI, no. 4, pp. 405-409.

Clements, Lydia.
1954 A Preliminary Study of Some Pleistocene Cultures of the California Desert. The Masterkey, vol. 28, no. 5, pp. 177-185. Southwest Museum, Los Angeles.

Clements, Thomas, and Lydia Clements.
1953 Evidence of Pleistocene Man in Death Valley, California. Geological Society of America Bulletin, vol. 64, no. 10, pp. 1189-1204. Baltimore.

Coe, Joffre Lanning.
1952 The Cultural Sequence of the Carolina Piedmont *in* Archaeology of the Eastern United States, pp. 301-311. J. B. Griffin, Editor, University of Chicago Press.

Colbert, Edwin H.
1950 The Fossil Vertebrates *in* The Stratigraphy and Archaeology of Ventana Cave, Arizona, pp. 126-147. University of New Mexico Press, Albuquerque.

Collins, Henry B., Jr.
1943 Eskimo Archaeology and Its Bearing on the Problem of Man's Antiquity in America: Recent Advances in American Archaeology. Proceedings of the American Philosophical Society, vol. 86, no. 2, pp. 220-235. Philadelphia.
1951 The Origin and Antiquity of the Eskimo. Smithsonian Report for 1950, pp. 423-467. Smithsonian Institution, Washington, D. C.
1953 Radiocarbon Dating in the Arctic. American Antiquity, vol. XVIII, no. 3, pp. 197-203.
1954 Arctic Area. Program of the History of America, vol. I, no. 2. Publicaciones del Instituto Panamericano de Geografia e Historia, no. 160. Mexico, D. F.

Cook, Harold J.
1927 New Geological and Palaeontological Evidence Bearing on the Antiquity of Mankind in America. Natural History, vol. XXVII, no. 3, pp. 240-247.
1928 A New Fossil Bison from Texas. Proceedings Colorado Museum of Natural History, vol. VIII, no. 3.
1931 More Evidence of the "Folsom Culture" Race. Scientific American, vol. 144, no. 2, February, pp. 102-103. New York.

Cook, Sherbourne F., and Robert F. Heizer.
1953a The Present Status of Chemical Methods for Dating Prehistoric Bone. American Antiquity, vol. XVIII, no. 4, pp. 354-358.
1953b Archaeological Dating by Chemical Analysis of Bone. Southwestern Journal of Anthropology, vol. 9, no. 2, pp. 231-238. Albuquerque.

Coon, Carleton S., Stanley Garn, and Joseph B. Birdsell.
1950 A Study of Problems of Race Formation in Man. Charles Thomas Co., Springfield, Illinois.

Cotter, John Lambert.
1937a The Occurrence of Flints and Extinct Animals in Pluvial Deposits near Clovis, New Mexico, pt. IV, Report on the Excavations at the Gravel Pit in 1936. Proceedings Philadelphia Academy Natural Sciences, vol. 89, pp. 2-16.
1937b The Significance of Folsom and Yuma Artifact Occurrences in the Light of Typology and Distribution. Twenty-fifth Anniversary Studies, Philadelphia Anthropological Society, vol. 1, pp. 22-35.

1938   The Occurrence of Flints and Extinct Animals in Pluvial Deposits near Clovis, New Mexico, pt. VI, Report on Field Season of 1937. Proceedings Philadelphia Academy Natural Sciences, vol. 90, pp. 113-117.

1954   Indications of a Paleo-Indian Co-Tradition for North America. American Antiquity, vol. XX, no. 1, p. 67.

Crane, H. R.
1955   Antiquity of the Sandia Culture: Carbon 14 Measurements. Science, vol. 122, no. 3172.

1956   University of Michigan Radiocarbon Dates, I. Science, vol. 124, pp. 664-672.

Cressman, L. S.
1937   The Wikiup Damsite No. 1 Knives. American Antiquity, vol. III, no. 1, pp. 53-67.

1944   Reply to A. D. Krieger's Review of L. S. Cressman's Archaeological Researches in the Northern Great Basin. American Antiquity, vol. X, no. 2, pp. 206-211.

1947   Further Information on Projectile Points from Oregon. American Antiquity, vol. XIII, no. 2, pp. 177-179.

1948   Odell Lake Site: A New Paleo-Indian Campsite in Oregon. American Antiquity, vol. XIV, no. 1, pp. 57-58.

1950   Review of An Ancient Site at Borax Lake, California, by Mark R. Harrington. American Anthropology, vol. 52, no. 1, pp. 91-93.

1951   Western Prehistory in the Light of Carbon 14 Dating. Southwestern Journal of Anthropology, vol. 7, no. 3, pp. 289-313. Albuquerque.

1956   Klamath Prehistory. Appendices by William G. Haag and William S. Laughlin. Transactions American Philosophical Society, New Series, vol. 46, pt. 4. Philadelphia.

Cressman, L. S., Howell Williams, and Alex D. Krieger.
1940   Early Man in Oregon: Archaeological Studies in the Northern Great Basin. University of Oregon Monographs. Studies in Anthropology, no. 3.

Cressman, L. S., and W. S. Laughlin.
1941   A Probable Association of Mammoth and Artifacts in the Willamette Valley, Oregon. American Antiquity, vol. VI, no. 4, pp. 339-342.

Cressman, L. S., and Collaborators.
1942   Archaeological Researches in the Northern Great Basin: with Collaboration of Frank C. Baker, Henry P. Hansen, Paul S. Conger, Robert F. Heizer. Carnegie Institute of Washington, Publication 538. Washington, D. C.

Crook, Wilson W., Jr.
1955   Reconsideration and Geologic Revaluation of the Famous Abilene, Texas, Sites. Panhandle-Plains Historical Review, XXVIII, pp. 38-62.

Crook, W. W., Jr., and R. K. Harris.
1952   Trinity Aspect of the Archaic: The Carrollton and Elam Foci. Bulletin Texas Archeological and Paleontological Society, vol. 23, pp. 7-38.

Cruxent, J. M., and Irving Rouse.
1956   A Lithic Industry of Paleo-Indian Type in Venezuela. American Antiquity, vol. XXII, no. 2, pt. 2, pp. 172-179.

Daugherty, Richard D.
1956a Archaeology of the Lind Coulee Site, Washington. Proceedings of the American Philosophical Society, vol. 100, no. 3, pp. 223-278. Philadelphia.

1956b Early Man in the Columbia Intermontane Province. Anthropological Papers, University of Utah, vol. 24. Salt Lake City.

Davis, E. Mott.

1953 Recent Data from Two Paleo-Indian Sites on Medicine Creek, Nebraska. American Antiquity, vol. XVIII, no. 4, pp. 380-386.

1954 The Culture History of The Central Great Plains Prior to the Introduction of Pottery. Ph. D. Thesis, Harvard University.

Davis, E. M., and C. B. Schultz.

1952 The Archaeological and Paleontological Salvage Program at the Medicine Creek Reservoir, Frontier County, Nebraska. Science, vol. 115, no. 2985, pp. 288-290.

de Laguna, Frederica.

1946 The Importance of the Eskimo in Northeastern Archaeology *in* Man in Northeastern North America, Frederick Johnson, Editor, Robert S. Peabody Foundation for Archaeology, vol. 3, Phillips Academy, Andover, Massachusetts.

1947 The Prehistory of Northern North America as seen from the Yukon. Memoirs of the Society for American Archaeology, vol. XII, no. 3, pt. 2.

De Terra, Helmut.

1951 Radiocarbon Age Measurements and Fossil Man in Mexico. Science, vol. 113, no, 2927, pp. 124-125.

De Terra, Helmut, Javier Romero, and T. D. Stewart.

1949 Tepexpan Man. Viking Fund Publications in Anthropology, no. 11. New York.

Dick, Herbert W.

1952 Evidences of Early Man in Bat Cave and on the Plains of San Augustin, New Mexico *in* Indian Tribes of Aboriginal America, vol. III, Proceedings 29th International Congress of Americanists, pp. 158-163. University of Chicago Press.

Di Peso, Charles C.

1953 Clovis Fluted Points from Southeastern Arizona. American Antiquity, vol. XIX, no. 1, pp. 82-85.

1955 Two Cerro Guaymas Clovis Fluted Points from Sonora, Mexico. The Kiva, pp. 13-15. Arizona State Museum, Tucson.

Dixon, Keith A.

1953 A "Sandia" Point from Long Valley, Mono County, California. The Masterkey, vol. XXVII, no. 3, pp. 97-104. The Southwest Museum, Los Angeles.

Dixon, Roland B.

1923 The Racial History of Man. Charles Scribner's Sons, New York.

Driver, Harold E.

1953 Statistics in Anthropology. American Anthropology, vol. 55, no. 1, pp. 42-59.

Duff, Wilson, and Charles E. Borden.

1954 A Scottsbluff Eden Point from British Columbia. Anthropology in British Columbia, no. 4, pp. 33-34.

Dumberge, J. H., and J. E. Potzger.

1956 Late Wisconsin Chronology of the Lake Michigan Basin Correlated with Pollen Studies. Geological Society of America Bulletin, vol. 67, no. 3, pp. 271-280.

Eardley, A. J.

1956 Basin Expansions and Stability in Levels of Lake Bonneville. Geological Society of America Bulletin, vol. 67, no. 12, pt. 2, p. 1689 (Abstract).

Eiseley, Loren C.

1939 Pollen Analysis and its Bearing upon American Prehistory: A Critique. American Antiquity, vol. V, no. 2, pp. 115-139.

1946 Men, Mastodons and Myth. The Scientific Monthly, vol. LXII, pp. 517-524. Washington.

1947   The Fire and The Fauna. American Anthropology, vol. 49, no. 4, pt. I, pp. 678-680.
1954   Man the Fire Maker. Scientific American, vol. 191, no. 3, pp. 52-57.

Engerrand, Jorge.
1912   La Huella mas Antigua quiza del Hombre en la Peninsula de Yucatan. Reseña de la 2n Sesion del XVII Congreso Internacional de Americanistas, Mexico, D. F.

Ericson, D. B.
1956   Late Pleistocene Climates and Deep Sea Sediments. Science, vol. 124, pp. 385-389.

Evans, Glen L.
1950   Late Quaternary Faunal Succession in the Southern High Plains (Abstract). Geological Society of America Bulletin, vol. 61, no. 12, pt. 2, pp. 1457-1458.
1951   Prehistoric Wells in Eastern New Mexico. American Antiquity, vol. XVII, no. 1, pt. 1, pp. 1-8.

Ewing, Maurice, and William L. Donn.
1956   A Theory of Ice Ages. Science, vol. 123, no. 3207, pp. 1061-1066.

Figgins, Jesse Dade.
1927   The Antiquity of Man in America. Natural History, vol. XXVII, no. 3, pp. 229-239.
1931   An Additional Discovery of the Association of a "Folsom" Artifact and Fossil Mammal Remains. Proceedings, Colorado Museum of Natural History, vol. X, no. 2, Denver.
1933   A Further Contribution to the Antiquity of Man in America. Proceedings Colorado Museum Natural History, vol. XII, no. 2.
1934   Folsom and Yuma Artifacts. Proceedings Colorado Museum Natural History, vol. XIII, no. 2.
1935a   Folsom and Yuma Artifacts: pt. II. Proceedings Colorado Museum Natural History, vol. XIV, no. 2.
1935b   New World Man. Proceedings Colorado Museum Natural History, vol. XIV, no. 1.

Fischel, Hans E.
1939   Folsom and Yuma Culture Finds. American Antiquity, vol. IV, no. 3, pp. 232-264.
1941   Supplementary Data on Early Man in America. American Antiquity, vol. VI, no. 4, pp. 346-348.

Flint, Richard Foster.
1947   Glacial Geology and the Pleistocene Epoch. John Wiley & Sons, Inc., New York.
1953   Probable Wisconsin Substages and Late Wisconsin Events in Northeastern United States and Southeastern Canada. Geological Society of America Bulletin, vol. 64, no. 8, pp. 897-919.
1955   Rates of Advance and Retreat of the Margin of the Late-Wisconsin Ice Sheet. American Journal of Science, vol. 253, no. 5, pp. 249-255. (Abstract).
1956   New Radiocarbon Dates and Late-Pleistocene Stratigraphy. American Journal of Science, vol. 254, no. 5, pp. 265-287. (Absract).
1957   Glacial and Pleistocene Geology. John Wiley and Sons, Inc., New York.

Flint, R. F., and W. A. Gale.
1955   Wisconsin Stratigraphy and Radiocarbon Dates at Searles Lake, California. Geological Society of America Bulletin, vol. 66, no. 12, pt. 2, pp. 1559-1560. (Abstract).

Forbis, Richard G.
1956   Early Man and Fossil Bison. Science, vol. 123, no. 3191, pp. 327-328. Lancaster, Pennsylvania.

Forbis, Richard G., and John D. Sperry.
1952 An Early Man Site in Montana. American Antiquity, vol. XVIII, no. 2, pp. 127-132.
Ford, James H., and Gordon R. Willey.
1941 An Interpretation of the Prehistory of the Eastern United States. American Anthropologist, vol. 43, no. 3, pp. 325-363.
Fowler, Melvin L.
1954 Some Fluted Projectile Points from Illinois. American Antiquity, vol. XX, no. 2, pp. 170-171.
Fowler, Melvin L., and Howard Winters.
1956 Modoc Rock Shelter: Preliminary Report. Illinois State Museum Report of Investigations, no. 4. Springfield, Illinois.
Garfield, Viola E., and Wilson Duff.
1951 Anthropological Research and Publication in Anthropology in British Columbia, no. 2, pp. 2-8, British Columbia Provincial Museum, Victoria.
Gebhard, Paul H.
1949 An Archaeological Survey of the Blowouts of Yuma County, Colorado. American Antiquity, vol. XV, no. 2, pp. 132-143.
Giddings, J. L., Jr.
1950a Early Man on the Bering Sea Coast. Annals of the New York Academy of Sciences, Series II, vol. 13, no. 1, pp. 18-21.
1950b Traces of Early Man on the North Bering Sea Coast. University Museum Bulletin, University of Pennsylvania, vol. 14, no. 4, pp. 3-13. Philadelphia.
1951 The Denbigh Flint Complex. American Antiquity, vol. XVI, no. 3, pp. 193-202.
1952 Ancient Bering Strait and Population Spread. Science in Alaska, Selected Papers of the Alaskan Science Conference, Henry Collins, Editor, Arctic Institute of North America, pp. 85-102.
1954 Early Man in the Arctic. Scientific American, vol. 190, no. 6, pp. 82-89.
1955 The Denbigh Flint Complex is not yet Dated. American Antiquity, vol. XX, no. 4, pp. 375-376.
Gidley, James W.
1929 Further Study of the Problem of Early Man in Florida. Smithsonian Institution Explorations and Field Work in 1928, pp. 13-20.
1930 Investigations of Early Man in Florida. Smithsonian Institution Explorations and Field Work in 1929, p. 37.
1931 Further Investigations and Evidence of Early Man in Florida. Smithsonian Institution Explorations and Field Work in 1930, pp. 41-44.
Gidley, James W., and Frederick B. Loomis.
1926 Fossil Man in Florida. American Journal of Science, 5th Series, vol. 12, September, pp. 254-265.
Gifford, D. S., and E. W. Gifford.
1949 The Cochise Culture Olivella. American Antiquity, vol. XV, no. 2, p. 163.
Gjessing, Gutorm.
1953 The Circumpolar Stone Age. Antiquity, vol. 27, pp. 131-136. Newbury, Berkshire, England.
Gladwin, Harold S.
1937 Excavations at Snaketown II: Comparisons and Theories. Medallion Papers no. XXVI, Gila Pueblo, Globe, Arizona.
Goggin, John M.
1949 Cultural Traditions in Florida Prehistory in The Florida Indian and His Neighbors, pp. 13-44. Winter Park, Florida.
1950 An Early Lithic Complex from Central Florida. American Antiquity, vol. XVI, no. 1, pp. 46-49.

Greenman, Emerson F.
1941   Sites on Abandoned Beaches of Lake Huron, Ontario. Society for American Archaeology Notebook, vol. 2, no. 2, pp. 26-27.
1948   The Killarney Sequence and its Old World Connections. Michigan Academy of Science, Arts, and Letters, Papers, vol. 32, pp. 313-319. Ann Arbor.
1955   Wave Action at George Lake 1, Ontario. American Antiquity, vol. XX, no. 4, pp. 376-377.
1957   An American Eolithic? American Antiquity, vol. XXII, no. 3, p. 298.

Greenman, Emerson F., and George M. Stanley.
1943   The Archaeology and Geology of Two Early Sites near Killarney, Ontario. Papers of the Michigan Academy of Science, Abstracts, and Letters, vol. 28, pp. 505-530.

Griffin, James B., Editor.
1952   Archaeology of Eastern United States. University of Chicago Press.

Griffin, James B.
1946   Cultural Change and Continuity in Eastern United States *in* Man in Northeastern North America, edited by Frederick Johnson. Papers of the Robert S. Peabody Foundation for Archaeology, vol. III. Phillips Academy, Andover, Massachusetts.
1952   Radiocarbon Dates for the Eastern United States *in* Archaeology of Eastern United States, Griffin, Editor, pp. 365-370. University of Chicago Press.
1955   Chronology and Dating Processes. Yearbook of Anthropology, pp. 133-147. Wenner-Gren Foundation, New York.

Griffin, John W.
1953   Prehistoric Florida: A Review *in* Archaeology of the Eastern United States, pp. 322-334. J. B. Griffin, Editor, University of Chicago Press.

Gross, Hugo.
1951   Mastodon, Mammoth, and Man in America. Texas Archeological and Paleontological Society Bulletin, vol. 22. Lubbock, Texas.

Haag, William G.
1942   Early Horizons in the Southeast. American Antiquity, vol. VII, no. 3, pp. 209-222.

Hack, John T.
1941   The Changing Physical Environment of the Hopi Indians of Arizona. Peabody Museum Papers, vol. 35, no. 1. Cambridge, Massachusetts.
1943   Antiquity of the Finley Site. American Antiquity, vol. VIII, no. 3, pp. 235-241.

Hamilton, A.
1951   America's Oldest House. Natural History, vol. XL, no. 8, October. American Museum of Natural History, New York.

Harbour, Jerry.
1956   Preliminary Geology of the Lucy Site. El Palacio, vol. 63, no. 2, pp. 50-52. Santa Fe, New Mexico.

Harp, Elmer, Jr.
1951   An Archaeological Survey in the Strait of Belle Isle Area. American Antiquity, vol. XVI, no. 3, pp. 203-220.
1957   Notes and News—Arctic Area. American Antiquity, vol. XXII, no. 4, p. 437.

Harrington, Mark Raymond.
1933   Gypsum Cave, Nevada. Southwest Museum Papers, no. 8, Los Angeles.
1934   A Camel Hunter's Camp in Nevada. The Masterkey, vol. VIII, no. 1, pp. 22-24. The Southwest Museum, Los Angeles.

1938a Pre-Folsom Man in California. The Masterkey, vol. XII, no. 6, pp. 173-175. Southwest Museum, Los Angeles.
1938b Folsom Man in California. The Masterkey, vol. XII, no. 4, pp. 133-137. Southwest Museum, Los Angeles.
1948a A New Pinto Site. The Masterkey, vol. XXII, no. 4, pp. 116-118. Southwest Museum, Los Angeles.
1948b America's Oldest Dwelling? The Masterkey, vol. XXII, no. 5. Southwest Museum, Los Angeles.
1948c An Ancient Site at Borax Lake, California. Southwest Museum papers, no. 16.
1951 Latest from Little Lake. The Masterkey, vol. XXV, no. 6, pp. 188-191. Southwest Museum, Los Angeles.
1954 The Oldest Camp-fires. The Masterkey, vol. XXVIII, no. 6, pp. 233-234. Southwest Museum, Los Angeles.
1955a Man's Oldest Date in America. Natural History, vol. 64, no. 10, pp. 513-517 and pp. 554-555.
1955b A New Tule Springs Expedition. The Masterkey, vol. XXIX, no. 4, pp. 112-113. Southwest Museum, Los Angeles.

Haury, Emil W.
1953 Artifacts with Mammoth Remains, Naco, Arizona, I: Discovery of the Naco Mammoth and the Associated Projectile Points. American Antiquity, vol. XIX, no. 1, pp. 1-14.
1956 The Lehner Mammoth Site. The Kiva, vol. 21, nos. 3 and 4, pp. 23-24. Arizona Archaeological and Historical Society, Tucson.

Haury, Emil W., and Collaborators.
1950 The Stratigraphy and Archaeology of Ventana Cave, Arizona. University of New Mexico Press, Albuquerque.

Haynes, C. V., Jr.
1955 Evidence of Early Man in Torrance County, New Mexico. Bulletin Texas Archeological and Paleontological Society, vol. 26, pp. 144-164, Austin.

Heizer, Robert F.
1938 A Complete Atlatl Dart from Pershing County, Nevada. New Mexico Anthropologist, vol. 2, pp. 68-71. Alburquerque.
1940a A Note on Folsom and Nepesta Points. American Antiquity, vol. VI, no. 1, pp. 79-80.
1940b The Archaeology of Central California, I: The Early Horizon. Anthropological Records, vol. 12, no. 1. University of California Press.
1941 Review of "Prehistoric Man of the Santa Barbara Coast" by David Banks Rogers. American Antiquity, vol. VI, no. 9, pp. 372-375.
1950 The Stanford Skull, A Probable Early Man from Santa Clara County, California. University of California Archaeological Survey Reports, no. 6, pp. 1-9. Berkeley.
1950a Observations on Early Man in California. Reports of the University of California Archaeological Survey Reports, no. 7, pp. 5-9. Berkeley.
1950b On the Methods of Chemical Analysis of Bone as an Aid to Prehistoric Culture Chronology. University of California Archaeological Survey Reports, no. 7, pp. 10-14.
1951a An Assessment of Certain Nevada, California, and Oregon Radiocarbon Dating: Frederick Johnson, Editor. American Antiquity, vol. XVII, no. 1, pt. 2, pp. 23-25.
1951b Preliminary Report on the Leonard Rockshelter Site, Pershing County, Nevada. American Antiquity, vol. XVII, no. 2, pp. 89-97.
1952 A Review of Problems in the Antiquity of Man in California. University of California Archaeological Survey Report, no. 16, pp. 3-17. Berkeley.
1953a Sites Attributed to Early Man in California. University of California Archaeological Survey Report, no. 22, pp. 1-4. Berkeley.

1953b Long Range Dating in Archaeology *in* Anthropology Today: A. L. Kroeber, Editor. University of Chicago Press.
1953c The Archaeology of the Napa Region. University of California Archaeological Reports, vol. 12, no. 6. Berkeley.

Heizer, Robert F., and F. Fenenga.
1939 Archaeological Horizons in Central California. American Anthropology, vol. 41, no. 3, pp. 378-399.

Heizer, Robert F., and Edwin M. Lambert.
1947 Observations on Archaeological Sites in Topanga Canyon, California. University of California Publications in American Archaeology and Ethnology, vol. 44, no. 2, pp. 237-258.

Heizer, Robert F., and S. F. Cook.
1949 A Comparative Analysis of Human Bone from Several Central California Sites. Manuscript.
1952 Fluorine and Other Chemical Tests of some North American Human and Animal Bones. American Journal of Physical Anthropology, vol. 10, no. 3, pp. 289-304.

Hewes, Gordon W.
1946 Early Man in California and the Tranquillity Site. American Antiquity, vol. XI, no. 4, pp. 209-212.

Hibben, Frank C.
1941 Evidences of Early Occupation of Sandia Cave, New Mexico, and Other Sites in the Sandia-Manzano Region. Smithsonian Miscellaneous Collections, vol. 99, no. 23.
1943 Evidences of Early Man in Alaska. American Antiquity, vol. VIII, no. 3, pp. 254-259.
1946 The First Thirty-eight Sandia Points. American Antiquity, vol. XI, no. 4, pp. 257-258.
1951 Sites of the Paleo-Indian in the Middle Rio Grande Valley. American Antiquity, vol. XVII, no. 1, pp. 41-46.
1955 Specimens from Sandia Cave and Their Possible Significance. Science, vol. 122, no. 3872, pp. 688-689.

Hoffman, Bernard G.
1952 Implications of Radiocarbon Datings for the Origin of the Dorset Culture. American Antiquity, vol. XVIII, no. 1, pp. 15-17.

Holder, Preston, and Joyce Wike.
1949 The Frontier Culture Complex: A Preliminary Report on a Prehistoric Hunters' Camp in Southwestern Nebraska. American Antiquity, vol. XIV, no. 4, pt. 1, pp. 260-265.

Hopkins, D. M., and J. L. Giddings, Jr.
1953 Geological Background of the Iyatayet Archaeological Site, Cape Denbigh, Alaska. Smithsonian Miscellaneous Collections, vol. 121, no. 11. Washington.

Hooton, Earnest A.
1933 Notes on Five Texas Crania. Bulletin Texas Archeological and Paleontological Society, vol. 5, pp. 25-39. Abilene.
1946 Up From the Ape (Revised Edition.) MacMillan Co., New York.

Horberg, Leland
1955 Radiocarbon Dates and Pleistocene Chronological Problems in the Mississippi Valley Regions. Journal of Geology, vol. 63, no. 3, pp. 278-286.

Howard, Edgar B.
1935a Evidence of Early Man in North America. The Museum Journal, University of Pennsylvania Museum, vol. XXIV, nos. 2-3. Philadelphia.
1935b Occurrence of Flints and Extinct Animals in Pluvial Deposits near Clovis, New Mexico, pt. 1, Introduction. Proceedings Philadelphia Academy Natural Sciences, vol. LXXXVII, pp. 299-303.

1936 An Outline of the Problem of Man's Antiquity in North America. American Anthropologist, New Series 38, pp. 394-413.

1937 The Emergence of a General Folsom Pattern. 25th Anniversary Studies, Philadelphia Anthropological Society, vol. I, pp. 111-115.

1939 Folsom and Yuma Points from Saskatchewan. American Antiquity, vol. IV, no. 3, pp. 277-279.

1943 The Finley Site: Discovery of Yuma Points, *in situ*, near Eden, Wyoming. American Antiquity, vol. VIII, no. 3, pp. 224-234.

Howard, Edgar B., Linton Satterthwaite, Jr., and Charles Bache.

1941 Preliminary Report on a Buried Yuma Site in Wyoming. American Antiquity, vol. VII, no. 1, pp. 70-74.

Howells, W. W.

1938 Crania from Wyoming Resembling "Minnesota Man." American Antiquity, vol. II, no. 4, pp. 318-326.

1940 The Origins of American Indian Race Types *in* The Maya and Their Neighbors, pp. 3-9. D. Appleton-Century Co., New York.

Hrdlicka, Ales.

1907 Skeletal Remains Suggesting or Attributed to Early Man in North America. Bureau of American Ethnology Bulletin 33, pp. 21-28. Washington, D. C.

1912 Early Man in South America (In collaboration with W. H. Holmes, Bailey Willis, Fred Eugene Wright, Clarence N. Fenner). Bureau of American Ethnology Bulletin 52. Washington, D. C.

1918 Recent Discoveries Attributed to Early Man in America. Bureau of American Ethnology Bulletin 66. Washington, D. C.

1923 Origin and Antiquity of the American Indian. Smithsonian Institution Annual Report, 1923, pp. 481-494. Washington, D. C.

1937a Early Man in America: What Have the Bones to Say? *in* Early Man, pp. 93-104. J. B. Lippincott Co., Philadelphia.

1937b The "Minnesota Man." American Journal of Physical Anthropology, vol. 22, pp. 175-199.

Hughes, Jack T.

1949 Investigation in Western South Dakota and Northeastern Wyoming. American Antiquity, vol. XIV, no. 4, pp. 266-277.

1950 An Experiment in Relative Dating of Archaeological Remains by Stream Terraces. Texas Archeological and Paleontological Society Bulletin, vol. 21, pp. 97-104.

Hunt, Alice P.

1950 Artifacts Associated with Pleistocene Deposits in the Denver Area, Colorado. Plains Archaeological News Letter, vol. 3, pp. 7-9.

Hunt, Charles B.

1950 Progress in Mapping Late Pleistocene and Recent Deposits in the Denver Area. Plains Archaeological Conference News Letter, vol. 3, no. 2, p. 10.

1953 Pleistocene-Recent Boundary in the Rocky Mountain Region. Geological Survey Bulletin 996-A, U. S. Government Printing Office, Washington, D. C.

1955 Radiocarbon Dating in the Light of Stratigraphy and Weathering Processes. The Scientific Monthly, vol. 81, no. 5, pp. 240-247.

1956 Geology of the Taylor Site *in* Archaeological Investigations on the Uncompahgre Plateau by H. M. Wormington and Robert H. Lister. Denver Museum of Natural History, Proceedings, no. 2.

Hurst, C. T.

1943 A Folsom Site in a Mountain Valley of Colorado. American Antiquity, vol. VIII, no. 3, pp. 250-253.

Hurt, Wesley R., Jr.

1949 Resemblances Between the Pre-Ceramic Horizons of the Southeast and Southwest. Paper read at 14th Annual Meeting of the Society for American Archaeology, May 13, Bloomington, Indiana.

1953   A Comparative Study of the Preceramic Occupations of North America. American Antiquity, vol. XVIII, no. 3, pp. 204-222.

Hurt, Wesley R., Jr., and Daniel McKnight.
1949   Archaeology of the San Augustin Plains: A Preliminary Report. American Antiquity, vol. XIV, no. 3, pp. 172-194.

Huscher, Harold.
1939   Influence of the Drainage Pattern of the Uncompahgre Plateau on the Movements of Primitive Peoples. Southwestern Lore, vol. V, no. 2. Gunnison, Colorado.

Irving, William.
1951   Archaeology in the Brooks Range of Alaska. American Antiquity, vol. XVII, no. 1, p. 52.
1955   Burins from Central Alaska. American Antiquity, vol. XX, no. 4, pp. 380-383.

Jenks, Albert E.
1936   Pleistocene Man in Minnesota: A Fossil *Homo Sapiens*. The University of Minnesota Press, Minneapolis, Minnesota.
1937   Minnesota's Brown's Valley Man and Associated Burial Artifacts. Memoirs American Anthropological Association, no. 49. Menasha, Wisconsin.
1938   A Reply to a Review by Dr. Ales Hrdlicka. American Anthropologist, April-June, vol. 40, no. 2, pp. 328-336.

Jenks, Albert E., and Lloyd A. Wilford.
1938   The Sauk Valley Skeleton. Bulletin Texas Archeological and Paleontological Society, vol. X, pp. 136-169. Abilene.

Jenks, Albert E., and Mrs. H. H. Simpson, Sr.
1941   Beveled Artifacts in Florida of the Same Type as Artifacts Found Near Clovis, New Mexico. American Antiquity, vol. VI, no. 4, pp. 314-319.

Jennings, Jesse D.
1953   Danger Cave: A Progress Summary. El Palacio, vol. 60, no. 5, pp. 179-213.

Jennings, Jesse D., and Edward Norbeck.
1955   Great Basin Prehistory: A Review. American Antiquity, vol. XXI, no. 1, pp. 1-11.

Jennings, Jesse D., Editor.
1956   The American Southwest: A Problem in Cultural Isolation *in* Seminars in Archaeology, Robert Wauchope, Editor. Memoirs of the Society for American Archaeology; American Antiquity, vol. XXII, no. 2, pt. 2.

Jepsen, Glenn L.
1951   Ancient Buffalo Hunters in Wyoming. News Letter no. 24, Archaeological Society of New Jersey, pp. 22-24.
1953a   Ancient Buffalo Hunters of Northwestern Wyoming. Southwestern Lore, vol. 19, no. 2, pp. 19-25. Boulder, Colorado.
1953b   Ancient Buffalo Hunters. Princeton Alumni Weekly, vol. 53, no. 25, pp. 10-12. Princeton, New Jersey.

Johnson, Frederick.
1946   An Archaeological Survey Along the Alaskan Highway, 1944. American Antiquity, vol. XI, no. 3, pp. 183-186.

Johnson, Frederick, Editor.
1946   Man in Northeastern North America. Papers of the Robert S. Peabody Foundation for Archaeology, vol. III. Andover, Massachusetts.
1951   Radiocarbon Dating. Memoirs of the Society for American Archaeology; American Antiquity, vol. XVII, no. 1, pt. 2.

Johnson, Frederick, and Frank C. Hibben.
1957   Radiocarbon Dates from Sandia Cave, Correction. Science, vol. 125, no. 3241, pp. 234-235.

Johnson, Ludwell H., III.
1952 Men and Elephants in America. Scientific Monthly, vol. 75, no. 4, pp. 215-221.

Johnston, W. A.
1933 Quaternary Geology of North America in Relation to the Migration of Man. American Aborigines, 5th Pacific Congress, D. Jenness, Editor, University of Toronto Press, pp. 11-45.

Judson, Sheldon.
1953 Geology of the San Jon Site, Eastern New Mexico. Smithsonian Miscellaneous Collections, vol. 121, no. 1, pp. 1-70. Washington, D. C.

Karlstrom, Thor N. V.
1956 The Problem of the Cochrane in Late Pleistocene Chronology. Geological Survey Bulletin 1021-J. U. S. Government Printing Office, Washington, D. C.
1957 Tentative Correlation of Alaskan Glacial Sequences, 1956. Science, vol. 125, no. 3237, pp. 73-74.

Karlstrom, Thor N. V., and Meyer Rubin.
1955 Radiocarbon Dating of the "Cochrane Readvance" in Canada. Geological Society of America Bulletin, vol. 66, no. 12, pt. 2, p. 1582, (Abstract).

Kelley, J. Charles.
1947 The Cultural Affinities and Chronological Position of the Clear Fork Focus. American Antiquity, vol. XIII, no. 2, pp. 97-108.
1951 Review of "The Stratigraphy and Archaeology of Ventana Cave, Arizona." American Antiquity, vol. XVII, no. 2, pp. 152-154.

Kelley, J. Charles, T. N. Campbell, and D. J. Lehmer.
1940 The Association of Archeological Material with Geological Deposits in the Big Bend Region of Texas. Bulletin Sul Ross State Teachers College, vol. XXI, no. 3, (Publications, West Texas Historical and Scientific Society, no. 10), Alpine.

Kidd, Kenneth E.
1951 Fluted Points in Ontario. American Antiquity, vol. XVI, no. 3, p. 260.

Kidder, A. V.
1938 Arrowheads or Dart Points. American Antiquity, vol. IV, no. 2, pp. 156-157.

Kleine, H. K.
1953 A Remarkable Paleo-Indian Site in Alabama. Tennessee Archaeologist, vol. 9, no. 2, pp. 31-37. Knoxville.

Kneberg, Madeline.
1952 The Tennessee Area in Archaeology of the Eastern United States, J. B. Griffin, Editor, pp. 190-198, University of Chicago Press.
1954 The Duration of the Archaic Tradition in the Lower Tennessee Valley. Southern Indian Studies. 10th Southeastern Conference, Archaeological Society of North Carolina, vol. VI, pp. 40-44, Chapel Hill.
1956 Some Important Projectile Point Types Found in the Tennessee Area. The Tennessee Archaeologist, vol. XII, no. 1, pp. 17-28, Knoxville.

Koch, Albert C.
1839 Evidences of the Contemporaneous Existence of Man with Mastodon in Missouri. American Journal of Science, vol. 36, pp. 198-200.
1860 Mastodon Remains in the State of Missouri, Together with Evidence of the Existence of Man Contemporaneously with the Mastodon. Trans. The Academy of Science of St. Louis, vol. I, pp. 61-64.

Krader, Lawrence.
1952 Neolithic Find in the Chukchi Peninsula. American Antiquity, vol. XVII, no. 3, pp. 261-262.

Krieger, Alex D.
1944a The Typological Concept. American Antiquity, vol. IX, no. 3, pp. 271-278.
1944b Review of Archaeological Researches in the Northern Great Basin, by Cressman, *et al.* American Antiquity, vol. IX, no. 3, pp. 351-359.
1946 Culture Complexes and Chronology in Northern Texas. University of Texas Publication 4640. Austin.
1947 Certain Projectile Points of the Early American Hunters. Texas Archeological and Paleontological Society Bulletin, vol. 18, pp. 7-27. Alpine.
1948 A Suggested General Sequence in North American Projectile Points. Sixth Plains Archeological Conference Proceedings; Anthropological Papers, University of Utah, vol. 11, pp. 117-124. Salt Lake City.
1950 Review of "Tepexpan Man," by de Terra, Romero, and Stewart. American Antiquity, vol. XV, no. 4, pt. 1, pp. 343-348.
1951a Review of "Prehistoria de Mexico," by Aveleyra. American Antiquity, vol. XVI, no. 4, pp. 357-358.
1951b Review of Early Man in the New World. American Antiquity, vol. XVII, no. 1, pp. 61-62.
1953 New World Culture History: Anglo-America *in* Anthropology Today. University of Chicago Press.
1954 A Comment on "Fluted Point Relationships," by John Witthoft. American Antiquity, vol. XIX, no. 3, pp. 273-275.

Krieger, Alex D., Editor.
Notes and News—Early Man.
1950a American Antiquity, vol. XVI, no. 2, pp. 181-182.
1950b American Antiquity, vol. XVI, no. 3, p. 285.
1951a American Antiquity, vol. XVII, no. 1, pp. 77-78.
1951b American Antiquity, vol. XVII, no. 2, pp. 175-176.
1951c American Antiquity, vol. XVII, no. 3, pp. 281-283, p. 287.
1952a American Antiquity, vol. XVIII, no. 1, pp. 90-91.
1952b American Antiquity, vol. XVIII, no. 2, pp. 189-190.
1953a American Antiquity, vol. XVIII, no. 3, pp. 289-291, p. 292.
1953b American Antiquity, vol. XIX, no. 1, pp. 100-101.
1954 American Antiquity, vol. XIX, no. 3, pp. 304-305.
1955a American Antiquity, vol. XX, no. 3, pp. 305-306.
1955b American Antiquity, vol. XXI, no. 2, p. 202.
1956 American Antiquity, vol. XXI, no. 3, p. 341.
1957a American Antiquity, vol. XXII, no. 3, pp. 321-323.
1957b American Antiquity, vol. XXII, no. 4, pp. 434-436.

Lance, John F.
1953 Artifacts with Mammoth Remains, Naco, Arizona, III: Description of the Naco Mammoth. American Antiquity, vol. XIX, no. 1, pp. 19-22.

Larsen, Helge.
1951 De Dansk-Amerikanske Alaska-ekspeditioner 1949-1951. Saetryk af Geografisk Tidsskrift 51 Bind.
1953 Archaeological Investigations in Alaska since 1939. Polar Record, vol. 6, pp. 593-607.

Laughlin, William S.
1951 Notes on an Aleutian Core and Blade Industry. American Antiquity, vol. XVII, no. 1, pp. 52-55.

Laughlin, William S., and Gordon H. Marsh.
1954 The Lamellar Flake Manufacturing Site on Anangula Island in the Aleutians. American Antiquity, vol. XX, no. 1, pp. 27-39.

Lee, Thomas E.
1954 The First Sheguiandah Expedition, Manitoulin Island, Ontario. American Antiquity, vol. XX, no. 2, pp. 101-111.
1955 The Second Sheguiandah Expedition, Manitoulin Island, Ontario, American Antiquity, vol. XXI, no. 1, pp. 63-71.

1956   Position and Meaning of a Radiocarbon Sample from the Shegui-
        andah Site, Ontario. American Antiquity, vol. XXII, no. 1, p. 79.
Leechman, Douglas.
1950   An Implement of Elephant Bone from Manitoba. American Antiq-
        uity, vol. XVI, no. 2, pp. 157-159.
Leighton, M. M.
1936   Geological Aspects of the Finding of Primitive Man Near Abilene,
        Texas: Preliminary Report. Medallion Papers, no. XXIV, Gila
        Pueblo, Globe, Arizona.
Leonard, A. B., and J. C. Frye.
1954   Ecological Conditions Accompanying Loess Deposition in the Great
        Plains Region of the United States. Journal of Geology, vol. 62,
        pp. 299-404.
Leverett, Frank.
1937   Personal letter to A. E. Jenks, December 11.
Leverett, Frank, and Frederick W. Sardeson.
1932   Quaternary Geology of Minnesota and Parts of Adjacent States.
        U. S. Geological Survey, Professional Paper 161, pp. 119-146.
Lewis, T. M. N.
1953   The Paleo-Indian Problem in Tennessee. The Tennessee Archaeologist,
        vol. IX, no. 2, pp. 38-40. Knoxville.
1954   Sandia Points. The Tennessee Archaeologist, vol. X, no. 1, pp.
        26-27. Knoxville.
Lewis, T. M. N., and Madeline Kneberg.
1947   The Archaic Horizon in Western Tennessee. Tennessee Anthropo-
        logical Papers, no. 2, Extension Series, vol. 23, no. 4, University of
        Tennessee, Knoxville.
1951   Early Projectile Point Forms, and Examples from Tennessee. The
        Tennessee Archaeologist, vol. VII, no. 1, pp. 6-19. Knoxville.
1954   Early Projectile Points from Bedford County. The Tennessee
        Archaeologist, vol. X, no. 1, pp. 21-23. Knoxville.
1955   Editors' Notes, The A. L. LeCroy Collection. The Tennessee
        Archaeologist, vol. XI, no. 2, pp. 75-82. Knoxville.
1956   The Paleo-Indian Complex on the LeCroy Site. The Tennessee
        Archaeologist, vol. XII, no. 1, pp. 5-11. Knoxville.
Libby, Willard F.
1955   Radiocarbon Dating. Second Edition. The University of Chicago
        Press.
Lister, Robert H.
1953   The Stemmed, Indented Base Point, a Possible Horizon Marker.
        American Antiquity, vol. XVIII, no. 3, pp. 264-265.
Logan, Wilfred D.
1952   Graham Cave, An Archaic Site in Montgomery County, Missouri.
        Memoir no. 2, Missouri Archaeological Society, Columbia.
Lopatin, Ivan A.
1939   Fossil Man in the Vicinity of Los Angeles, California. Proceedings
        Sixth Pacific Science Congress, vol. IV, pp. 177-181. Berkeley,
        California.
Lorenzo, Jose J.
1953   A Fluted Point from Durango, Mexico. American Antiquity, vol.
        XVIII, no. 4, pp. 394-395.
Lougee, Richard J.
1953   A Chronology of Post Glacial Time in Eastern North America.
        The Scientific Monthly, vol. 76, no. 5, pp. 259-276. Lancaster,
        Pennsylvania.
Lucas, Barbara.
1951   Tree-holes at the Stahl Site. The Masterkey, vol. XXV, no. 6,
        pp. 191-193.

McCary, Ben C.
1947 A Survey and Study of Folsom-like Points found in Virginia. Quarterly Bulletin Archaeological Society of Virginia, vol. II, no. 1, Charlottesville, Virginia.
1948 A Report on Folsom-like Points found in Granville County, North Carolina. Quarterly Bulletin Archaeological Society of Virginia, vol. III, no. 1. Charlottesville, Virginia.
1951 A Workshop Site of Early Man in Dinwiddie County, Virginia. American Antiquity, vol. XVII, no. 1, pt. 1, pp. 9-17.
1954 Survey of Virginia Fluted Points, nos. 226-231. Archaeological Society of Virginia, Quarterly Bulletin, vol. VII, no. 3, pp. 14-16.
1956 Survey of Virginia Fluted Points, Nos. 231-263. Archaeological Society of Virginia, Quarterly Bulletin, Charlottesville, Virginia.

McCown, Theodore D.
1939 That Magic Word, Solutrean. American Antiquity, vol. V, no. 2, pp. 150-152.
1941 The Antiquity of Man in the New World. American Antiquity, vol. VI, no. 3, pp. 203-213.
1950 The Stanford Skull: The Physical Characteristics. University of California Archaeological Survey Reports, no. 6, pp. 10-17. Berkeley.

McKern, W. C.
1939 The Midwestern Taxonomic Method as an Aid to Archaeological Culture Study. American Antiquity, vol. 4, no. 4, pp. 301-313.
1942 The First Settlers of Wisconsin. Wisconsin Magazine of History, vol. 26, no. 2, pp. 153-169. Madison.

MacGowan, Kenneth.
1950 Early Man in the New World. The MacMillan Co., New York.

MacNeish, Richard S.
1950 A Synopsis of the Archaeological Sequence in the Sierra de Tamaulipas. Revista Mexicana de Estudios Antropologicos, Tomo XI, pp. 79-96, Mexico, D. F.
1951 An Archaeological Reconnaissance in the Northwest Territories. National Museum of Canada Bulletin 123, pp. 24-41. Ottawa.
1952 A Possible Early Site in the Thunder Bay District, Ontario. Annual Report National Museum of Canada, Bulletin 126, pp. 28-47. Ottawa.
1953 Archaeological Reconnaissance in the MacKenzie River Drainage. National Museum of Canada Bulletin 128, pp. 1-17. Ottawa.
1954 The Pointed Mountain Site near Fort Liard, Northwest Territories, Canada. American Antiquity, vol. XIX, no. 3, pp. 234-253.
1955 Ancient Maize in Mexico. Archaeology, vol. 8, no. 2, pp. 108-115. Cambridge.
1956a Two Archaeological Sites on Great Bear Lake, Northwest Territories. Annual Report of the National Museum of Canada, Bulletin 136, pp. 54-82. Ottawa.
1956b The Engigstciak Site on the Yukon Arctic Coast. Anthropological Papers, University of Alaska, vol. 4, no. 2, pp. 91-111. Fairbanks.

Mahan, E. C.
1954 A Survey of Paleo-Indian and Other Early Flint Artifacts from
1955 Sites in Northern, Western, and Central Alabama. The Tennessee Archaeologist, vol. X, no. 2; vol. XI, no. 1, no 2. Knoxville.
1956 A Survey of Paleo-American Points from Alabama. The Tennessee Archaeologist, vol. XII, no. 1, pp. 12-14, vol. XII, no. 2, pp. 28-31.

Maldonado-Koerdell, Manuel
1947 Antecedentes del Descubrimiento del Hombre de Tepexpan. Anthropos, vol. I, no. 1, pp. 1-4. Mexico, D. F.
1948a Los Vertebrados Fosiles del Cuaternario en Mexico. Revista de la Sociedad Mexicana de Historia Natural, vol. 9, nos. 1 and 2, pp. 1-35. Mexico, D. F.
1948b Bibliografia Mexicana de Prehistoria. Sobretiro de "Boletin Bibliografico de Antropologia Americana," vol. X. Mexico.

1949 Las Industrias Prehistoricas de Mexico. Instituto Nacional de Antropologia y Historia, Anales, vol. 3, pp. 9-16. Mexico, D. F.

Maldonado-Koerdell, Manuel, and Luis Aveleyra A. de Anda.

1949 Nota Preliminar sobre dos Artefactos del Pleistoceno Superior Hallados en la Region de Tequixquiac, Mexico, *in* Tomo Especial de Homenaje al Dr. Edward Seler. El Mexico Antiguo, tomo 7. Mexico, D. F.

Mangelsdorf, Paul C., and C. Earle Smith, Jr.

1949 New Archaeological Evidence on Evolution in Maize. Botanical Museum Leaflets, Harvard University, vol. XIII, no. 6, pp. 213-247. Cambridge, Massachusetts.

Martin, Paul S., George I. Quimby, and Donald Collier.

1947 Indians Before Columbus: Twenty Thousand Years of North American History Revealed by Archaeology. University of Chicago Press.

Martin, Paul S., John B. Rinaldo, and Ernst Antevs.

1949 Cochise and Mogollon Sites, Pine Lawn Valley, Western New Mexico. Fieldiana: Anthropology, vol. 38, no. 1. Chicago Natural History Museum.

Martin, Paul, and John Rinaldo

1950 Sites of the Reserve Phase, Pine Lawn Valley, Western New Mexico. Fieldiana: Anthropology, vol. 38, no. 3. Chicago Natural History Museum.

Martin, Paul S., *et al.*

1952 Mogollon Cultural Continuity and Change: The Stratigraphic Analysis of Tularosa and Cordova Caves. Fieldiana: Anthropology, vol. 40. Chicago Natural History Museum.

Martinez del Rio, Pablo

1952a El Mamut de Santa Isabel Iztapan. Cuadernos Americanos, Mexico, D. F.

1952b Los Origines Americanos, 3rd Edition. Mexico, D. F.

Mather, John R.

1954 The Effect of Climate on the New World Migration of Primitive Man. Southwestern Journal of Anthropology, vol. 10, no. 3, pp. 304-321. Albuquerque.

May, Irving.

1955 Isolation of Organic Carbon from Bones for C-14 Dating. Science, vol. 121, no. 3143, pp. 508-509.

Mayer-Oakes, William.

1952 A Central American Clue to Early Man. Carnegie Magazine, June, pp. 189-191. Carnegie Museum, Pittsburgh, Pennsylvania.

Meighan, Clement W.

1955a Report on the Great Basin Archaeological Conference. American Antiquity, vol. XX, no. 3, pp. 308-312.

1955b Archaeology of the North Coast Ranges, California. University of California Archaeological Survey, Report no. 30, pp. 1-39. Berkeley.

Meldgaard, Jorgen.

1952 A Paleo-Eskimo Culture in West Greenland. American Antiquity, vol. XVII, no. 3, pp. 222-230.

Meserve, F. G., and E. H. Barbour.

1932 Association of an Arrow Point with Bison Occidentalis in Nebraska. Nebraska State Museum Bulletin vol. 1, pp. 239-242.

Miller, Carl F.

1950 Early Cultural Horizons in the Southeastern United States. American Antiquity, vol. XV, no. 4, pp. 273-288.

1956 Life 8000 years ago uncovered in an Alabama Cave. National Geographic Magazine, vol. CX, no. 4, pp. 542-558, National Geographic Society, Washington, D. C.

Montagu, M. F. Ashley.
  1944 An Indian Tradition Relating to the Mastodon. American Anthropologist, vol. 46, no. 4, pp. 568-571.

Montagu, M. F. Ashley, and C. Bernard Peterson.
  1944 The Earliest Account of the Association of Human Artifacts with Fossil Mammals in North America. American Philosophical Society Proceedings, vol. 87, no. 5, pp. 407-419. Philadelphia.

Mooser, Federico, Sidney E. White, and Jose L. Lorenzo.
  1956 La Cuenca de Mexico: Consideraciones Geologicas y Arqueologicas. Instituto Nacional de Antropologia e Historia. Mexico, D.F.

Morgan, Richard G.
  1953 Outline of Cultures in the Ohio Region *in* Archaeology of the Eastern United States, J. B. Griffin, Editor. University of Chicago Press.

Moss, John Hall.
  1951 (In collaboration with Kirk Bryan, G. William Holmes, Linton Satterthwaite, Jr., Henry P. Hansen, C. Bertrand Schultz, W. D. Frankforter.) Early Man in the Eden Valley. Museum Monographs, The University Museum, University of Pennsylvania, Philadelphia.
  1952 The Antiquity of the Finley (Yuma) Site, Example of the Geologic Method of Dating *in* Indian Tribes of Aboriginal America, Selected Papers of the XXIX International Congress of Americanists. University of Chicago Press.

Movius, Hallam L., Jr.
  1949 The Lower Palaeolithic Cultures of Southern and Eastern Asia. Transactions, American Philosophical Society, New Series, vol. 38, pt. 4, pp. 329-420.

Mulloy, William.
  1954 The McKean Site in Northeastern Wyoming. Southwestern Journal of Anthropology, vol. 10, no. 3, pp. 432-460. Albuquerque.

Nelson, N. C.
  1933 The Antiquity of Man in America in the Light of Archaeology. The American Aborigines, Their Origin and Antiquity. Diamond Jeness, Editor, pp. 87-130. University of Toronto Press.
  1936 Review of "Evidence of Early Man in North America" by E. B. Howard. American Antiquity, vol. I, no. 3, pp. 237-239.
  1937a Review of "Additional Information on the Folsom Complex" by F. H. H. Roberts, Jr. American Antiquity, vol. II, no. 4, pp. 317-326.
  1937b Notes on Cultural Relations between Asia and America. American Antiquity, vol. II, no. 4, pp. 367-372.

Newman, Marshall T.
  1953 The Applications of Ecological Rules to the Racial Anthropology of the Aboriginal New World. American Anthropologist, vol. 55, no. 3, pp. 311-327.

Oakley, K.P.
  1951 The Fluorine-dating Method. Yearbook of Physical Anthropology, vol. 5, (for 1949), pp. 44-52. New York.

Oetteking, B.
  1930 Skeletal Remains from Texas. Notes, Museum of the American Indian, Heye Foundation, vol. VIII, no. 3. New York.

Okladnikov, A. P.
  1950 Lenskie Drevnosti—Materialy po Istorri Yakutii. Institut Istorii Material'noy Kul'tury imeni N. Ya. Marra. Akademia Nauk S.S.S.R., vol. 3.
  1955 IAkutiia do Prisoedineniia k Russkomu Gosudarstvu. Akademia Nauk S.S.S.R., Institut Iazyka, Literatury i Istorii, Iakutskogo filiala, AN S.S.S.R. Istorieea Iakutskoi A.S.S.R., Tom. 1

Orr, Phil C.

1952 Review of Santa Barbara Channel Archaeology. Southwestern Journal of Anthropology, vol. 8, no. 2, pp. 211-226. Albuquerque.

1956a Radiocarbon Dates from Santa Rosa Island, I. Santa Barbara Museum of Natural History, Anthropology, Bulletin 2.

1956b Pleistocene Man in Fishbone Cave, Pershing County, Nevada. Nevada State Museum, Department of Archaeology, Bulletin 2. Carson City.

Osborne, Douglas.

1956 Early Lithic in the Pacific Northwest. Research Studies of the State College of Washington, vol. XXIV, no. 1, pp. 38-44. Pullman.

Petri, B. E.

1916 Report on a Voyage to the Baikal Lake in the Summer of 1916. Report of the Russian Academy of Sciences (in Russian).

Pewé, Troy L.

1954 The Geological Approach to Dating Archaeological Sites. American Antiquity, vol. XX, no. 1, pp. 51-61.

Phillips, Philip, and Gordon R. Willey.

1953 Method and Theory in American Archaeology: An Operational Basis for Culture-Historical Integration. American Anthropologist, vol. 55, no. 5, pt. 1, pp. 615-631.

Preston, Richard S., Elaine Person, and E. S. Deevey.

1955 Yale Natural Radiocarbon Measurements II. Science, vol. 122, no. 3177, pp. 954-960.

Pringle, R. W., et al.

1957 Radiocarbon Age Estimates Obtained by an Improved Liquid Scintillation Technique. Science, vol. 125, no. 3237, pp. 69-70.

Quimby, George I.

1952 The Archaeology of the Upper Great Lakes Area in Archaeology of the Eastern United States: J. B. Griffin, Editor. University of Chicago Press.

1954a Cultural and Natural Areas before Kroeber. American Antiquity, vol. XIX, no. 4, pp. 317-331.

1954b The Old Copper Assemblage and Extinct Animals. American Antiquity, vol. XX, no. 2, pp. 169-170.

1955 Reply to Homer Aschmann's Comments on "Cultural and Natural Areas before Kroeber." American Antiquity, vol. XX, no. 4, pp. 378-379.

1956 The Locus of the Natchez Pelvis Find. American Antiquity, vol. XXII, no. 1, pp. 77-78.

Rainey, Froelich.

1939 Archaeology in Central Alaska. Anthropological Papers, American Museum of Natural History, vol. XXXVI. New York.

1940 Archaeological Investigations in Central Alaska. American Antiquity, vol. V, no. 4, pp. 299-308.

1953 The Significance of Recent Archaeological Discoveries in Inland Alaska in Asia and North America: Transpacific Contacts; Marian W. Smith, Editor. Memoir no. 9, Society for American Archaeology, vol. XVIII, no. 3, pt. 2, pp. 43-46.

Rau, Charles.

1873 North American Stone Implements. Annual Report, Smithsonian Institution for 1872, pp. 395-408, Washington, D. C.

Ray, Cyrus N.

1929 A Differentiation of the Prehistoric Cultures of the Abilene Section. Texas Archeological and Paleontological Society, vol. 1, pp. 7-22 Abilene.

1930 Report on some Recent Archaeological Researches in the Abilene Section. Texas Archeological and Paleontological Society, vol. 2, pp. 45-58. Abilene.

1934   Flint Cultures of Early Man in Texas. Texas Archeological and Paleontological Society, vol. 5, pp. 107-111. Abilene.
1937   Late Discoveries in the Abilene Region. Texas Archeological and Paleontological Society, vol. 9, pp. 192-217. Abilene.
1938   The Clear Fork Culture Complex. Texas Archeological and Paleontological Society, vol. 10, pp. 193-207. Abilene
1940   The Deeply Buried Gibson Site. Texas Archeological and Paleontological Society, vol. 12, pp. 223-237. Abilene.
1942   Ancient Artifacts and Mammoth's Teeth of the McLean Site. Texas Archeological and Paleontological Society, vol. 14, pp. 137-146. Abilene.
1945   Stream Bank Silts of the Abilene Region. Texas Archeological and Paleontological Society, vol. 16, pp. 117-147. Abilene.
1948   The Facts Concerning the Clear Fork Culture. American Antiquity, vol. XIII, no. 4, pt. 1, pp. 320-322.

Ray, Cyrus N., and Kirk Bryan.
1938   Folsomoid Point found in Alluvium Beside a Mammoth's Bones. Science, New Series, vol. 88, no. 2281, September 16, pp. 257-258.

Ray, Cyrus N., and E. B. Sayles.
1941   An Agreement on Abilene Region Terminology. Texas Archeological and Paleontological Society, vol. 13, pp. 175-176. Abilene.

Renaud, E. B.
1931   Prehistoric Flaked Points from Colorado and Neighboring Districts. Proceedings, Colorado Museum Natural History, vol. X, no .2.
1932   Yuma and Folsom Artifacts, New Material. Proceedings, Colorado Museum Natural History, vol. XI, no. 2.
1936   Southern Wyoming and Southwest South Dakota. The Archaeological Survey of the High Western Plains: 7th Report. University of Denver.
1938   The Black's Fork Culture of Southwest Wyoming. The Archaeological Survey of the High Western Plains: 10th Report. University of Denver.
1940   Further Research in the Black's Fork Basin, Southwest Wyoming, 1938-1939. The Archaeological Survey of the High Western Plains: 12th Report. University of Denver.

Rex González, Alberto.
1952   Antiguo Horizonte Perceramico en las Sierras Centrales de la Argentina. Runa: Archivo para las Ciencias del Hombre, vol. 5, pp. 110-133, Buenos Aires.

Richards, Horace G.
1951   The Vindication of Natchez Man. Frontiers, vol. 15, no. 5, pp. 139-140. Philadelphia Academy of Natural Sciences.

Ritchie, William A.
1951   Ground Slates: Eskimo or Indian? Pennsylvania Archaeologist, vol. 21, nos. 3-4, pp. 46-52, Philadelphia.
1953   A Probable Paleo-Indian Site in Vermont. American Antiquity, vol. XVIII, no. 3, pp. 249-258.
1957   Traces of Early Man in the Northeast. New York State Museum and Science Service, Bull. No. 358, Albany.

Ritzenthaler, R. E., and Paul Scholz.
1946   The Osceola Site, an "Old Copper" Site near Potosi, Wisconsin. The Wisconsin Archaeologist, vol. 27, no. 3, pp. 53-70, Milwaukee.

Ritzenthaler, R. E., and W. L. Wittry.
1952   The Oconto Site—An Old Copper Manifestation. The Wisconsin Archaeologist, vol. 33, no. 4, pp. 199-223, Milwaukee.

Roberts, Frank H. H., Jr.
1935   A Folsom Complex: Preliminary Report on Investigations at the Lindenmeier Site in Northern Colorado. Smithsonian Miscellaneous Collections, vol. 94.

1936 Additional Information on the Folsom Complex: Report on the Second Season's Investigations at the Lindenmeier Site in Northern Colorado. Smithsonian Miscellaneous Collections, vol. 95, no. 10.
1937a New World Man. American Antiquity, vol. 11, no. 3, pp. 172-177.
1937b New Developments in the Problem of the Folsom Complex. Smithsonian Institution Explorations and Field Work in 1936, pp. 67-74.
1937c The Folsom Problem in American Archaeology in Early Man. J. B. Lippincott & Co., Philadelphia.
1940 Developments in the Problem of the North American Paleo-Indian in Essays in Historical Anthropology of North America. Smithsonian Miscellaneous Collections, vol. 100, pp. 51-116.
1942 Archeological and Geological Investigations in the San Jon District, Eastern New Mexico. Smithsonian Miscellaneous Collections, vol. 103, no. 4.
1943 "A New Site" in Notes and News. American Antiquity, vol. VIII, no. 3, p. 300.
1945 A Deep Burial in the Clear Fork of the Brazos River. Texas Archeological and Paleontological Society Bulletin, vol. 13, pp. 9-30. Abilene.
1951a The Early Americans. Scientific American, vol. 184, no. 2, pp. 15-19.
1951b Radiocarbon Dates and Early Man in Radiocarbon Dating; Johnson, Editor. American Antiquity, vol. XVII, no. 1, pt. 2, pp. 20-22.
1953 Recent Developments in the Early Man Problem in the New World. Eastern States Archaeological Federation Bulletin, no. 12, pp. 9-11. Trenton, New Jersey.

Rogers, David Banks.
1929 Prehistoric Man of the Santa Barbara Coast. Santa Barbara Museum of Natural History.

Rogers, Malcolm J.
1939 Early Lithic Industries of the Lower Basin of the Colorado River and Adjacent Desert Areas. San Diego Museum Papers, no. 3.

Rolfe, B. N.
1955 Paleopedologic Study at the Lindenmeier Site, Colorado. Geological Society Bulletin, vol. 66, no. 12, pt. 2, p. 1609, (Abstract).

Roosa, William B.
1956a Preliminary Report on the Lucy Site. El Palacio, vol. 63, no. 2, pp. 36-49. Santa Fe, New Mexico.
1956b The Lucy Site in Central New Mexico. American Antiquity, vol. XXI, no. 3, p. 310.

Roosa, William B., and Stewart L. Peckham.
1954 Notes on the Third Interglacial Artifacts. American Antiquity, vol. XIX, no. 3, pp. 280-281.

Rouse, Irving.
1950 Vero and Melbourne Man: A Cultural and Chronological Interpretation. New York Academy of Sciences, Transactions Series 2, vol. 12, no. 7, pp. 220-224. New York.
1951 A Survey of Indian River Archaeology, Florida. Yale University Publications in Anthropology, no. 44.
1952 The Age of the Melbourne Interval. Texas Archeological and Paleontological Society Bulletin, vol. 23, pp. 293-299. Lubbock.

Rouse, Irving, and José M. Cruxent
1957 Further Comments on the Finds at El Jobo, Venezuela. American Antiquity, vol. XXII, no. 4, pp. 412.

Rowe, Paul R.
1952 Early Horizons in Mills County, Iowa: Part I, Evidences of Early Man. Iowa Archaeological Society Journal, vol. I, no. 3, pp. 6-13; vol. II, no. 1, pp. 3-10.

Rubin, Meyer, and Hans E. Suess
1956   U. S. Geological Survey Radiocarbon Dates III. Science, vol. 123, no. 3194, pp. 442-448. Washington.

Sanford, John T.
1935   The Richmond Mastodon. Proceedings of the Rochester Academy of Science, vol. 7, no. 5, pp. 135-156.

Sauer, Carl O.
1948   Environment and Culture During the Last Deglaciation. American Philosophical Society Proceedings, vol. 92, no. 1, pp. 65-77.

Sayles, E. B.
1935   An Archaeological Survey of Texas. Medallion Papers, no. XVI. Gila Pueblo, Globe, Arizona.
1945   The San Simon Branch, Excavations at Cave Creek and in the San Simon Valley, I: Material Culture. Medallion Papers, no. XXXIV. Gila Pueblo, Globe, Arizona.

Sayles, E B., and Ernst Antevs.
1941   The Cochise Culture. Medallion Papers, no. XXIV. Gila Pueblo, Globe, Arizona.
1955   Report given at the 1955 Great Basin Archaeological Conference. American Antiquity, vol. XX, no. 3, p. 311.

Scharf, David.
1935   The Quaternary History of the Pinto Basin *in* The Pinto Basin Site. Southwest Museum Papers, no. 9, pp. 11-19. Los Angeles.

Schultz, C. Bertrand.
1932   Association of Artifacts and Extinct Mammals in Nebraska. Nebraska Museum, Bulletin 33, vol. 1, pp. 171-183.
1943   Some Artifact Sites of Early Man in the Great Plains and Adjacent Areas. American Antiquity, vol. VIII, no. 3, pp. 242-249.

Schultz, C. Bertrand, and L. C. Eiseley.
1935   Paleontological Evidence of the Antiquity of the Scottsbluff Basin Quarry and its Associated Artifacts. American Anthropologist, New Series, vol. 3, no. 2, pp. 306-318.
1936   An Added Note on the Scottsbluff Quarry. American Anthropologist, vol. 3, no. 3, pp. 521-524.

Schultz, C. Bertrand, and W. D. Frankforter.
1948   Preliminary Report on the Lime Creek Sites: New Evidence of Early Man in Southwestern Nebraska. Bulletin of the University of Nebraska State Museum, vol. III, no. 4, pp. 43-62. Lincoln.

Schultz, C. Bertrand, Gilbert S. Lueninghoener, and W. D. Frankforter.
1948   Preliminary Geomorphological Studies of the Lime Creek Area. Bulletin of the University of Nebraska State Museum, vol. III, no. 4, pp. 31-42. Lincoln.
1951   A Graphic Resume of the Pleistocene of Nebraska (with notes on the fossil mammalian remains). University of Nebraska State Museum Bulletin, vol. III, no. 6.

Scott, William B.
1937   A History of Land Mammals in the Western Hemisphere. Macmillan Co., New York.

Sears, Paul B.
1951   Climate and Culture: New Evidence. Science, vol. 114, no. 2950, pp. 46-47.

Sellards, E. H.
1917   On the Association of Human Remains and Extinct Vertebrates at Vero, Florida. Journal of Geology, vol. 25, no. 1, pp. 4-24.
1937   The Vero Finds in the Light of Present Knowledge *in* Early Man, pp. 193-210. J. B. Lippincott & Co., Philadelphia.
1938   Artifacts Associated with Fossil Elephant. Bulletin Geological Society of America, vol. 49, July, pp. 999-1010.

1940a Early Man In America: Index to Localities, and Selected Bibliography. Bulletin Geological Society of America, vol. 51, pp. 373-432.
1940b Pleistocene Artifacts and Associated Fossils from Bee County, Texas. Bulletin Geological Society of America, vol. 51, pp. 1627-1657.
1941 Stone Images from Henderson County, Texas. American Antiquity vol. VII, no. 1, pp. 29-38.
1947 Early Man In America: Index to Localities, and Selected Bibliography, 1940-1945. Bulletin Geological Society of America, vol. 58, pp. 955-978.
1952 Early Man In America. University of Texas Press, Austin.
1955 Fossil Bison and Associated Artifacts from Milnesand, New Mexico. American Antiquity, vol. XX, no. 4, pp. 336-344.

Sellards, E. H., Glen L. Evans, and Grayson E. Meade.
1947 Fossil Bison and Associated Artifacts from Plainview, Texas, with Description of Artifacts by Alex D. Krieger. Bulletin Geological Society of America, vol. 58, pp. 927-954.

Shippee, J. M.
1948 Nebo Hill, A Lithic Complex in Western Missouri. American Antiquity, vol. XIV, no. 1, pp. 29-32.
1950 An Oblique Parallel Flaked Point from Missouri. American Antiquity, vol. XVI, no. 2, p. 164.
1955 Cave Investigations. Missouri Archaeological Society Newsletter no. 94. Columbia, Missouri.
n. d. The Diagnostic Point Type of the Nebo Hill Complex. Paper presented at Conference for Plains Archaeology, Lincoln, Nebraska, November 28, 1953.

Simpson, George Gaylord.
1933 A Nevada Fauna of Pleistocene Type and Its Probable Association with Man. American Museum of Natural History Novitates No. 667. New York.

Simpson, Ruth D.
1947 A Classic Folsom from Lake Mohave. The Masterkey, vol. 21, pp. 24-25.
1949 The Plot Thickens at Little Lake. The Masterkey, vol. 23. no. 1, January.
1954 A Friendly Critic Visits Texas Street. The Masterkey, vol. 28, no. 5, pp. 174-176. The Southwest Museum, Los Angeles.
1955 Hunting Elephants in Nevada. The Masterkey, vol. 29, no. 4, pp. 114-116. The Southwest Museum, Los Angeles.
1956 Introduction to Early Western American Prehistory. Bulletin Southern California Academy of Sciences, vol. 55, pt. 2, pp. 61-71. Los Angeles.

Skarland, Ivar, and J. L. Giddings, Jr.
1948 Flint Stations in Central Alaska. American Antiquity, vol. XIV, no. 2, pp. 116-120.

Skinner, Morris F., and Ove C. Kaisen.
1947 The Fossil Bison of Alaska and Preliminary Revision of the Genus. Bulletin American Museum Natural History, vol. 89, Article 3.

Smith, Arthur George.
1952 A Fluted Point from Long Island, New York. American Antiquity, vol. XVII, no. 3, p. 262.

Smith, Elmer R.
1941 Archaeology of Deadman Cave, Utah. Bulletin University of Utah, vol. XXXII, no. 4.
1952 The Archaeology of Deadman Cave: A Revision. University of Utah Anthropological Papers, no. 10. Salt Lake City.

Smith, Phillip S.
1937 Certain Relations Between Northwestern America and Northeastern Asia *in* Early Man, pp. 105-114. J. B. Lippincott & Co., Philadelphia.

Soday, Frank J.
  1952 A New Paleo-Indian Site. Dallas Archaeological Society Record, vol. II, no. 2, pp. 6-9. Dallas, Texas.
  1954 The Quad Site: A Paleo-Indian Village in Northern Alabama. The Tennessee Archaeologist, vol. 10, no. 1, pp. 1-20. Knoxville.

Sokoloff, V. P., and J. Luis Lorenzo.
  1953 Modern and Ancient Soils at some Archaeological Sites in the Valley of Mexico. American Antiquity, vol. XIX, no. 1, pp. 50-55.

Solecki, Ralph S.
  1950a A Preliminary Report of an Archaeological Reconnaissance of the Kukpowruk and Kokolik Rivers in Northwest Alaska. American Antiquity, vol. XVI, no. 1, pp. 66-68.
  1950b Archeology and Geology in Northwestern Alaska. The Earth Science Digest, vol. IV, no. 7. Revere, Massachusetts.
  1951a Notes on Soil Analysis and Archaeology. American Antiquity, vol. XVI, no. 3, pp. 254-256.
  1951b Notes on Two Archaeological Discoveries in Northern Alaska, 1950. American Antiquity, vol. XVII, no. 1, pp. 55-57.
  1951c Archeology and Ecology of the Arctic Slope of Alaska. Smithsonian Report for 1950, pp. 469-495. Smithsonian Institution, Washington, D. C.
  1954 A Fluted Point from Dickson County, Tennessee. The Tennessee Archeologist, vol. 10, no. 2. Knoxville.
  1955 Lamellar Flakes versus Blades: A Reappraisal. American Antiquity, vol. XX, no. 4, pp. 393-394.

Solecki, Ralph S., and Robert J. Hackman.
  1951 Additional Data on the Denbigh Flint Complex in Northern Alaska. Journal Washington Academy of Sciences, vol. 41, no. 3, pp. 85-88.

Stephenson, Robert L.
  1950 Culture Chronology in Texas. American Antiquity, vol. XVI, no. 2, pp. 151-157.

Steward, Julian H.
  1933 Archaeological Problems of the Northern Periphery of the Southwest. Museum of Northern Arizona, Bulletin 5. Flagstaff.
  1937 Ancient Caves of the Great Salt Lake Region. Bureau of American Ethnology Bulletin no. 116. Washington, D. C.
  1940 Native Cultures of the Intermountain (Great Basin) Area. Smithsonian Miscellaneous Collections, vol. 100, pp. 445-502.

Stewart, T. D.
  1945 Report on the J. C. Putnam Skeleton from Texas. Texas Archeological and Paleontological Society Bulletin, vol. 16, pp. 21-35. Abilene.
  1946 A Re-examination of the Fossil Human Skeletal Remains from Melbourne, Florida in Further Data on the Vero Skull. Smithsonian Miscellaneous Collections, vol. 106, no. 10. Washington, D. C.
  1949 The Development of the Concept of Morphological Dating in Connection with Early Man in America. Southwestern Journal of Anthropology, vol. 5, no. 1. Albuquerque.

Stock, Chester, and Francis D. Bode.
  1937 The Occurrence of Flints and Extinct Animals in Pluvial Deposits near Clovis, New Mexico: Part III, Geology and Vertebrate Paleontology of the Late Quaternary. Proceedings Philadelphia Academy of Natural Sciences, vol. LXXXVIII, pp. 219-241.

Strong, William Duncan.
  1930 A Stone Culture of Northern Labrador and Its Relation to the Eskimo-like Cultures of the Northeast. American Anthropologist, vol. 32, pp. 126-144.
  1935 An Introduction to Nebraska Archeology. Smithsonian Miscellaneous Collections, vol. 93, no. 10.
  1947 Review of "Indians Before Columbus" by Martin, Quimby, and Collier. American Antiquity, vol. XIII, no. 2, pp. 184-189.

Suess, H. E.
1954   U. S. Geological Survey, Radiocarbon Dates I. Science, vol. 120, pp. 467-473.
1956   Absolute Chonology of the Last Glaciation. Science, vol. 123, no. 3192, pp. 355-357.

Suhm, Dee Ann, and Alex D. Krieger, with the collaboration of Edward B. Jelks.
1954   An Introductory Handbook of Texas Archaeology. Bulletin Texas Archeological Society, vol. 25. Austin.

Tanton, T. L.
1931   Fort William and Port Arthur, and Thunder Cape Map Areas, Thunder Bay District, Ontario, Canada. Department of Mines, Geological Survey Memoir 167. Ottawa.

Thomas, Edward S.
1952   The Orleton Farms Mastodon. Ohio Journal of Science, vol. 52, no. 1, pp. 1-5.

Thompson, Raymond M.
1948   Notes on the Achaeology of the Utukok River, Northwestern Alaska. American Antiquity, vol. XIV, no. 1, pp. 62-65.

Thompson, Raymond H.
1954   Archaic Culture in Kentucky. (Abstract by Joffre Coe.) Southern Indian Studies. 10th Southeastern Conference. Archaeological Society of North Carolina, vol. VI, pp. 7-8, Chapel Hill.

Treganza, A. E.
1947   Notes on the San Dieguito Lithic Industry of Southern California and Baja California *in* Observations on Archaeological Sites in Topanga Canyon, California. University of California Publications in American Archaeology and Ethnology, vol. 44, no. 2, pp. 253-255. Berkeley.
1952   Archaeological Investigations in the Farmington Reservoir Area, Stanislaus County, California. Reports of the University of California Archaeological Survey, no. 14, Berkeley.

Treganza, A. E., and R. F. Heizer.
1953   Additional Data on the Farmington Complex: A Stone Implement Assemblage of Probable Early Postglacial Date from Central California. Reports of the University of California Archaeological Survey, no. 22, pp. 28-38. Berkeley.

Wauchope, Robert (Editor).
1956   Seminars In Archaeology. Memoirs of the Society for American Archaeology, no. 11. American Antiquity, vol. XXII, no. 2, pt. 2.

Webb, William S.
1950   The Carlson Annis Mound. University of Kentucky Reports in Anthropology, vol. 7, pp. 265-354. Lexington.
1951   The Parrish Village Site: Site 45, Hopkins County, Kentucky. University of Kentucky Reports in Anthropology, vol. 7, no. 6. Lexington.

Webb, William, and David L. DeJarnette.
1942   An Archaeological Survey of Pickwick Basin in the Adjacent Portion of the States of Alabama, Mississippi, and Tennessee. Bureau of American Ethnology Bulletin 129.

Wedel, Waldo R.
1947   Culture Chronology in the Central Great Plains. American Antiquity, vol. XII, no. 3, pp. 148-155.

Weidenreich, Franz.
1939   On the Earliest Representations of Modern Mankind Recovered in the Soil of East Asia. Peking Natural History Bulletin, vol. 13, pp. 161-174.

Weiner, J. S., K. P. Oakley, and W. E. LeGros Clark.
1953   The Solution of the Piltdown Problem. Bulletin of the British Museum (Natural History) Geology, vol. 2, no. 3, pp. 141-146.

Wendorf, Fred, and Tully Thomas.
1951   Early Man Sites near Concho, Arizona. American Antiquity, vol. XVII, no. 2, pp. 107-113.

Wendorf, Fred, Alex D. Krieger, Claude C. Albritton, T. D. Stewart.
1955   The Midland Discovery. University of Texas Press, Austin.

Wheat, Joe Ben.
1940   Preliminary Report on Excavation of the Hodges Site. Bulletin Texas Archeological and Paleontological Society, vol. 12, pp. 195-216.
1953   An Archeological Survey of the Addicks Dam Basin, Southeast Texas. River Basin Surveys, Papers nos. 1-6, Bureau of American Ethnology Bulletin 154, pp. 143-252. Smithsonian Institution, Washington, D. C.

Wheeler, Richard P.
1954   Selected Projectile Point Types of the United States: II. Bulletin Oklahoma Anthropological Society, vol. 2, pp. 1-6. Norman.

Wheeler, S. M.
1942   Archaeology of Etna Cave, Lincoln County, Nevada. Nevada State Park Commission, Carson City.

Whitaker, Thomas W., Hugh C. Cutler, and Richard S. MacNeish.
1957   Cucurbit Materials from Three Caves near Ocampo, Tamaulipas. American Antiquity, vol. XXII, no. 4, pp. 352-358.

Wilford, Lloyd A.
1955   A Revised Classification of the Prehistoric Cultures of Minnesota. American Antiquity, vol. XXI, no. 2, pp. 130-142.

Willey, Gordon R.
1952   Review of "A Survey of Indian River Archaeology" by Irving Rouse. American Antiquity, vol. XVIII, no. 1, pp. 75-77.

Willey, Gordon R., and Philip Phillips.
1955   Method and Theory in American Archaeology II: Historical-Developmental Interpretation. American Anthropologist, vol. 57, no. 4, pp. 723-819.

Williams, Stephen.
1957   The Island 35 Mastodon: Its Bearing on the Age of Archaic Cultures in the East. American Antiquity, vol. XXII, no. 4, pp. 359-371.

Witthoft, John.
1950   Notes on Pennsylvania Fluted Points. Pennsylvania Archaeology Bulletin, vol. XX, nos. 3 and 4.
1952   A Paleo-Indian Site in Eastern Pennsylvania: An Early Hunting Culture. Proceedings American Philosophical Society, vol. 96, no. 4, pp. 464-495. Philadelphia.
1954   A Note on Fluted Point Relationships. American Antiquity, vol. XIX, no. 3, pp. 271-273.
1954a   A Brief History of the Indian Hunter. Pennsylvania Game News, vol. XXV, nos. 6-9.
1955   Texas Street Artifacts. New World Antiquity, vol. 2, no. 9, pp. 132-133. Markham House Press, London.

Wittry, Warren L., and Robert E. Ritzenthaler.
1956   The Old Copper Complex: An Archaic Manifestation in Wisconsin. American Antiquity, vol. XXI, no. 3, pp. 244-254.

Woodbury, George and Edna.
1935   Prehistoric Skeletal Remains from the Texas Coast. Medallion Papers, no. XVIII, Gila Pueblo, Globe, Arizona.

Wormington, H. M.
1948 A Proposed Revision of Yuma Point Terminology. Proceedings of the Colorado Museum of Natural History, vol. XVIII, no. 2. Denver.
1953a Origins: Indigenous Period. Program of the History of America, vol. 1, no. 1. Publicaciones del Instituto Panamericano de Geografia e Historia, no. 153. Mexico, D. F.
1953b Der urgeschichtliche Mensch in Nordamerika und die Leitformen seiner Kulturen. Quartär, Bd. VI, 1, pp. 1-18.

Wormington, H. M. and Robert H. Lister
1956 Archaeological Investigations on the Uncompahgre Plateau in West Central Colorado, Denver Museum of Natural History, Proceedings, No. 2.

Wright, H. E., and Meyer Rubin.
1956 Radiocarbon Dates of Mankato Drift in Minnesota. Science, vol. 124, no. 3223, pp. 625-626.

INDEX

A

Abilene points, 116
Abilene, Texas, 47, 113, 116
Abrading stones, 120, 122, 138, 143
Academy of Natural Sciences, Philadelphia, 47
Adzes, 65, 100, 150
Agate Basin points, 99, 107, 141, 142, 268, 269
Agate Basin Site, 141
Agogino, George, 180
Alabama, 72, 81, 91, 148, 149
Alabama Archaeological Society, 81
Alaska, 9, 42, 48, 83, 109, 112, 124, 140, 207, 208, 212, 214-215, 216, 250, 253, 254
Alberta, Canada, 29, 42, 90, 99, 109, 112, 123, 124, 132-134, 135, 210, 217-218
Alberta points, 133, 134, 135
Albritton, C. C., 41, 241, 245
Albuquerque Gravel Pit, 176
Aleutian Islands, 212, 214, 249
Algonquin lake stages, 206
Allen, H. H., 123
Allen, Jimmy, 127, 144
Jimmy Allen Site, Wyo., 144-146, 237
Allen Site, Nebr., 137
Alleröd period, 18
Allison, V. C., 102
Alluvial Sequence, 221
Almagre Complex, 202
Altithermal Period, 10, 14, 20, 51, 64, 115, 122, 126, 132, 150, 157, 165, 168, 175, 179, 180, 183, 190, 191, 193, 202, 203, 215, 227, 240, 245
Amaranth, 180
Amargosa I, 178
Amargosa II, 179, 180, 193
Amargosa III, 179
American Museum of Natural History, 197
Amsden, C. E., 162, 165
Amurian, 256
Anaktuvuk Pass, 214
Anaktuvuk River, 215
Ananiuliak Island, 214
Anastasia Formation, 226
Anathermal Period, 10, 160, 163, 165, 191, 193, 199, 227, 231
Andersen, Harold, 104, 130
Andersen, Perry, 104, 130
Anderson, A. W., 47
Anderson Basin, 47
Angeles Mesa, 231

Angostura points, 66, 95, 107, 138, 139, 140, 141, 212, 217, 268, 269
Angus, Nebraska, 43
Antevs, Ernst, 10, 15, 18, 48, 50, 51, 56, 59, 60, 63, 115, 155, 160, 162, 163, 165, 167, 168, 169, 171, 172, 173, 174, 175, 191, 235
Antelope, 244
Antler, 149, 150, 152, 186, 204, 233
Archaeological Society of Virginia, 71, 81
Archaic Stage, defined, 4
Archaic, eastern U. S., 4, 47, 64, 65, 66, 67, 72, 74, 83, 101, 102, 116, 123, 148-150, 152, 199, 206, 227, 228, 229, 230, 248, 258
Archaic, Mexico, 240, 241,
Arctic Ocean, 11, 252
Arellano, A. R. V., 92, 238, 241
Argentina, 99, 203
Arizona, 41, 42, 43, 53, 54, 56, 59, 169, 171, 177, 221
Arizona State Museum, 53, 55, 177
Arkansas, 23, 102, 114, 123
Arroyo cutting, 9
Aschman, H., 84
Asia, 1, 83, 99, 249, 250, 251, 252, 253, 254, 255, 256, 257, 259
Athapaskans, 208
Atlantis, 249
Atlatls, 29, 51, 191
Atlatl spur, 184
Atlatl weights, 74, 149
Atrisco Focus, 177
Augustin points, 174
Auriferous gravels, 164
Australasia, 256
Aveleyra A. de Anda, Luis, 92, 93, 95, 110, 200
Awls, 37, 51, 65, 138, 150, 184, 217
Axes, 74, 146, 150, 219, 220

B

Bache, C., 124
Baggerly, C., 224
Bags, 51
Baja California, 84
Balls, grooved, 138, 160
Bannerstones, 152
Barcena, M., 200
Barbeau Creek Rockshelter, 147
Barbour, E. H., 113, 118
Bartlett, K., 221
Basal grinding, 38, 60, 62, 65, 66, 71, 72, 84, 86, 95, 108, 112, 120, 122, 141, 146, 169, 187, 263, 265, 267, 269